Hesi A2 Full Study Guide

From Stress to Success

Master Your Exam Preparation and Secure Your Nursing Career with Up-to-Date Practice Tests to Achieve Top Scores on Your First Attempt

ATPB Academy

Hesi A2 Full Study Guide

Printed in the United States of America

ISBN: 979-8323099436

Welcome to Your HESI A2 Journey!

Thank you for selecting our book as your guide to prepare for the HESI A2 exam, and we are honored that you have chosen to trust us! We understand how important this step is in your educational and professional journey, and we are here to support you every step of the way.

In these pages, you will find a comprehensive collection of resources, insights, and practice materials designed to enhance your understanding and boost your confidence as you prepare for the exam. I understand the many responsibilities you have to manage between work, personal and family commitments; finding adequate time to prepare for the exam is a significant challenge. For this very reason, we have created a manual that offers you a comprehensive study guide, with the goal of making it easier for you to prepare. Our goal is to provide you with the most relevant and up-to-date information to help you succeed.

We are committed to supporting your learning journey beyond this book. We invite you to join our exclusive Facebook support group, where you can connect with fellow aspirants, receive exam updates, discover new questions, and gain additional tips to enhance your preparation. To join, simply scan the QR code found below, and take your exam preparation to the next level.

Your success is our priority, and we are always here to help. Together, let's make your first attempt at the HESI A2 exam a **resounding success!**

Additionally, at the end of this book, you'll find a second QR code. Scanning this will allow you to download some fantastic bonuses that we've specially prepared for our students. Be sure not to miss out on them!

TABLE OF CONTENT

SECTION 5 - BIOLOGY

SECTION 6 - CHEMISTRY

SECTION 7 - HUMAN ANATOMY AND PHYSIOLOGY

SECTION 8 - PHYSICS

HERE'S HOW YOU CAN REALLY MAKE A DIFFERENCE!

Dear Reader,

Before we dive into your exam preparation, I'd like to ask for a moment of your time. As you're likely aware, reviews are vital for a book's growth and relevance, ensuring it remains current and continues to incorporate new content and insights.

Consider this: we're quick to leave a review when dissatisfied, yet we often overlook this when our expectations are met. Sharing positive, detailed feedback about what stood out and how it benefitted you is just as crucial.

Your review is incredibly important to me and the team dedicated to supporting our readers and students daily. Please, could you spare a few minutes to write a review? Your effort will greatly influence the ongoing success of our initiative and assist other students who, like you, are facing such a crucial examination.

It's super easy to leave a review: simply scan the QR code below to be taken directly to the Amazon page where you can share your thoughts on the book. We thank you wholeheartedly. Your input is the highest form of appreciation for our hard work and commitment to this project.

INTRODUCTION

HOW TO USE THIS BOOK

Before diving into this book, understanding how to effectively use it is crucial. Doing so will help optimize your study time and enhance your performance. Pay close attention to my suggestions on study strategies, recommended routines to follow at the end of each chapter, and tips that have proven successful for both myself and others preparing for this exam.

A common question I encounter is: How much time is needed to prepare for this exam? Unfortunately, the answer isn't one-size-fits-all. The time required to prepare for the HESI A2 exam varies significantly based on individual factors such as your existing knowledge, learning style, and the specific requirements of the nursing program you're aiming to enter.

Here are some guidelines to help you determine the necessary preparation time:

- **Assess your starting point:** If you have a strong background in the subjects covered by the HESI A2, such as math, biology, chemistry, anatomy, and physiology, you might need less time to prepare. On the other hand, if these areas are unfamiliar or challenging, you might need more time.
- **Individual learning pace**: Some individuals can quickly grasp and remember information, while others may need more time for thorough study and review.
- **Study habits and schedules:** Your available study time can significantly impact your preparation length. Part-time study due to other commitments will extend your preparation compared to those who can study full-time.
- **Test-taking skills:** If you're adept at taking tests, your focus may be more on content review. Conversely, if standardized tests are usually difficult for you, additional time to hone test-taking strategies may be beneficial.

Considering these guidelines, learning time can be categorized into three broad areas:

1. **Short-term preparation**: For those with solid subject knowledge and strong test-taking skills, 4-6 weeks of preparation, dedicating a few hours daily, may suffice.
2. **Medium-term preparation:** A 2-3 month preparation period could be suitable for those somewhat familiar with the content but needing in-depth review, especially when balancing other commitments.
3. **Long-term preparation:** A preparation period of 3-6 months may be necessary for those requiring extensive review or with limited daily study time.

In my experience, the average person I assist spends **about 2 months preparing for the exam** to achieve a good level of readiness.

WHAT THE EXAM CONSISTS OF

In this section, we delve into the specifics of the HESI A2 exam and its composition. The Health Education Systems, Inc. Admission Assessment (HESI A2) plays a pivotal role for aspiring nursing students, evaluating their academic readiness for nursing programs. It ensures applicants possess the fundamental competencies crucial for success in their nursing education.

The HESI A2 exam is comprehensively designed to span a broad array of topics, providing an in-depth evaluation of a candidate's skills. Typically, the exam encompasses the following sections:

- **Mathematics**: This segment evaluates essential mathematical abilities critical for tasks like dosage calculations in nursing. It consists of 50 questions on subjects including basic arithmetic, fractions, proportions, ratios, and elementary algebra. Participants are allotted approximately 50 minutes to complete this portion.
- **Reading Comprehension:** Essential for understanding patient documentation and medical literature, this section comprises about 47-50 questions with a 60-minute time frame. It assesses the ability to grasp key ideas, identify main themes, and make logical inferences from written material.
- **Vocabulary and General Knowledge**: Comprising 50-55 questions to be answered in 50 minutes, this section evaluates the candidate's grasp of general language and terms commonly used in healthcare settings.
- **Grammar:** A 50-question section allotted 50 minutes, focusing on fundamental grammar rules, sentence structure, and common grammatical errors, reflecting the importance of clear communication in nursing.
- **Biology**: This 25-30 question section, with a 25-minute duration, tests basic biological concepts, vital for understanding body systems and functions in nursing practice.
- **Chemistry**: Sometimes included, this section has 25-30 questions and lasts about 25 minutes, covering foundational chemistry concepts.
- **Anatomy and Physiology**: Critical for all nursing students, this section includes 25-30 questions and takes about 25 minutes, testing knowledge of the human body's structure and function.
- **Physics**: Included in some versions of the exam, it consists of 25-30 questions and has a similar 25-minute duration, covering basic physics principles.

These sections will be thoroughly and clearly analyzed throughout the book. However, I want to address the classic questions that are likely already on your mind. Ninety percent of students share these common concerns, so it's beneficial to answer these questions in this initial part of the textbook. That way, once we dive into the study material, you'll already have a clear understanding.

HOW TO REGISTER FOR THE HESI A2 EXAM

To register and pay for the HESI exam, you must have an Evolve account with Elsevier. Then, visit the Evolve homepage, accessible via the following link: **https://evolve.elsevier.com/cs/**

- Select "**I'm a student**"
- Select "Register for Distance Testing" under HESI Secured Exams
- On the HESI Registration page, click "**Register**" to add the HESI Registration to your cart.
- Click Redeem/Checkout.
- Enter your name, email address, and password to create your Evolve account.
- Read the Registered User Agreement.
- Click "Yes, I accept" and then click Submit.
- After registration, the HESI Assessment-Student Access link will appear under the My Content section of your Evolve account.
- Choose a test date.
- Navigate to the Evolve student homepage.
- Click "Login" to access your Evolve account.
- Under the HESI Assessment section, click "Student Access."
- On the HESI Student Access page, click the "Payments" tab.
- Enter the payment ID corresponding to your selected test date and click "Search."
- Ensure the information in Section 2 matches your chosen test date.
- Fill in the billing information in Section 3 and your email address in Section 4.
- Use the billing name and address that matches the credit card you plan to use for the HESI exam payment.
- Click "Proceed to Checkout" to input your credit card details.

Once your payment is successfully processed, a receipt verifying the transaction will be immediately available and saved within the "Payment History" section of your account. Please note, the transaction record will display the username tied to your Evolve account, rather than the credit card holder's name.

AFTER HOW LONG DO I RECEIVE THE RESULTS?

The HESI A2 exam results are typically available immediately after you finish the test. However, in cases where there are essay components or sections necessitating manual review, processing the results for these parts may take a bit longer.

WHAT SHOULD I DO AFTER RECEIVING MY RESULTS?

First, thoroughly review your score report to gauge your performance across different sections. If your scores align with the prerequisites of your chosen nursing program, you may proceed with your application. Otherwise, use the insights from your report to pinpoint areas needing improvement should you consider retaking the exam.

IMPORTANT: Confirm that your scores are forwarded to the relevant institutions if not done so automatically.

HOW LONG ARE MY SCORES VALID?

The validity of HESI A2 exam scores can vary based on the policies of the specific nursing program or institution you're applying to. Typically, most nursing programs accept scores as valid for 1 to 2 years from the test date.

WHAT TO BRING AND WHAT NOT TO BRING TO THE EXAM

What You Can Bring:

- **Photo Identification**: You must bring a valid, government-issued photo ID that includes your photograph and signature, such as a driver's license, passport, state ID, or military ID.
- **Confirmation of Registration**: Some testing centers may require proof of exam registration, like a confirmation email or letter.
- **Required Materials**: Bring any materials specified by the testing center or nursing program, such as specific documents.
- **Essentials**: Dress comfortably for the testing center environment. You might be allowed to bring a sweater or jacket if the room tends to be cold.

What You Cannot Bring:

- **Electronic Devices**: Cell phones, smartwatches, calculators (unless otherwise specified), PDAs, and other electronic devices are generally prohibited.
- **Personal Items**: Bags, purses, wallets, and coats usually need to be stored away from the testing area.
- **Study Materials**: Books, notes, papers, or any study aids are not allowed in the testing space.
- **Food and Beverages**: Typically not allowed in the testing room, though some centers might have a designated space for a water bottle.
- **Other Items**: Hats, hoods, and any headgear (except for religious reasons) are often not allowed.

WHAT HAPPENS IF I DON'T PASS THE EXAM?

Not passing the HESI A2 exam doesn't mark the end of your nursing program aspirations. Review the retake policy specific to your program; most allow retakes but may require a waiting period between attempts, often around 60 days. Utilize this time to thoroughly prepare for your next attempt, concentrating on weaker areas. Explore different study materials, including guides, online resources, or tutoring, to strengthen your understanding and performance.

WHERE CAN YOU TAKE THE TEST?

The HESI A2 exam is offered at various locations, tailored to the requirements of the nursing school or educational institution you're applying to. Common venues for taking the exam include:

- **On-Campus Testing Centers**: Many colleges and universities with nursing programs provide the HESI A2 exam right on campus. These dedicated testing centers are fully equipped for standardized exam administration.

- **Third-Party Testing Centers**: The exam might also be conducted at independent testing centers that handle a wide range of professional and academic assessments. These centers cater to students who cannot access a campus that administers the test.

- **Prometric Test Centers**: Sometimes, the HESI A2 is offered through Prometric, known for delivering testing and assessment services. Prometric centers offer a consistent, professional testing atmosphere and are located across many cities and countries, making them accessible to a broad range of candidates.

These tips may seem basic, but they have made a significant difference for many of my students preparing for the exam. I've gathered the most common and effective advice to help you navigate your exam day successfully:

1. **Plan Your Trip**: Familiarize yourself with the route and travel time to the exam center well in advance. Last-minute rushes can lead to unnecessary stress, negatively impacting your exam performance. Stay focused and plan ahead.

2. **Arrival Time**: Make it a point to arrive early at the exam center. There are two key reasons for this: first, latecomers may not be allowed to take the exam; second, arriving early can help you start the exam in a more relaxed state.

3. **Check in Advance**: A few days before the exam, verify the list of items allowed and prohibited at the exam center. Relying on second-hand information could lead you to accidentally bring a banned item, resulting in penalties.

4. **Breaks**: Learn about the exam center's policy on breaks during the exam, especially regarding eating, drinking, or restroom visits. Research indicates that our ability to concentrate peaks for about 65 minutes, followed by the need for a 5-minute break to reset. If you notice your focus waning after 65 minutes, consider taking a short break if the rules allow.

By keeping these tips in mind, you can approach your exam day with greater confidence and calm, setting the stage for your best performance.

HOW IS THIS BOOK STRUCTURED

This book is designed to streamline your study process. Each section begins with targeted content, outlining essential information to answer typical test questions.

NOTE: The questions on the HESI A2 exam may closely resemble those in this book, with minor variations in numbers or wording. Thus, if you perform well on these practice questions, you're likely to do well on the actual exam. **Approximately 15% of the exam questions are updated regularly**; this figure is based on anecdotal evidence rather than an official statistic.

At the end of each chapter, you'll find multiple-choice questions and their correct answers. This allows you to gauge your understanding and identify areas for improvement. If you're not satisfied with your performance, revisit the section before moving on to ensure you've addressed any uncertainties or knowledge gaps.

TIPS FOR TEST PREPARATION

Back when I was a student juggling college classes and work, I developed certain routines that significantly boosted my study efficiency. Now, as a tutor aiding students in their academic journeys, I want to share the most effective strategies to help you excel in any exam. Let's explore these tips together:

Understand Your Learning Type

Each individual absorbs and processes information differently, and these differences significantly influence how one should approach studying for a comprehensive exam like the HESI A2. Broadly categorized into visual, auditory, kinesthetic, and reading/writing preferences, learning styles offer insight into the methods and techniques that will best support your study efforts.

- Visual learners thrive on imagery and spatial understanding. If you're a visual learner, incorporating diagrams, charts, and color-coded notes into your study materials can greatly enhance your retention of complex concepts, particularly in sections like Anatomy and Physiology.

- Auditory learners, on the other hand, benefit from listening and speaking as primary modes of learning. Engaging in group discussions, listening to recorded lectures, or even explaining topics out loud to yourself can significantly reinforce your understanding of the material.

- Kinesthetic learners excel when they can manipulate the material and engage in hands-on activities. Creating physical models, performing experiments, or even walking while reviewing flashcards can make study sessions more productive for kinesthetic individuals.

- Lastly, reading/writing learners find their strength in the written word, preferring to absorb information through reading and summarizing texts. If this resonates with you, extensive note-taking, creating detailed outlines, and rewriting your notes could be particularly effective strategies.

By identifying your learning type, you can tailor your HESI A2 exam preparation to suit your innate preferences, making your study time not only more efficient but also more enjoyable. Experiment with different strategies within your learning domain to find what works best for you, and remember, flexibility is key.

Make Study Your Priority

This pivotal approach is not about relentless hours of hitting the books; it's about smart, focused, and consistent effort integrated into your daily routine. In the realm of competitive exams like the HESI A2, where a broad spectrum of knowledge is assessed, prioritizing your study is the linchpin for success.

Allocate specific time blocks dedicated solely to studying each day. These periods should be free from distractions and other commitments, allowing you to fully immerse in the material. It's not the quantity but the quality of time spent that matters. Use a planner or digital calendar to schedule these study sessions, treating them with the same importance as any other critical appointment. Furthermore, assess your weekly and monthly schedule to identify areas where you can reallocate time towards your preparation. This might mean sacrificing some leisure activities or social engagements temporarily. Remember, this is a short-term investment for a long-term gain.

Create Your Ideal Work Environment

Creating your ideal work environment is a critical step in optimizing your HESI A2 exam preparation. The space where you study can significantly impact your concentration, retention, and overall learning efficiency. As a tutor, I've seen firsthand how a thoughtfully arranged study area can enhance a student's focus and productivity.

Firstly, select a location that minimizes distractions. This could be a quiet room in your home, a library, or any other place where you can study uninterrupted for extended periods. Ensure your chosen spot has adequate lighting to reduce eye strain, especially during long study sessions. Comfort is another key factor. Invest in a comfortable chair and a desk that allows you to maintain good posture. Physical discomfort can be a major distraction and hinder your ability to focus. Organize your study materials neatly within reach. A clutter-free desk can help declutter your mind, making it easier to concentrate on the task at hand. Consider using organizers or shelves to keep your textbooks, notes, and other study aids well-arranged.

Lastly, personalize your study space with elements that boost your motivation. This could be inspirational quotes, a small plant, or anything that creates a positive and motivating atmosphere.

The Night Before the Exam

On the eve of the exam, resist the urge to cram. Instead, do a light review of your notes, focusing on key concepts and areas you feel confident about. This reinforces your knowledge without overwhelming your brain. Ensure you have all necessary items for the exam day prepared—identification, confirmation of registration, and any allowed materials. Then, engage in a relaxing activity to ease your mind, such as meditation, a leisurely walk, or listening to calming music. A healthy, light dinner and a good night's sleep are paramount. Aim for 7-8 hours of rest to ensure your mind and body are rejuvenated.

The Day of the Exam

Wake up early to avoid rushing, which can spike your stress levels. Have a nutritious breakfast that includes a balance of protein, complex carbs, and hydration to fuel your body and brain. Reviewing notes should be minimal; instead, focus on deep breathing or visualization techniques to maintain calmness. Arrive at the testing center early to acclimate to the environment and center yourself before the exam begins.

SECTION 1 - MATHEMATICS
UNDERSTANDING NUMBERS

Numbers are the building blocks of mathematics, a language through which we express quantities, measurements, and the relationships between objects. This chapter will delve into the essence of numbers, their properties, and their significance in various mathematical operations, setting a strong foundation for your HESI A2 math preparation.

THE NATURE OF NUMBERS

Numbers are categorized into several types, each serving distinct purposes. At the most basic level, we have natural numbers (1, 2, 3, ...), which we use for counting objects. Extending this category by including zero gives us the whole numbers (0, 1, 2, 3, ...). When we incorporate negatives, we step into the realm of integers (... -3, -2, -1, 0, 1, 2, 3 ...). Further, numbers like ½ and 0.75, which can be expressed as fractions or decimals, are known as rational numbers. In contrast, numbers like π (pi) and $\sqrt{2}$, which cannot be precisely expressed as fractions, are irrational numbers. The collection of rational and irrational numbers forms the set of real numbers, encompassing all the number types we use in daily mathematics.

The following table provides an overview of the different types of numbers, their descriptions, and examples, offering a clear understanding of the fundamental building blocks of mathematics:

NUMBER TYPE	DESCRIPTION	EXAMPLES
Natural Numbers	Positive integers (1, 2, 3, ...), used for counting objects	1, 2, 100, 999
Whole Numbers	Natural numbers including zero (0, 1, 2, 3, ...)	0, 1, 20, 100
Integers	Whole numbers and their negatives (... -3, -2, -1, 0, 1, 2, 3 ...)	-10, -1, 0, 1, 10
Rational Numbers	Numbers that can be expressed as fractions or decimals (½, 0.75)	1/4, 0.5, 0.333...
Irrational Numbers	Numbers that cannot be expressed precisely as fractions (π, $\sqrt{2}$).	π (3.14159...), $\sqrt{2}$ (1.41421...)
Real Numbers	All rational and irrational numbers, encompassing all number types used in daily mathematics.	All of the above

BASE 10 AND NUMBER VALUES

The numeral system most commonly used worldwide is the base-10 or decimal system, rooted in our ten digits (0 through 9). The value of a number in this system is determined by its position or place value. For example, in the number 345, the '5' is in the 'ones' place, the '4' is in the 'tens' place, and the '3' is in the 'hundreds' place. Each position represents a power of 10, with the rightmost digit being 10^0 (ones), the next to the left being 10^1 (tens), and so on. This positional system allows us to understand and manipulate numbers with ease, performing operations like addition, subtraction, multiplication, and division.

THE NUMBER LINE

The number line is a fundamental visual representation in mathematics that illustrates the ordering of numbers along a straight line. Each point on the line corresponds to a unique number, with zero typically positioned at the center, positive numbers extending indefinitely to the right, and negative numbers to the left. This linear model helps in understanding basic arithmetic operations, such as addition and subtraction, as movements along the line. The number line also provides a clear framework for grasping concepts like absolute value, distance between numbers, and the idea of infinity. Its simplicity and versatility make it an indispensable tool in teaching and learning mathematics across all levels.

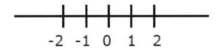

-2 -1 0 1 2

The symbols ">" and "<" are fundamental in mathematics, representing the relationships of greater than and less than, respectively. When we say "a > b," we mean that "a" is greater than "b," indicating that on the number line, "a" is positioned to the right of "b." Conversely, "a < b" signifies that "a" is less than "b," placing "a" to the left of "b" on the number line. These symbols are pivotal in expressing inequalities, comparing quantities, and establishing order among numbers. Their proper use enables precise communication in mathematical reasoning, problem-solving, and data analysis, making them essential tools in the mathematical lexicon.

THE ABSOLUTE VALUE OF A NUMBER

The absolute value of a number represents its distance from zero on the number line, disregarding its direction or sign. It is denoted by two vertical bars surrounding the number, for example, $|x|$. This mathematical concept is fundamental in understanding the inherent magnitude of a number without considering its positivity or negativity. For instance, the absolute values of both -5 and 5 are 5, as each is five units away from zero. Absolute values are extensively used in various mathematical disciplines, including algebra and geometry, to solve equations involving distances and to ensure calculations yield non-negative results, reflecting real-world distances or quantities that cannot be negative.

OPERATIONS WITH NUMBERS

Mastering the basic operations with numbers is essential. Addition is the process of combining quantities, subtraction is determining the difference between quantities, multiplication is repeated addition, and division is splitting into equal parts or groups. These operations are the core actions we perform with numbers and are subject to various properties such as the commutative, associative, and distributive properties, which you will explore further in this book. Let's now examine these operations in detail.

BASIC ARITHMETIC OPERATIONS

ADDITIONS

Addition is one of the four basic arithmetic operations, representing the process of combining two or more numbers or quantities to form a total or sum. It is the most fundamental and frequently used operation in mathematics, serving as the cornerstone for more complex mathematical concepts and operations. The symbol "+" denotes addition, and the numbers involved in the operation are called "addends," while the result is known as the "sum."

How Addition is Done
Addition can be performed with any set of numbers: whole numbers, decimals, fractions, and even negative numbers. The process involves combining the values of the addends to arrive at the sum. For whole numbers, addition usually starts from the rightmost digits (the units) and proceeds to the left, summing corresponding digits in each column.

Rules of Addition
1. **Commutative Property:** Addition is commutative, meaning the order of the addends does not affect the sum. For example, 4 + 5 is equal to 5 + 4.

2. **Associative Property**: Addition is associative, which allows for the grouping of addends in any manner without affecting the sum. For instance, (2 + 3) + 4 equals 2 + (3 + 4).

3. **Identity Property:** The sum of any number and zero is the number itself. For example, 7 + 0 equals 7.

4. **Addition of Negative Numbers:** When adding a negative number, it is equivalent to subtracting its absolute value from the other number. For instance, 5 + (-3) is the same as 5 - 3.

How Carryover Works

Carryover, or "carrying," is a concept applied in addition when the sum of a column exceeds the value that can be represented in a single digit (more than 9 in base-10 numeral system). The excess is carried over to the next left column. This is best illustrated through multi-digit addition.

For example, when adding 378 and 469:

$$
\begin{array}{cccc}
1 & 1 & & \\
3 & 7 & 8 & + \\
4 & 6 & 9 & \\
\hline
8 & 4 & 7 &
\end{array}
$$

- **Units Column:** Start with the rightmost column (units). 8 + 9 = 17. Write down 7, carry over 1 to the tens column.
- **Tens Column:** Add the tens, including the carryover: 7 (from 378) + 6 (from 469) + 1 (carryover) = 14. Write down 4, carry over 1 to the hundreds column.
- **Hundreds Column:** Add the hundreds, including the carryover: 3 + 4 + 1 (carryover) = 8.
- **The sum is 847.**

Advanced Concepts
- **Addition of Decimals:** Align the decimal points and proceed with the addition as with whole numbers. Carryover applies to the left of the decimal point in the same way.
- **Addition of Fractions:** Ensure the fractions have a common denominator, add the numerators, and keep the denominator the same. Simplify if necessary.

SUBTRACTIONS

Subtraction is a basic arithmetic operation that represents the process of removing one quantity from another to find the difference between them. This operation is symbolized by the minus sign "-". In subtraction, the number from which another number is to be subtracted is called the "minuend," the number that is to be subtracted is called the "subtrahend," and the result is known as the "difference."

How Subtraction is Done

Subtraction can be applied to various types of numbers, including whole numbers, fractions, and decimals. The operation involves taking the value of the subtrahend away from the minuend. For whole numbers, subtraction typically starts from the rightmost digits (the units) and proceeds to the left, subtracting the corresponding digits in each column.

Rules of Subtraction

1. **Non-Commutative Nature:** Unlike addition, subtraction is not commutative; changing the order of the numbers changes the result. For instance, 5 - 3 does not equal 3 - 5.
2. **Subtracting Zero:** Subtracting zero from any number leaves the number unchanged. For example, 7 - 0 equals 7.
3. **Subtracting from Zero:** Subtracting any positive number from zero gives a negative result. For instance, 0 - 4 equals -4.
4. **Subtracting a Negative Number:** Subtracting a negative number is the same as adding its absolute value. For example, 5 - (-3) is the same as 5 + 3.

How Tens Borrowing Works

Borrowing, or "regrouping," is a method used in subtraction when a digit in the minuend is smaller than the corresponding digit in the subtrahend. The process involves borrowing a value from the next higher place value to make the subtraction possible.

For example, when subtracting 465 from 802:

$$
\begin{array}{r}
1 \\
7\,9 \\
8\,0\,2\, - \\
4\,6\,5\, = \\
\hline
3\,3\,7
\end{array}
$$

1. **Units Column**: Start with the rightmost column. 2 (in 802) is smaller than 5 (in 465), so we need to borrow. We turn the 0 in the tens place of 802 into a 9 and add 10 to the 2, making it 12. Now, 12 - 5 = 7.
2. **Tens Column**: After borrowing, we have 9 in the tens place of 802. 9 - 6 = 3.
3. **Hundreds Column**: Move to the leftmost column. 8 - 4 = 4.
4. **The difference is 337.**

Advanced Concepts

- **Subtraction of Decimals:** Align the decimal points and proceed with the subtraction as with whole numbers. Borrowing applies across the decimal point in the same way as with whole numbers.

- **Subtraction of Fractions:** Ensure the fractions have a common denominator, then subtract the numerators while keeping the denominator the same. Simplify the fraction if possible.

MULTIPLICATION

Multiplication is a fundamental arithmetic operation that simplifies the process of repeated addition. It involves combining equal groups to find the total quantity. In essence, to multiply means to add a number to itself a certain number of times, as specified by another number. The symbols commonly used to denote multiplication are "×" or "*".

How Multiplication is Done
Multiplication can be performed with various types of numbers: whole numbers, fractions, decimals, and even negative numbers. The numbers involved in multiplication are called "factors," and the result of multiplying these factors is known as the "product." In its simplest form, multiplication combines two factors, but it can involve several factors.

For example, multiplying 3 by 4 (written as 3 × 4) means adding 3 to itself 4 times: 3 + 3 + 3 + 3, which equals 12. Thus, the product of 3 and 4 is 12.

Multiplication Example
Suppose I have 122 packs of pills, and each pack contains 12. How many pills will I have in total?

```
  1  2  2  x
        1  2
  2  4  4  +
1  2  2
1  4  6  4
```

1. Multiply the number 122 by 2 (the unit digit of 12). That gives us 244.
2. Multiply the number 122 by 1 (the tens digit of 12), but since it's in the tens place, you actually multiply by 10, making it equivalent to multiplying by 120. This gives us 1220.
3. Add the two products together: 244 (step 1) + 1220 (step 2) equals 1464.
4. So, the result of multiplying 122 by 12 is 1464.

Rules of Multiplication

1. **Commutative Property:** Multiplication is commutative; changing the order of the factors does not change the product. For instance, 4×5 equals 5×4.
2. **Associative Property:** Multiplication is associative; when multiplying three or more numbers, the way the numbers are grouped does not affect the product. For example, $(2 \times 3) \times 4$ equals $2 \times (3 \times 4)$.
3. **Distributive Property:** Multiplication over addition follows the distributive property. For instance, $3 \times (4 + 5)$ equals $(3 \times 4) + (3 \times 5)$.
4. **Multiplication by One:** Any number multiplied by one remains unchanged. For example, 7×1 equals 7.
5. **Multiplication by Zero:** Any number multiplied by zero results in zero. For example, 9×0 equals 0.
6. **Multiplying Negative Numbers:** The product of two negative numbers is positive, while the product of a positive number and a negative number is negative. For example, $(-3) \times (-4)$ equals 12, and $(-3) \times 4$ equals -12.

Multiplication Table for 10 Numbers

A multiplication table is a useful tool for quickly finding the product of two numbers. Here is the multiplication table for numbers 1 through 10:

X	1	2	3	4	5	6	7	8	9	10
1	1	2	3	4	5	6	7	8	9	10
2	2	4	6	8	10	12	14	16	18	20
3	3	6	9	12	15	18	21	24	27	30
4	4	8	12	16	20	24	28	32	36	40
5	5	10	15	20	25	30	35	40	45	50
6	6	12	18	24	30	36	42	48	54	60
7	7	14	21	28	35	42	49	56	63	70
8	8	16	24	32	40	48	56	64	72	80
9	9	18	27	36	45	54	63	72	81	90
10	10	20	30	40	50	60	70	80	90	100

DIVISION

Division is one of the four fundamental operations in arithmetic, serving as the counterpart to multiplication. It involves splitting a quantity (the dividend) into a specified number of equal parts (the divisor), resulting in a quotient. Division can be conceptualized as the process of determining how many times one number is contained within another or how a quantity can be evenly distributed.

How Division is Done

Division can be applied to various types of numbers, including whole numbers, fractions, and decimals. The process differs slightly depending on the nature of the numbers involved, but the basic principle remains the same: dividing the dividend by the divisor to obtain the quotient. For whole numbers, division may also result in a remainder if the division is not exact.

For example, dividing 20 by 4 (written as $20 \div 4$ or $\frac{20}{4}$) asks how many times 4 is contained within 20, which is 5 times. Thus, the quotient is 5.

Division Example

Suppose we want to divide the following numbers: 78 by 5. Below, I will explain the process of dividing these two numbers.

```
7  8  |  5
5           1  5
2  8
2  5
   3
```

1. **Divide**: Look at the first digit of 78. Since 5 doesn't go into 7 evenly, you consider the first two digits, 78. Five goes into 78 a total of 15 times, because 5 times 15 is 75.
2. **Multiply**: Multiply 15 (the quotient) by 5 (the divisor) to get 75.
3. **Subtract**: Subtract 75 from 78 to get 3.
4. **Bring down**: Since there are no more digits to bring down, you're left with a remainder of 3.

So, when you divide 78 by 5, you get a quotient of 15 with a remainder of 3. In decimal form, this operation would require you to extend the division to include tenths, hundredths, etc., until you reach a stopping point or a repeating decimal pattern. But simply put, 78 divided by 5 gives you 15 with a remainder of 3, or 15.6 as a decimal.

Rules of Division

1. **Non-Commutative Nature**: Unlike addition and multiplication, division is not commutative; changing the order of the numbers changes the result. For instance, $10 \div 2$ does not equal $2 \div 10$.
2. **Division by One:** Dividing any number by one leaves the number unchanged. For example, $9 \div 1$ equals 9.
3. **Division by Zero:** Division by zero is undefined. For instance, $5 \div 0$ has no meaning in standard arithmetic, as no number can be multiplied by zero to yield 5.
4. **Zero Divided by Any Number:** Zero divided by any non-zero number is always zero. For example, $0 \div 5$ equals 0.
5. **Dividing Negative Numbers:** The quotient of two negative numbers is positive, while the quotient of a positive number and a negative number (or vice versa) is negative. For example, $(-10) \div (-2)$ equals 5, and $10 \div (-2)$ equals -5.

Division Techniques

- **Long Division:** This method involves a step-by-step process where the dividend is divided by the divisor one digit at a time, subtracting the product of the divisor and the current quotient digit from the part of the dividend considered at each step.
- **Short Division:** A simpler form of long division suitable for simpler problems or when the divisor is a single digit.
- **Division with Remainders:** When the dividend does not divide evenly by the divisor, the division results in a quotient and a remainder. For example, $13 \div 4$ equals 3 with a remainder of 1.
- **Division of Fractions:** To divide by a fraction, multiply by its reciprocal. For instance, dividing by $\frac{1}{2}$ (which is $1 \div 2$) is the same as multiplying by its reciprocal, $\frac{2}{1}$.

EXPONENTS

Exponents, a fundamental concept in mathematics, represent a compact and powerful way to express repeated multiplication of the same number. An exponent denotes how many times a base number is multiplied by itself. For instance, in the expression 53 (read as "five to the power of three" or "five cubed"), the base is 5, and the exponent is 3, indicating that 5 is multiplied by itself three times: $5 \times 5 \times 5 = 125$

How Exponents Work

The operation involving exponents consists of two main components: the base and the exponent. The base is the number being multiplied, and the exponent tells us how many times the base is used as a factor in the multiplication.

The expression a^n, where

- **a** is the base
- **n** is the exponent

means a multiplied by itself n times.

ORDER OF FOUR FUNDAMENTAL OPERATIONS

The order of the four fundamental operations—addition, subtraction, multiplication, and division—is a cornerstone of arithmetic and essential for solving mathematical expressions correctly. This hierarchy is governed by the convention known as the order of operations, which dictates the sequence in which these operations should be performed to achieve the correct result.

The order of operations is commonly remembered by the acronym **PEMDAS**, which stands for

Parentheses, Exponents, Multiplication and Division (from left to right), and **Addition and Subtraction** (from left to right). This rule ensures that calculations are performed in a standardized manner, preventing ambiguity in mathematical expressions.

- **Parentheses (P):** Operations enclosed in parentheses are performed first. If an expression contains nested parentheses, the innermost set is solved first, moving outward. This rule also applies to brackets and braces.
- **Exponents (E):** Once parentheses are resolved, attention shifts to exponents, including powers and roots. These operations are executed next, before any multiplication, division, addition, or subtraction.
- **Multiplication and Division (MD):** These operations are performed third, proceeding from left to right in the expression. It's crucial to note that multiplication and division are considered equal in the order of operations. Therefore, when they appear together, they are carried out sequentially from left to right, regardless of which comes first.
- **Addition and Subtraction (AS):** Finally, addition and subtraction are performed, also from left to right. Similar to multiplication and division, addition and subtraction are treated as equals in the order of operations hierarchy. When they occur together, they are resolved in the order they appear, from left to right.

Importance of the Order of Operations

Adhering to the order of operations is vital for ensuring the consistency and accuracy of mathematical calculations. Ignoring this order can lead to significant errors and misunderstandings, especially as expressions become more complex. For example, in the expression $3 + 4 \times 2$, applying the order of operations means performing the multiplication first ($4 \times 2 = 8$), then the addition ($3 + 8$), yielding 11 as the correct result. Neglecting the order and adding 3 and 4 first would incorrectly give 14.

FRACTIONS DECIMALS PERCENTAGES RATIO AND PROPORTIONS

Fractions and decimals are two essential representations of numbers that fall between whole numbers, expressing parts of a whole. A fraction is composed of two integers - a numerator displayed above a line (or slash), and a denominator below. For example, $\frac{3}{4}$ represents three parts out of four equal parts of a whole. Decimals, on the other hand, use a point to separate the whole number part from the fractional part, such as 0.75, which is another way to represent, $\frac{3}{4}$. Both forms are interchangeable and widely used in various contexts, offering flexibility in mathematical calculations and problem-solving.

FRACTIONS

Fractions represent a way to express parts of a whole, a concept integral to mathematics and its applications in various fields. A fraction consists of two parts: a numerator, indicating the number of parts considered, and a denominator, signifying the total number of equal parts into which the whole is divided. The fraction is written with the numerator above a horizontal line (or slash) and the denominator below, as in, $\frac{3}{4}$ which reads as "three fourths" or "three over four."

Understanding Fractions

Fractions are used when whole numbers are insufficient to describe quantities that are less than one or between two whole numbers. They are essential in measuring, cooking, and numerous scientific calculations, providing precision in representing parts of a whole.

Basic Operations with Fractions

Fractions can be added, subtracted, multiplied, and divided, but these operations follow specific rules:

- **Addition and Subtraction:** To add or subtract fractions, they must have a common denominator. If they don't, you must first find the least common denominator (**LCD**), convert the fractions to have this common denominator, and then add or subtract the numerators. For example, to add $\frac{1}{4}$ and $\frac{1}{3}$, convert to a common denominator of 12, resulting in $\frac{3}{12} + \frac{4}{12} = \frac{7}{12}$

- **Multiplication:** To multiply fractions, simply multiply the numerators together and the denominators together. For example, $\frac{2}{3} \times \frac{3}{4} = \frac{6}{12}$, which can be simplified to $\frac{1}{2}$

- **Division:** To divide fractions, multiply the first fraction by the reciprocal of the second. For example, $\frac{3}{4} \div \frac{2}{3} = \frac{3}{4} \times \frac{3}{2} = \frac{9}{8}$

Simplifying Fractions

Simplifying fractions involves reducing them to their simplest form, where the numerator and denominator are the smallest integers possible. This is done by dividing both the numerator and the denominator by their greatest common divisor (GCD). For instance, $\frac{8}{12}$ can be simplified to $\frac{2}{3}$ by dividing both the numerator and denominator by 4.

Mixed Numbers and Improper Fractions

A mixed number combines a whole number with a fraction, such as $2\frac{1}{2}$, representing two whole units and half of another. An improper fraction, where the numerator is larger than the denominator (like $\frac{5}{2}$), can also express this quantity. Converting between these forms is a common practice in mathematics, especially in calculations involving measurements.

Rules of Fractions

Understanding the properties and rules governing fractions is crucial:

1. **Equivalent Fractions**: Different fractions can represent the same quantity, such as $\frac{1}{2}$, $\frac{2}{4}$, and $\frac{3}{6}$. Multiplying or dividing both the numerator and denominator by the same number creates these equivalent fractions.

2. **Comparing Fractions**: To compare fractions, they must have a common denominator. The fraction with the larger numerator is greater if the denominators are the same.

Determining which fraction is smaller or larger involves comparing their values. Here's how you can do it:

1. **Common Denominator Method**: The most straightforward way to compare fractions is to convert them to have a common denominator. Once the fractions have the same denominator, the fraction with the larger numerator is the larger fraction. For example, to compare $\frac{3}{4}$ and $\frac{5}{6}$, you might convert them to have a common denominator of 12, resulting in $\frac{9}{12}$ and $\frac{10}{12}$ respectively. Since $\frac{10}{12}$ has the larger numerator, $\frac{5}{6}$ is the larger fraction.

2. **Cross-Multiplication**: Another method is cross-multiplication, which doesn't require finding a common denominator. You cross-multiply the fractions, meaning you multiply the numerator of the first fraction by the denominator of the second and vice versa. If the product from the first fraction is larger, then the first fraction is larger. For instance, comparing $\frac{3}{4}$ and $\frac{5}{6}$, you would calculate 3×6 and 4×5. Since 18>20 is false, $\frac{3}{4}$ is smaller than $\frac{5}{6}$.

3. **Visual Representation**: For simpler fractions, drawing a visual representation can help. If you divide a shape into equal parts and shade the corresponding number of parts for each fraction, the fraction that covers more of the shape is the larger fraction.

4. **Decimal Conversion**: Converting fractions to decimals provides a direct comparison. Divide the numerator by the denominator for each fraction and compare the decimal values. The larger decimal corresponds to the larger fraction. For example, $\frac{3}{4}$ =0.75 and 6 ≈ 0.833. Since 0.833 is greater than 0.75, $\frac{5}{6}$ is the larger fraction.

DECIMALS

Decimals are a method of expressing fractions and real numbers that are not whole numbers, using a base-10 system. A decimal number is composed of a whole number part and a fractional part, separated by a decimal point (in many countries, a comma is used). For example, in the decimal 23.45, 23 is the whole number part, and 45 is the fractional part, representing $\frac{45}{1000}$.

Understanding Decimals

The position of a digit in a decimal number determines its value. Immediately to the right of the decimal point are the tenths, followed by the hundredths, thousandths, and so on, each position representing a successive power of $\frac{1}{10}$. For instance, in 0.789, 7 is in the tenths place, 8 is in the hundredths place, and 9 is in the thousandths place, meaning the number is equivalent to $\frac{7}{10}$ + $\frac{8}{100}$ + $\frac{9}{1000}$.

Operations with Decimals

Decimals can be added, subtracted, multiplied, and divided using rules similar to those for whole numbers, with special attention to the placement of the decimal point.

1. **Addition and Subtraction**: To add or subtract decimals, align the decimal points and then proceed as with whole numbers. Adjust the numbers by adding zeros if necessary to ensure each number has the same number of digits after the decimal point.

2. **Multiplication**: When multiplying decimals, ignore the decimal points and multiply the numbers as if they were whole numbers. Then, in the product, place the decimal point so that the number of digits after it is equal to the sum of the digits after the decimal points in the factors.

3. **Division**: To divide by a decimal, you must first convert the divisor into a whole number by "moving" the decimal point to the right. You must then move the decimal point in the dividend the same number of places to the right, ensuring the quotient reflects the correct value.

Rules of Decimals

Decimals follow certain rules that help in their manipulation and understanding:

- **Zeroes at the End**: Adding zeroes to the end of a decimal does not change its value. For example, 0.80 is the same as 0.8.

- **Zeroes at the Beginning**: Zeroes before the first non-zero digit in the fractional part do not add value but indicate precision. For example, 0.05 is five hundredths.

- **Repeating Decimals**: Some fractions, when converted into decimals, result in an infinitely repeating pattern of digits. These are denoted by a line or dot over the repeating digits. For instance, $\frac{1}{3}$ is represented as 0.333..., with the 3s repeating indefinitely.

Converting Between Fractions and Decimals

Conversion between fractions and decimals is a common task. To convert a fraction to a decimal, divide the numerator by the denominator. To convert a decimal to a fraction, consider the place value of the last digit, use it as the denominator (with the corresponding power of 10), and the entire decimal sequence as the numerator, simplifying if possible.

Converting a Fraction to a Decimal

Example: Convert the fraction $\frac{3}{4}$ to a decimal.

- Step 1: Understand the fraction. The fraction $\frac{3}{4}$ means 3 divided by 4.

- Step 2: Perform the division. Divide the numerator (3) by the denominator (4) using long division or a calculator.

- Step 3: Write the result. Dividing 3 by 4 gives 0.75. So, $\frac{3}{4}$ =0.75.

Converting a Decimal to a Fraction

Example: Convert the decimal 0.25 to a fraction.

- Step 1: Understand the decimal. The decimal 0.25 represents 25 hundredths or 25 parts out of 100.

- Step 2: Write as a fraction. Knowing that "hundredths" means $\frac{25}{100}$, you can start with the fraction

- Step 3: Simplify the fraction. Both the numerator (25) and the denominator (100) can be divided by 25, which simplifies the fraction to $\frac{1}{4}$

- So, 0.25 equals $\frac{1}{4}$ in fraction form.

PERCENTAGES

Percentages are a versatile and widely used mathematical concept that express numbers as a fraction of 100. The term "percent" comes from the Latin "per centum," meaning "by the hundred." The symbol for percent is "%." For example, saying "25%" is equivalent to stating "25 per 100".

Understanding Percentages

Percentages offer a way to compare quantities of different sizes on a common scale and are fundamental in expressing proportions, ratios, and fractions in a more understandable format. For instance, saying that 50% of a class passed an exam gives a clear picture that half of the class succeeded, irrespective of the class size.

Calculating Percentages

Calculating percentages involves understanding three key components: the part, the whole, and the percentage. The basic formula for finding the percentage is:

$$\text{Percentage} = \left(\frac{Part}{Whole}\right) \times 100$$

- **Finding the Percentage**: To find what percentage one number is of another, divide the "part" by the "whole" and then multiply by 100. For example, to find what percentage 20 is of 80, divide 20 by 80 and multiply by 100, which equals 25%.

- **Finding the Part**: To find the part when the whole and the percentage are known, multiply the whole by the percentage (expressed as a decimal). For instance, to find 30% of 150, multiply 150 by 0.30, which gives 45.

- **Finding the Whole**: To find the whole when the part and the percentage are known, divide the part by the percentage (expressed as a decimal). For example, if 40 is 25% of a number, divide 40 by 0.25 to get 160.

Rules of Percentages

Several rules simplify calculations and manipulations involving percentages:

1. **Percent Increase and Decrease**: To calculate a percent increase, subtract the original number from the new number, divide by the original number, and multiply by 100. The process is similar for a percent decrease, but you start with the decreased amount.
2. **Converting Between Percentages and Decimals**: To convert a percentage to a decimal, divide by 100. To convert a decimal to a percentage, multiply by 100.
3. **More than 100%**: Percentages can exceed 100%, indicating more than the whole. For example, 150% of a number is one and a half times the whole.
4. **Compound Percentages**: Applying multiple percentage changes sequentially involves calculating each change based on the previous result, not the original amount.

PROPORTIONS

Proportions are mathematical expressions that denote the equality of two ratios or fractions. They are fundamental in understanding how different quantities relate to each other in terms of size, quantity, or scale. A proportion states that two ratios are equivalent, allowing for the comparison of parts to wholes across different contexts. The notation **a:b = c:d (read as "a is to b as c is to d")** embodies the concept of proportion, where a and d are the extremes, and b and c are the means.

Understanding Proportions

At the heart of proportions is the concept of similarity and equivalence. When we say two ratios are proportional, we mean that they scale or resize by the same factor. For instance, if the ratio of boys to girls in one class is the same as the ratio in another class, we can say the gender distribution is proportional between the two classes.

Setting Up Proportions

To solve problems involving proportions, one typically sets up an equation that represents the equality of two ratios. For example, if 3 out of 4 apples are red, and you have 12 apples in total, you can set up the proportion $\frac{3}{4} = \frac{x}{12}$ to find out how many apples are red. Solving the proportion gives the value of x, which represents the part of the second ratio that corresponds to the part of the first.

Rules of Proportions

Several rules and properties are crucial for working with proportions:

1. **Cross Multiplication**: The most common method to solve proportions is cross multiplication, which involves multiplying the means and then the extremes. If a:b = c:d, then ad = bc. This property allows for the easy calculation of unknown variables in a proportion.
2. **Inverse Proportions**: In some cases, quantities are inversely proportional, meaning as one quantity increases, the other decreases at a rate that maintains a constant product. This is expressed as ab = k, where k is a constant.
3. **Unitary Method**: This involves finding the value of a single unit (1) from a given proportion and then scaling up to find the value corresponding to a larger quantity. It is particularly useful in problems involving rates or prices.
4. **Scaling Up and Down**: Proportions allow for the scaling of quantities. If you know the ratio and one quantity, you can scale up or down to find equivalent amounts in different situations.

EQUATIONS

Equations are mathematical statements asserting the equality of two expressions, typically involving variables and constants. Solving an equation entails finding the value(s) of the variable(s) that make the statement true. Equations are solved by manipulating the expressions on either side of the equals sign to isolate the variable.

Types of equations vary in complexity, from simple linear equations (e.g.,2x+3=7), where the variable is raised to the power of one, to quadratic equations (ax2 +bx+c=0), and more complex polynomial, exponential, and logarithmic equations, each requiring specific methods for finding solutions.

ONE-STEP LINEAR EQUATIONS

One-step linear equations are the simplest form of linear equations, involving a single operation to solve for the variable. These equations are structured around the basic arithmetic operations: addition, subtraction, multiplication, or division. The primary characteristic of one-step linear equations is that they require only one step to isolate the variable and find its value, making them an essential foundational concept in algebra.

Understanding One-Step Linear Equations

A one-step linear equation looks like $ax=b$, $x+a=b$, $x-a=b$, or $\frac{x}{a} = b$, where x is the variable we aim to solve for, and a and b are known constants. The equation expresses a balance between two expressions: whatever operation is applied to one side must also be applied to the other to maintain equality.

Solving One-Step Linear Equations

The solution involves performing the inverse operation to both sides of the equation to isolate the variable on one side. Here's how it's done for each type of operation:

1. **Addition**: If the equation involves adding a number to the variable, such as $x+a=b$, subtract a from both sides to isolate x. The solution will be $x=b-a$.

2. **Subtraction**: If the equation involves subtracting a number from the variable, such as $x-a=b$, add a to both sides to isolate x. The solution will be $x=b+a$.

3. **Multiplication**: For equations where the variable is multiplied by a number, $ax=b$, divide both sides by a to solve for x. The solution is $x = \frac{b}{a}$.

4. **Division**: If the variable is divided by a number, $\frac{a}{x} = b$, multiply both sides by a to isolate x. The solution is $x = \frac{a}{b}$.

Example Problems
- **Addition**: Solve $x+4=10$. Subtract 4 from both sides to get $x=10-4$, hence $x=6$.
- **Subtraction**: Solve $x-5=3$. Add 5 to both sides to find $x=3+5$, resulting in $x=8$.
- **Multiplication**: Solve $3x=12$. Divide both sides by 3, yielding $x= \frac{12}{3}$, so $x=4$.
- **Division**: Solve $\frac{x}{2} =5$. Multiply both sides by 2 to get $x=5\times2$, which gives $x=10$.

Tips for Solving One-Step Linear Equations
1. Ensure you perform the inverse operation on both sides of the equation to maintain balance.
2. Check your solution by substituting the value of x back into the original equation to see if it holds true.
3. Practice with a variety of equations to become familiar with different scenarios and inverse operations.

TWO-STEP LINEAR EQUATIONS

Two-step linear equations are slightly more complex than one-step equations as they require two operations to isolate the variable and solve the equation. These equations typically involve a combination of addition or subtraction and multiplication or division. The structure of a two-step linear equation might look like ax+b=c or a(x+b)=c, where a, b, and c are constants, and x is the variable we aim to solve for.

Understanding Two-Step Linear Equations

The essence of two-step linear equations lies in performing two inverse operations in a specific order to isolate the variable. The goal is to "undo" what has been done to the variable, step by step, to get the variable x on one side of the equation and its solution on the other. The presence of two operations makes these equations a crucial step in building algebraic problem-solving skills.

Solving Two-Step Linear Equations

The process of solving two-step linear equations generally follows these steps:

1. **Eliminate the Constant Term:** The first step usually involves getting rid of the addition or subtraction term that is not attached to the variable. This is done by performing the inverse operation on both sides of the equation. For instance, if 5x+7=22, you would subtract 7 from both sides to eliminate the constant term: 5x+7−7=22−7, simplifying to 5x=15.
2. **Isolate the Variable**: Once the constant term is eliminated, the next step is to isolate the variable by performing the inverse of the multiplication or division operation. Continuing with the example 5x=15, you would divide both sides by 5 to solve for x: $\frac{5x}{5} = \frac{15}{5}$, resulting in x=3.

Example Problems

- Solve 2x−4=10: First, add 4 to both sides to eliminate the constant term: 2x−4+4=10+4, simplifying to 2x=14. Next, divide both sides by 2 to isolate x=7.
- Solve $\frac{x}{3}$ +5=8: Start by subtracting 5 from both sides to remove the constant term: $\frac{x}{3}$ =3. Then, multiply both sides by 3 to isolate x: x=9.

Tips for Solving Two-Step Linear Equations

1. Always perform the same operation on both sides of the equation to maintain equality.
2. Keep track of positive and negative signs, especially when dealing with subtraction or when negative numbers are involved.
3. After solving the equation, check your solution by substituting the value of x back into the original equation to verify its accuracy.

STANDARD UNIT OF MEASUREMENT

The standard unit of measurement provides a consistent reference for quantifying physical properties such as length, mass, volume, and temperature. Globally, the International System of Units (SI) is recognized as the official standard, comprising basic units like the meter for length, kilogram for mass, second for time, and Kelvin for temperature. These standards ensure uniformity and precision in measurements across different regions and disciplines, facilitating scientific research, trade, and daily activities. Adopting standard units eliminates confusion and enhances communication, enabling accurate comparison and replication of measurements in various contexts.

LENGT CONVERSION

Length conversion involves changing a measurement from one unit of length to another within the same system of measurement, such as converting from centimeters to meters, or between systems, like converting inches to centimeters. Understanding how to convert between these units is crucial in fields ranging from construction and manufacturing to science and everyday life, ensuring clear communication and precision.

How Length Conversion Works

Length conversion is based on predefined equivalence between different units of length. In the metric system, units are based on powers of 10, making conversions straightforward. For example, 1 meter (m) is equal to 100 centimeters (cm), 1000 millimeters (mm), and so forth. To convert from a larger unit to a smaller unit, you multiply by a factor of 10 for each step down. Conversely, to convert from a smaller unit to a larger unit, you divide by the same factor.

Example: Converting Centimeters to Meters

Suppose you want to convert 150 centimeters to meters.

1. Identify the conversion factor: Since 1 meter is equal to 100 centimeters, the conversion factor from centimeters to meters is $\frac{1}{100}$.
2. Apply the conversion factor: Divide the number of centimeters by 100 to find the equivalent length in meters.
3. Perform the conversion: $150 \text{cm} \div 100 = 1.5 \text{m}$

Thus, 150 centimeters is equal to 1.5 meters.

Metric Units of Length

Here's a table of common metric units of length, from smallest to largest, along with their equivalences:

UNIT	ABBREVIATION	EQUIVALENT IN METERS (M)
Millimeter	mm	0.001m
Centimeter	cm	0.01 m
Decimeter	dm	0.1 m
Meter	m	1 m
Decameter	dam	10 m
Hectometer	hm	100 m
Kilometer	km	1000 m

This table is instrumental for performing conversions within the metric system by moving the decimal point the appropriate number of places based on the unit.

Additional Tips for Length Conversion
- **Remember the prefixes:** Metric units use prefixes to denote different scales, with each prefix representing a power of 10. Familiarizing yourself with these can make conversions more intuitive.
- **Use conversion tools for non-metric units:** When converting between metric and non-metric units (like inches to centimeters), it's often easiest to use a conversion tool or formula, as these conversions are not based on powers of 10.
- **Practice with real-world examples:** Applying what you've learned to real-life situations, such as measuring objects or distances, can reinforce your understanding and ability to convert between units.

IMPERIAL MEASUREMENT SYSTEM

The system of measurement involving feet, yards, and other non-metric units is commonly known as the Imperial or US customary system. This system is predominantly used in the United States and a few other countries for everyday measurements. Unlike the metric system, which is based on powers of 10, the Imperial system uses predefined conversion factors between units that are not as straightforward.

Understanding the Imperial System of Length
In the Imperial system, units of length include inches, feet, yards, and miles, among others. Each unit has a specific conversion factor relative to the others. For instance, there are 12 inches in a foot, 3 feet in a yard, and 1,760 yards in a mile.

Key Units and Conversions

1. **Inch (in):** The inch is a small unit of length used for measuring lengths and distances comparable to the width of a human thumb.
2. **Foot (ft):** One foot consists of 12 inches. The foot is commonly used for measuring height, shorter distances, and objects.
3. **Yard (yd):** One yard equals 3 feet or 36 inches. Yards are used in measuring larger areas, like fields or fabric lengths.
4. **Mile (mi):** One mile is equivalent to 5,280 feet or 1,760 yards. Miles are used for long distances, such as in road measurements.

Example: Converting Feet to Yards

To illustrate, let's convert 10 feet to yards.

1. **Identify the conversion factor:** Since 1 yard is equal to 3 feet, the conversion factor from feet to yards is $\frac{1}{3}$.
2. **Apply the conversion factor:** Divide the number of feet by 3 to find the equivalent length in yards.
3. **Perform the conversion:** 10ft÷3=3.3yd

Therefore, 10 feet is approximately 3.33 yards.

Table of Imperial Length Units

Here's a simplified table outlining the relationship between common Imperial units of length:

UNIT	EQUALS
1 Inch	1/12 Foot
1 Foot	12 Inches
1 Yard	3 Feet / 36 Inches
1 Mile	1,760 Yards / 5,280 Feet

Tips for Using the Imperial System

- Memorize key conversions: Knowing the basic conversions by heart can significantly streamline calculations.
- Use conversion tools for complex conversions: For conversions between the metric and Imperial systems or for large quantities, using a conversion calculator or tool can ensure accuracy.
- Practice with real-world examples: Applying these conversions to everyday situations, such as measuring rooms, distances, or objects, can reinforce understanding and proficiency.

SECTION 1 - MATHEMATICS 37

VOLUME AND WEIGHT CONVERSION

Volume and weight conversion is the process of changing measurements from one unit to another within the same category (volume or weight) or between the two. These conversions are crucial in various fields, including cooking, science, and international trade, ensuring accuracy and standardization.

Volume Conversion

Volume measures the space occupied by a substance or object, commonly expressed in liters, milliliters, gallons, quarts, pints, and cups, among other units. The metric system (liters, milliliters) and the Imperial/US customary system (gallons, quarts, pints, cups) are the two main systems used for volume measurements.

Example: Converting Liters to Gallons

Suppose you want to convert 5 liters to gallons.

1. **Identify the conversion factor:** 1 liter is approximately equal to 0.264172 gallons.
2. **Apply the conversion factor:** Multiply the number of liters by the conversion factor to find the equivalent volume in gallons.
3. **Perform the conversion:** 5L × 0.264172 gallons/L = 1.32086 gallons

Thus, 5 liters is approximately equal to 1.32 gallons.

Weight Conversion

Weight measures the heaviness of an object, commonly expressed in kilograms, grams, pounds, and ounces. Like volume, weight conversion can occur within the same system or between metric and Imperial/US customary systems.

Example: Converting Pounds to Kilograms

To convert 10 pounds to kilograms:

1. **Identify the conversion factor:** 1 pound is approximately equal to 0.453592 kilograms.
2. **Apply the conversion factor:** Multiply the number of pounds by the conversion factor to find the equivalent weight in kilograms.
3. **Perform the conversion:** 10lb × 0.453592kg/lb = 4.53592kg

Therefore, 10 pounds is approximately equal to 4.54 kilograms.

Hesi A2 Study Guide

Table of Common Volume and Weight Measurements

Here's a simplified table outlining some common volume and weight units and their equivalences:

Volume Unit:

METRIC	US CUSTOMARY
1 Liter (L)	0.264172 Gallons (gal)
1 Milliliter (mL)	0.033814 Ounces (oz)

Weight Unit:

METRIC	US CUSTOMARY
1 Kilogram (kg)	2.20462 Pounds (lb)
1 Gram (g)	0.035274 Ounces (oz)

Tips for Volume and Weight Conversion

- **Use conversion tools for accuracy:** Especially for complex conversions or when precision is crucial, using a digital conversion tool or calculator can ensure accuracy.
- **Understand the context:** Some conversions might require additional considerations, such as the density of a substance when converting between volume and weight.
- **Practice with real-life examples:** Applying conversions to everyday scenarios, such as cooking, shopping, or science experiments, can reinforce understanding and accuracy.

TEMPERATURE CONVERSION

Temperature conversion is essential in various contexts, including cooking, weather reporting, and scientific research, to understand and communicate temperature readings accurately across different measurement systems. The three primary temperature scales used globally are Celsius (°C), Fahrenheit (°F), and Kelvin (K). Each scale has its application areas, with Celsius commonly used in most countries, Fahrenheit primarily in the United States, and Kelvin in scientific contexts.

How Temperature Conversion Works

Converting temperatures between Celsius, Fahrenheit, and Kelvin involves specific formulas that account for the scales' starting points and the size of their degrees. The formulas for converting between these scales are as follows:

- **Celsius to Fahrenheit:** $°F=(°C×9/5)+32$

- **Fahrenheit to Celsius:** $°C=(°F-32)×5/9$

- **Celsius to Kelvin:** $K=°C+273.15$

- **Kelvin to Celsius:** $°C=K-273.15$

- **Fahrenheit to Kelvin:** $K=(°F-32)×5/9+273.15$

- **Kelvin to Fahrenheit:** $°F=(K-273.15)×9/5+32$

Example: Converting Celsius to Fahrenheit and Kelvin

Suppose you have a temperature of 25°C and want to convert it to Fahrenheit and Kelvin.

Celsius to Fahrenheit
1. Apply the conversion formula: Use $°F=(°C×9/5)+32$.
2. Substitute the given value: Plug 25°C into the formula to get $°F=(25×9/5)+32$.
3. Calculate: Perform the multiplication and addition to find $°F=45+32=77°F$.

Thus, 25°C is equivalent to 77°F.

Celsius to Kelvin
1. Apply the conversion formula: Use $K=°C+273.15$.
2. Substitute the given value: Plug 25°C into the formula to get $K=25+273.15$.
3. Calculate: Add to find $K=298.15$.

Therefore, 25°C is equivalent to 298.15K.

Table of Temperature Conversion Formulas

FROM / TO	Celsius (°C)	Fahrenheit (°F)	Kelvin (K)
Celsius (°C)	-	$°F=(°C×9/5)+32$	$K=°C+273.15$
Fahrenheit (°F)	$°C=(°F-32)×5/9$	-	$K=(°F-32)×5/9+273.15$
Kelvin (K)	$°C=K-273.15$	$°F=(K-273.15)×9/5+32$	-

Tips for Temperature Conversion
- **Remember the conversion formulas:** Familiarize yourself with the basic formulas for converting temperatures between Celsius, Fahrenheit, and Kelvin.
- **Use conversion tools for convenience:** For quick conversions, especially in complex calculations, digital temperature conversion tools or calculators can be very helpful.
- **Practice with real-world examples:** Apply these conversions to situations like cooking recipes from different countries, interpreting weather forecasts, or conducting experiments to reinforce understanding.

SECTION 1 - MATHEMATICS PRACTICE QUIZ

1 - Simplify the fraction $\frac{18}{24}$ to its lowest terms.

A. $\frac{7}{8}$

B. $\frac{4}{5}$

C. $\frac{3}{4}$

2 - Solve for x in the equation 3x−5=16.
A. x = 7
B. x = 3
C. x = 12
D. x = 1

3 - Convert 25% to a decimal
A. 0.25
B. 0.025
C. 2.5
D. 0.205

4 - In a classroom, the ratio of boys to girls is 3:2. If there are 15 boys, how many girls are there?
A. 10
B. 14
C. 11
D. 6

5 - What is the result of multiplying 14 x 31?
A. 343
B. 434
C. 424
D. 433

6 - What is 888 minus 331?

A. 550

B. 553

C. 555

D. 557

7 - If a surgical caps costs $60 and is on sale for 20% off, what is the sale price?

A. 42

B. 38

C. 48

D. 12

8 - What is 12345 ÷ 123?

A. 100

B. 94.25

C. 100.36

D. 105

9 - Convert 100°F to Celsius

A. 33.12°C

B. 37.78°C

C. 42.58°C

D. 37.99°C

10 - Add 1.25 and 2.75

A. 4

B. 4.25

C. 3.75

D. 3

11 - Convert 80 grams to ounces

A. 2.12 oz

B. 4.22 oz

C. 142.08 oz

D. 2.82 oz

12 - Solve for x if 4x+16=40

A. 6.5

B. 6

C. 12

D. 3

13 - A package of syringes costs $30 and contains 12 syringes. How much does a single syringe cost?

A. 2

B. 2.5

C. 3

D. 3.5

14 - Add $3\frac{1}{2}$ **and** $2\frac{2}{3}$

A. $6\frac{1}{6}$

B. $2\frac{2}{5}$

C. 12

15 - Every day, a warehouse employee dispatches 25 boxes, each adorned with 3 shipping labels. Given a stock of 500 shipping labels, how long will it take to deplete this supply? Please provide the answer rounded to the nearest full day.

A. 7

B. 9

C. 6

D. 5

16 - When you roll a die, what is the probability of getting a 6?

A. 10%

B. 14%

C. 16.6%

D. 6.6%

17 - What is the 65% of 865.12

A. 302.8

B. 305

C. 312.9

D. 298.12

18 - Solve for x if 12 +3x=40

A. 9.18

B. 5.32

C. 9.33

D. 10.5

19 - How many liters in 500 milliliters?

A. 1.5 liters

B. 5 liters

C. 0.5 liters

D. 0.05 liters

20 - Find x: 12:x=41:13

A. 3.2

B. 3.12

C. 3.5

D. 3.8

21 - Solve the equation: 6(x+5)-2 = 5(x-3)+2

A. 41

B. -14

C. -41

D. 12

22 - If quotient is 2 and 6 is the dividend, what is the divisor?

A. 12

B. 6

C. 2

D. 3

23 - If you have to give an injection of 200mg but the medicine you were given is in grams, how many grams of medicine should you give?

A. 0.2

B. 0.002

C. 2

D. 0.02

24 - Round 7.046 to the nearest tenth

A. 6

B. 7

C. 8

D. 10

25 - Convert 30°C to Kelvin.

A. 303.15

B. 303.75

C. 303.25

SECTION 1 - MATHEMATICS PRACTICE QUIZ - ANSWER KEY

1 - Simplify the fraction $\frac{18}{24}$ to its lowest terms.
C) $\frac{3}{4}$

2 - Solve for x in the equation 3x−5=16.
A) x = 7. Add 5 to both sides and then divide by 3, 3x=21 so x=7

3 - Convert 25% to a decimal
A) 0.25. To convert a percentage to a decimal, divide by 100, so $\frac{25}{100}$ =0.25

4 - In a classroom, the ratio of boys to girls is 3:2. If there are 15 boys, how many girls are there?
A) 10 girls. Use the ratio 3:2 to set up a proportion with the boys, $\frac{3 \text{ boys}}{2 \text{ girls}} = \frac{15 \text{ boys}}{x \text{ girls}}$ so x=10

5 - What is the result of multiplying 14 x 31?
B) 434

6 - What is 888 minus 331?
D) 557

7 - If a surgical caps costs $60 and is on sale for 20% off, what is the sale price?
C) 48$. 20% of 60$=12$, so the cost is 60$-12$=48$

8 - What is 12345 ÷ 123?
C) 100.36

9 - Convert 100°F to Celsius
B) 37.78°C. Use the formula °C=(°F-32) x 5/9

10 - Add 1.25 and 2.75
A) 4

11 - Convert 80 grams to ounces
D) 2.82 oz. To convert 80 grams to ounces we need to multiply 80 x 0.03527396194958

12 - Solve for x if 4x+16=40
B) 6

13 - A package of syringes costs \$30 and contains 12 syringes. How much does a single syringe cost?

B) 2.5

14 - Add $3\frac{1}{2}$ **and** $2\frac{2}{3}$

A) $6\frac{1}{6}$ Convert mixed numbers to improper fractions, add, then convert back.

15 - Every day, a warehouse employee dispatches 25 boxes, each adorned with 3 shipping labels. Given a stock of 500 shipping labels, how long will it take to deplete this supply? Please provide the answer rounded to the nearest full day.

A) 7. Each box takes 3 labels, 25 boxes = 75 labels so 500/75= 6.67 = 7

16 - When you roll a die, what is the probability of getting a 6?

C) 16.6%. The die has 6 faces, so it is (1 in 6) %.

17 - What is the 65% of 865.12

A) 302.8

18 - Solve for x if 12 +3x=40

C) 9.33

19 - How many liters in 500 milliliters?

C) 0.5 Liters. To convert from milliliters to liters, simply divide by 1000

20 - Find x: 12:x=41:13

D) 3.8.

21 - Solve the equation: 6(x+5)-2 = 5(x-3)+2

C) -41. First applies the distributive property so 6x+30-2=5x-15+2, So x=-41

22 - If quotient is 2 and 6 is the dividend, what is the divisor?

D) 3

23 - If you have to give an injection of 200mg but the medicine you were given is in grams, how many grams of medicine should you give?

A) 0.2

24 - Round 7.046 to the nearest tenth

B) 7

25 - Convert 30°C to Kelvin

A) 303.15. Use the formula: °K=°C+273.15

SECTION 2 - READING COMPREHENSION

Reading comprehension stands as a cornerstone of the HESI A2 exam, designed to evaluate a candidate's ability to digest, understand, and analyze written information. This capacity is essential not only for academic success in nursing and healthcare programs but also for professional proficiency in these fields, where understanding written instructions, patient records, and scholarly articles is part of daily operations.

This section of your preparation book aims to provide an in-depth overview of the Reading Comprehension section, detailing its structure, the variety of passages presented, and the question formats you will encounter.

STRUCTURE OF THE READING COMPREHENSION SECTION

The Reading Comprehension section is meticulously structured to assess a wide range of skills, from basic understanding to complex analysis and inference. Typically, this section includes multiple passages, each followed by a series of questions related to the text. The number of passages and questions can vary, but the goal remains consistent: to evaluate the test-taker's ability to process written information accurately.

Candidates are expected to demonstrate a comprehensive grasp of the material, including identifying main ideas, key details, and underlying themes. The ability to infer meanings and conclusions from the text is also tested, requiring a deep engagement with the material beyond surface-level understanding.

Types of Passages

The passages included in the Reading Comprehension section cover a broad spectrum of topics, reflecting the diverse reading one might encounter in healthcare education and practice. These can range from narrative passages, which may recount personal experiences or historical events, to expository texts that explain concepts or processes. Technical passages, particularly pertinent to the healthcare field, focus on specific medical or scientific topics, requiring candidates to navigate specialized vocabulary and complex ideas.

The variety ensures that the test assesses general reading skills and the ability to comprehend the types of materials relevant to nursing and healthcare studies. This diversity also means that successful candidates must be versatile readers, comfortable with different styles and subjects.

Question Formats

The questions following each passage are designed to cover a broad range of comprehension skills:

- **Multiple-Choice Questions**: The most common format, where candidates select the best answer from several options. These questions may ask for the main idea of the passage, meanings of words in context, or details about specific points.
- **True/False or Yes/No Questions**: These questions require candidates to judge the accuracy of statements based on the information in the passage.
- **Fill-in-the-Blank:** Occasionally, questions may ask candidates to complete sentences or summaries based on the passage, testing their ability to recall specific details.
- **Sequencing**: Some questions might ask candidates to arrange events or steps in a process in the correct order, assessing their understanding of the passage's structure and logic.

MAIN IDEA

The ability to discern the main idea of a text is a pivotal skill in reading comprehension, especially in the context of the HESI A2 exam. This skill allows readers to grasp the essence of a passage, understand its purpose, and anticipate the author's direction. Identifying the main idea is not just about recognizing explicit statements but also about inferring the underlying theme that ties the passage together. This section delves into strategies to help candidates pinpoint the primary theme or central thought of any passage, thereby enhancing their reading comprehension capabilities for the exam and beyond.

Understand the Structure

Recognizing the structure of a passage is your first step towards identifying its main idea. Most texts follow a logical format where the introduction presents the topic, the body elaborates on it with supporting details, and the conclusion sums it up. Often, the main idea is explicitly stated in the introductory sentences or the conclusion. In cases where it is not directly stated, understanding the structure can guide you towards inferring the main theme.

Look for Repetitive Themes

Authors tend to reiterate the central theme of their text through repeated concepts or keywords throughout the passage. By noting these repetitions, you can gather clues about the main idea. These recurring elements are not mere coincidences but deliberate attempts to emphasize the core message.

Summarize the Passage

Attempt to summarize the passage in your own words, focusing on capturing the essence in a single sentence. This exercise forces you to distill the information presented into its most basic form, shedding light on the main idea. If you struggle to summarize the entire passage in one sentence, you likely haven't fully grasped the primary theme yet.

SUPPORTING DETAILS

Mastering the identification of supporting details is crucial in enhancing reading comprehension skills for the HESI A2 exam and beyond. Supporting details play a vital role in reinforcing, illustrating, or explaining the main idea of a passage. They are the building blocks that flesh out the narrative or argument, providing evidence, examples, explanations, and other elements that give depth and clarity to the central theme. In this section of Chapter 2, we will delve into strategies to help candidates effectively recognize and evaluate these supporting details.

Understand the Relationship Between the Main Idea and Supporting Details

The first step in identifying supporting details is to clearly understand the main idea of the passage. Once the main theme is identified, supporting details can be seen as the evidence that backs up or explains this idea. They are usually presented as facts, statistics, anecdotes, examples, or other forms of data that relate directly to the main idea, providing a foundation for it.

Differentiate Between Main Ideas and Supporting Details

It's crucial to distinguish between the main idea, which is the overarching theme of the passage, and supporting details, which are provided to back up or illustrate the main idea. Supporting details can include examples, statistics, or anecdotes, which, while informative, serve the purpose of reinforcing the main theme rather than representing it.

Look for Signal Words

Authors often use specific signal words or phrases to introduce supporting details. Words such as "for example," "in addition," "furthermore," "specifically," and "for instance," serve as cues that a supporting detail is being presented. Recognizing these signal words can help readers anticipate and identify the information that supports the main idea.

EXAMPLE OF IDENTIFYING ITS MAIN IDEA AND SUPPORTING DETAILS.

Staying hydrated is essential for maintaining good health. The human body consists of about 60% water, which plays a crucial role in various bodily functions, including temperature regulation, joint lubrication, and nutrient transportation. Health experts recommend drinking at least eight glasses of water daily to prevent dehydration, which can lead to tiredness, confusion, and in severe cases, heatstroke. While all fluids contribute to hydration, water is preferable as it provides the necessary hydration without extra calories, sugars, or additives found in other beverages. Additionally, eating fruits and vegetables with high water content, such as cucumbers and watermelons, can also help maintain hydration levels.

Identifying the Main Idea

Main Idea: The primary theme of the passage is the critical importance of staying hydrated for overall health.

The main idea is derived from the passage's focus on explaining why hydration is vital, touching upon the role of water in the body and the consequences of dehydration. The recommendation for daily water intake further emphasizes the central message regarding hydration's significance.

Identifying Supporting Details

- **Bodily Functions**: Water's role in temperature regulation, joint lubrication, and nutrient transportation supports the main idea by detailing how hydration affects bodily functions.
- **Recommendation for Daily Intake**: The specific recommendation to drink at least eight glasses of water daily provides a concrete action supporting the main idea, suggesting how to stay hydrated.
- **Consequences of Dehydration**: Mentioning tiredness, confusion, and heatstroke as possible outcomes of dehydration reinforces the importance of hydration by illustrating the risks of neglecting it.
- **Preference for Water:** The passage notes that, despite all fluids contributing to hydration, water is preferable due to the absence of calories, sugars, or additives, further supporting the main idea by advocating for the healthiest hydration method.
- **Hydrating Foods:** Highlighting fruits and vegetables with high water content as alternatives to direct water intake offers additional support for the main idea, suggesting diverse methods to achieve hydration.
  -

INFERENCES

The ability to make inferences is as critical as understanding directly stated information. Inferences are reasoned conclusions or judgments drawn from evidence and reasoning rather than from explicit statements. This skill allows readers to "read between the lines," understanding the author's intentions, the underlying themes, or the future implications of the present situation, even when these are not directly spelled out. Mastering inference techniques enriches reading comprehension and equips test-takers with the analytical skills necessary for the nuanced understanding required in healthcare settings.

Understand the Context

The first step in making accurate inferences is to fully understand the context of the passage. Context provides the background information necessary to make educated guesses about unstated details. Pay attention to the setting, the tone, and the purpose of the text, as these elements can offer significant clues about the underlying messages.

Analyze the Evidence

Evidence within the text, such as descriptions, actions, dialogue, or events, can serve as a basis for inferences. When making an inference, look for patterns or relationships between pieces of information presented in the passage. Consider how these elements interact and what they suggest about the characters, the situation, or the author's message.

Ask Questions

Asking questions is a powerful strategy for generating inferences. While reading, ask yourself questions like: What is the author implying here? Why did the character act in this way? What could happen next? These questions prompt deeper engagement with the text and encourage the synthesis of information to form inferences.

Use Prior Knowledge

Applying your own experiences and prior knowledge to the information provided in the passage can aid in making inferences. Relating the text to real-world knowledge or similar situations enhances understanding and allows for more accurate conclusions.

CONTEXTUAL MEANING

Understanding the contextual meaning of words or phrases is a pivotal skill. It involves discerning the intended meaning of a word not just from its dictionary definition but from how it's used within the text's specific circumstances. This skill is crucial, as many words in the English language have multiple meanings, which can change based on context. Moreover, in healthcare and nursing fields, where terminology can be highly specialized, grasping the contextual meaning can significantly impact comprehension and, consequently, the quality of care. Here are effective methods to master this essential skill.

Examine Surrounding Sentences

Often, the sentences surrounding an unfamiliar word or phrase provide clues about its meaning. Authors typically offer explanations, synonyms, or examples in the text that can illuminate the intended usage. When you encounter a word whose meaning isn't immediately clear, look at the preceding and following sentences for context. This broader view can reveal how the word fits into the overall message.

Identify the Part of Speech

Understanding the role of a word in a sentence can give insights into its meaning. For example, is the word functioning as a verb, suggesting action? Or is it a noun, indicating a person, place, or thing? The part of speech can narrow down the possible meanings and guide you toward the correct interpretation based on how it's used in context.

Look for Contrast and Comparison Clues

Authors often use contrast (e.g., however, but, yet) and comparison (e.g., like, as, similar to) to define or clarify terms. These clues can help determine the meaning of words by comparing or contrasting them with something more familiar. Pay attention to these signals, as they can be explicit guides to understanding.

LOGICAL CONCLUSIONS

Logical conclusions are the cornerstone of advanced reading comprehension, especially in the context of the HESI A2 exam. This skill involves the ability to draw reasoned deductions that are not directly stated in the text but are implied by the information presented. It requires synthesizing the passage's content to arrive at insights or understandings that reflect the deeper implications of the text. Mastering this skill is particularly vital in healthcare and nursing education, where professionals often need to make informed decisions based on reading and interpreting complex information. Here are several approaches to enhance your ability to make logical conclusions from reading passages.

Understand the Passage Structure
A deep understanding of the passage's structure can significantly aid in drawing logical conclusions. Recognizing the introduction, development, and conclusion of the argument or narrative helps in piecing together the author's intent and the text's direction. This structural awareness serves as a foundation for inferring conclusions that are logically consistent with the presented information.

Identify Key Statements and Ideas
Focus on identifying the passage's key statements and ideas. These elements are the building blocks of the author's argument or the story's plot. By understanding these core components, you can more easily infer logical conclusions that align with the author's objectives or the narrative's trajectory.

Look for Patterns and Relationships
Detecting patterns in the data or relationships between ideas within the passage is crucial for making logical deductions. Whether it's cause and effect, compare and contrast, or sequence of events, recognizing these patterns allows you to anticipate outcomes or implications that are suggested but not explicitly stated.

Use Critical Thinking Skills
Applying critical thinking is imperative when drawing conclusions. Question the text, evaluate the evidence, and consider alternative interpretations. This analytical approach ensures that your deductions are well-reasoned and grounded in the passage's content, rather than being based on assumptions or external knowledge.

EFFECTIVE READING STRATEGIES

To excel in the Reading Comprehension section of the HESI A2 exam, adopting effective reading strategies is paramount. These strategies not only aid in understanding and retaining information but also in efficiently navigating through the exam's passages and questions.

Active Reading is the cornerstone of comprehension. It involves more than just passively reading the words on a page; it's about engaging with the text. Summarizing sections in your own words, questioning the author's intent, and predicting future content are practices that encourage deeper interaction with the material. This methodical approach not only enhances understanding but also significantly improves retention of information.

Skimming and Scanning are time-saving techniques that are particularly useful in a timed exam. Skimming allows you to quickly read through a passage to grasp the general idea, while scanning involves looking over the text to find specific information, such as names, dates, or key terms. Both skills are invaluable when you need to locate information quickly without reading every word in detail.

Note-Taking is an essential strategy for breaking down complex passages. By jotting down key points and drawing connections between ideas, you create a visual representation of the text's structure, making it easier to navigate and understand. This can be especially helpful for long or dense passages where important details might otherwise be lost or overlooked.

Vocabulary Building plays a critical role in reading comprehension. A robust vocabulary allows you to easily understand the context and the specific meanings of words without getting bogged down by unfamiliar terms. Expanding your vocabulary through reading varied materials and practice can significantly aid in deciphering context clues, enabling a smoother and more confident reading experience.

Together, these strategies form a comprehensive toolkit for tackling the Reading Comprehension section of the HESI A2 exam. By actively engaging with texts, efficiently identifying key information, systematically organizing thoughts through note-taking, and continuously building vocabulary, candidates can elevate their reading comprehension skills, paving the way for success not only in the exam but in their future academic and professional endeavors in healthcare.

SECTION 2 - READING COMPREHENSION PRACTICE QUIZ

Sample Reading Test

Annually, an increasing number of "baby boomers" turn 70, qualifying for Medicare. The Census Bureau noted that as of July 2013, about 14% of the U.S. population was 65 or older, a figure expected to rise above 20% by 2060. Rising health care expenses and greater health needs among the elderly highlight the critical role of Medicare. Medicare Part A covers hospital stays, while Part B covers doctor visits and outpatient services. In 2008, Medicare Part D was introduced, significantly aiding seniors with prescription drug costs.

Before Medicare Part D, many seniors struggled financially with the cost of medications. Now, the challenge often lies in choosing the most suitable Part D plan for prescription coverage. Despite Part D's benefits, uncertainties remain since not every drug is covered under each plan, necessitating annual plan reviews. Seniors with multiple health issues might not find a plan covering all their medications. Furthermore, after reaching a spending threshold of $2,750 on drugs, most plans enter a coverage gap, or "donut hole," where patients must cover a significant portion of their drug costs until they reach $4,200 out-of-pocket, leading some to reduce or cease their medications to save money.

While Medicare provides excellent health care for seniors, it does so at a significant financial cost. It serves as a reminder for younger generations to invest in preventive health measures to secure a healthier future in their later years.

1 - What is the main idea of the passage?

A. Seniors face a significant financial challenge due to the high prices of prescription medications.

B. Medicare Part D complements Part A and B by making prescription medications and healthcare more accessible to the elderly.

C. Medicare Part D is problematic and offers no advantages.

D. Seniors with Medicare Part D coverage have no issues with prescription medication costs.

2 - Which of the following is not mentioned as a detail in the text?

A. Enrollment in Medicare Part D is mandatory for seniors.

B. The elderly population over 70 years old will grow by 2060.

C. There is a coverage gap known as the "donut hole" in Medicare Part D.

D. Medicare Part A and Part B contribute to covering hospital and doctor expenses.

3 - How is the term "behoove" used in the concluding section?

A. To grow

B. To advise others

C. To be accountable

D. To be essential

4 - What is the main goal of the author in crafting this piece?

A. To convince the elderly to opt into Medicare Part D

B. To examine the features of Medicare Part D

C. To educate individuals on how to sign up for Medicare

D. To provide amusement to those outside the healthcare industry

5 - How would you describe the essay's tone?

A. Prudent

B. Confrontational

C. Gloomy

D. Empathetic

6 - Which of the following statements is an opinion?

A. The steep prices of prescription medications have burdened many seniors.

B. Each Medicare Part D plan does not cover every prescription medication

C. In 2008, Medicare legislation offering prescription benefits was passed by Congress.

D. Elderly individuals contribute a monthly premium for Part D coverage.

7 - What conclusion is unlikely to be drawn by the reader?

A. Early preventive care might reduce the risk of diseases common in older age.

B. The coverage gap known as the "donut hole" poses a significant financial challenge to many seniors.

C. The majority of Americans will never utilize Medicare and its components.

D. It's possible for some elderly individuals to switch their Part D plans annually.

8 - Select the most accurate recap of the passage.

A. Upon reaching the age of 70, seniors enroll in Medicare Parts A, B, and D, which offer up to $2,750 in medical coverage annually. For those with multiple health conditions, the coverage extends to $4,200. The prescription drug coverage from Part D significantly eases the lives of seniors.

B. Medicare Parts A, B, and D provide seniors with coverage for hospital costs, doctor visits, outpatient services, and prescription drugs. While Part D has many advantages, there are still issues related to the diversity of plans and their specific medication coverages, along with the financial implications of the "donut hole." Nonetheless, seniors fare better with Medicare's support.

C. The group known as "baby boomers" constitutes the largest portion of seniors in need of health care, set to represent more than 20% of the population by 2050. Despite Medicare's challenges, Part D guarantees necessary medical coverage for all senior

D. As the American population ages, the demand for health care increases. By enrolling in Medicare Parts A, B, and D, seniors can alleviate some of the financial strains associated with health care costs. These Medicare components are designed to help seniors manage the expenses of hospitalization, outpatient services, and medications.

Sample Reading Test

Recent findings reveal a troubling rise in credit card debt among senior citizens, attributed to inadequate retirement savings and escalating costs of medications not included in Medicare coverage. Despite the prominence of Medicare's prescription drug benefits in the last presidential election debate, legislative action has been lacking.

Consequently, a portion of the elderly population is allocating 45% to 55% of their income to pharmaceutical expenses. Combined with the costs of utilities, housing, and food, many seniors find themselves reliant on credit cards. SRI Consulting Business Intelligence, located in Princeton, reports a significant increase in the average debt for households with members aged 65 and older — from $6,000 in 1994 to $25,000 in 2002, marking a 205% rise.

This surge in debt can be partly attributed to a lack of understanding about credit card operations, particularly the fact that minimum payments typically only cover the interest charges. Increasingly, seniors are departing from the traditionally conservative stance on borrowing, embracing the common American practice of purchasing on credit.

There's a pressing need for Congress to enact legislation to reduce prescription drug prices for the elderly. It's unjust for individuals who have contributed a lifetime of work to face financial hardship in their retirement years. We urge you to contact your congressional representatives and advocate for the implementation of necessary reforms.

9 - What is the main idea of the text?

A. Seniors struggle with the heavy financial load of prescription medication costs.

B. From 1994 to 2002, there was a 205% increase in credit card debt among the elderly.

C. Today's senior citizens have not accumulated sufficient funds for their retirement.

D. Multiple factors contribute to the prevalent issue of credit card debt among senior citizens.

10 - Which detail is not mentioned in the text?

A. Inadequate retirement savings by seniors.

B. Seniors allocating funds for gambling activities.

C. Prescription medication expenses significantly impacting seniors' budgets.

D. Misunderstandings among seniors regarding the functionalities of credit cards.

11 - In the context of the first paragraph, what does "accruing" mean?

A. To grow or accumulate over time.

B. To cling or attach oneself in a dependent or parasitic manner.

C. To cause irritation or annoyance.

D. To convey a particular emotion.

12 - What was the author's main intent in composing this essay?

A. To educate.

B. To convince.

C. To amuse.

13 - How would you describe the overall mood of the essay?

A. Motivational

B. Hopeful

C. Gloomy

D. Irate

14 - Which of the following is a subjective statement?

A. An unprecedented number of seniors are facing credit card debt.

B. The steep prices of prescription medications are contributing to the growing credit card debt among seniors.

C. It is imperative for Congress to pass legislation on Medicare to decrease the cost of prescription drugs.

D. A lack of understanding about credit card mechanics leads some seniors into debt.

15 - What could not be concluded by the reader from the essay?

A. Some seniors struggle to manage their bill payments.

B. Seniors should prevent their children from utilizing their credit cards.

C. A lack of adequate retirement planning is evident among some seniors.

D. Necessities and basic living expenses force some seniors to rely on credit cards.

SECTION 2 - READING COMPREHENSION PRACTICE QUIZ - ANSWER KEY

1 - What is the main idea of the passage?
  B) Medicare Part D complements Part A and B by making prescription medications and healthcare more accessible to the elderly.

2 - Which of the following is not mentioned as a detail in the text?
  A) Enrollment in Medicare Part D is mandatory for seniors.

3 - How is the term "behoove" used in the concluding section?
  D) To be essential

4 - What is the main goal of the author in crafting this piece?
  B) To examine the features of Medicare Part D

5 - How would you describe the essay's tone?
  A) Prudent

6 - Which of the following statements is an opinion?
  A) The steep prices of prescription medications have burdened many seniors.

7 - What conclusion is unlikely to be drawn by the reader?
  C) The majority of Americans will never utilize Medicare and its components.

8 - Select the most accurate recap of the passage.
  B) Medicare Parts A, B, and D provide seniors with coverage for hospital costs, doctor visits, outpatient services, and prescription drugs. While Part D has many advantages, there are still issues related to the diversity of plans and their specific medication coverages, along with the financial implications of the "donut hole." Nonetheless, seniors fare better with Medicare's support.

9 - What is the main idea of the text?
  D) Multiple factors contribute to the prevalent issue of credit card debt among senior citizens.

10 -Which detail is not mentioned in the text?
  B) Seniors allocating funds for gambling activities.

11 - In the context of the first paragraph, what does "accruing" mean?
  A) To grow or accumulate over time.

12 - What was the author's main intent in composing this essay?

B) To convince.

13 - How would you describe the overall mood of the essay?

C) Gloomy

14 - Which of the following is a subjective statement?

C) It is imperative for Congress to pass legislation on Medicare to decrease the cost of prescription drugs.

15 - What could not be concluded by the reader from the essay?

B) Seniors should prevent their children from utilizing their credit cards.

SECTION 3 - VOCABULARY AND GENERAL KNOWLEDGE

ROOT WORDS

Root words are the core component of many medical terms, providing the basic meaning upon which prefixes and suffixes are added to form complete words. In medical terminology, root words typically originate from Latin or Greek and often represent a body part, condition, or procedure. Learning root words can greatly facilitate the comprehension and retention of medical terminology, as they serve as building blocks for constructing various terms.

Root words are significant in medical terminology for several reasons. Firstly, they provide a foundation upon which prefixes and suffixes can be added to create specific medical terms. For example, the root word "**cardi-**" refers to the heart. When combined with the suffix "**-ology**" (meaning the study of), it forms the term "cardiology," which refers to the study of the heart and its diseases. Similarly, the addition of the suffix "**-itis**" (indicating inflammation) to "**cardi-**" results in "carditis," denoting inflammation of the heart.

To illustrate the significance of root words, consider the root word "**derm-**" derived from the Greek word for skin. This root word is found in various medical terms related to the skin, such as "dermatology" (the study of skin diseases) and "dermatitis" (inflammation of the skin). By understanding the root word "derm-," healthcare professionals can quickly identify and comprehend terms related to dermatology, thereby enhancing their ability to diagnose and treat skin conditions.

Here is a table summarizing the main root words

ROOT WORD	MEANING	EXAMPLE TERMS
Cardio-	Heart	Cardiovascular (related to the heart and blood vessels)
		Cardiopulmonary (related to the heart and lungs)
Cardi-	Heart	Cardiology (study of the heart)
		Cardiac (related to the heart)
Derm-	Skin	Dermatology (study of the skin)
		Dermatitis (inflammation of the skin)
Gastr-	Stomach	Gastritis (inflammation of the stomach)
		Gastroenterology (study of the digestive system)
Gastro-	Stomach	Gastrointestinal (related to the stomach and intestines)
		Gastroscopy (examination of the stomach)
Gynec-	Female	Gynecology (study of the female reproductive system)

		Gynecologist (physician specializing in women's health)
Hepato-	Liver	Hepatology (study of the liver)
		Hepatic (related to the liver)
Hemo-	Blood	Hematology (study of blood)
		Hemorrhage (excessive bleeding)
Nephro-	Kidney	Nephrology (study of the kidneys)
		Nephritis (inflammation of the kidneys)
Neuro-	Nerve	Neurology (study of the nervous system)
		Neurological (related to the nervous system)
Ortho-	Straight, Correct	Orthopedic (related to the musculoskeletal system)
		Orthodontist (specialist in aligning teeth)
Osteo-	Bone	Osteoporosis (condition of porous bones)
		Osteopathy (treatment involving manipulation of bones)
Pulmo-	Lung	Pulmonology (study of the lungs)
		Pulmonary (related to the lungs)
Psych-	Mind, Soul	Psychology (study of the mind and behavior)
		Psychiatric (related to mental illness)
Rhin-	Nose	Rhinitis (inflammation of the nose)
		Rhinoplasty (surgical reconstruction of the nose)

PREFIXES AND SUFFIXES

Understanding common prefixes and suffixes is essential for decoding medical terms. These word parts are added to the beginning (prefix) or end (suffix) of a root word to modify its meaning. Here are some of the most common prefixes and suffixes used in medical terminology:

Prefixes

PREFIX	MEANING	EXAMPLE TERMS
Anti-	Against or opposing	Antifungal
Bi-	Two or double	Bifocal
Hyper-	Above or excessive	Hyperactive
Hypo-	Below or deficient	Hypoglycemia
Inter-	Between or among	Interact
Macro-	Large or long	Macroscopic
Micro-	Small or microscopic	Microscope

Poly-	Many or excessive	Polyuria
Sub-	Below or under	Subcutaneous
Trans-	Across or through	Transdermal

Suffixes:

SUFFIXES	MEANING	EXAMPLE TERMS
-ectomy	Surgical removal	Appendectomy
-emia	Condition of the blood	Anemia
-itis	Inflammation	Bronchitis
-ology	Study of	Cardiology
-oma	Tumor or mass	Carcinoma
-opathy	Disease or disorder	Neuropathy
-osis	Abnormal condition or increase	Osteoporosis
-ostomy	Surgical opening	Colostomy
-otomy	Surgical incision	Tracheotomy
-plasty	Surgical repair or reconstruction	Rhinoplasty

SECTION 3 - VOCABULARY AND GENERAL KNOWLEDGE

PRACTICE QUIZ

1 - What does the prefix "hyper-" mean in medical terminology?

A. Below

B. Above

C. Around

D. Without

2 - Which suffix is commonly used to denote inflammation?

A. -itis

B. -emia

C. -ectomy

D. -osis

3 - The term "cardiologist" refers to a specialist in:

A. Digestive system disorders

B. Heart diseases

C. Bone disorders

D. Respiratory disorders

4 - What is the medical term for the voice box?

A. Trachea

B. Larynx

C. Pharynx

D. Epiglottis

5 - Which of the following prefixes means "within" or "inside"?

A. Inter-

B. Peri-

C. Intra-

D. Sub-

SECTION 3 - VOCABULARY AND GENERAL KNOWLEDGE

PRACTICE QUIZ - ANSWER KEY

1 - What does the prefix "hyper-" mean in medical terminology?

B) Above

2 - Which suffix is commonly used to denote inflammation?

A) -itis

3 - How is the term "behoove" used in the concluding section?

B) Heart diseases

4 - What is the main goal of the author in crafting this piece?

B) Larynx

5 - How would you describe the essay's tone?

C) Intra-

SECTION 4 - GRAMMAR

COMMON SPELLING, PLURALES AND SUFFIXES RULES

Spelling

Understanding and applying common spelling rules can significantly enhance your writing skills and confidence. Although English spelling can seem irregular, there are several guidelines that can help you navigate the complexities of the language. Here are some essential spelling rules and tips:

- **I before E, except after C:** This rule applies in words where the sound is 'ee', such as in "believe" (i before e) and "receive" (e after c). However, be aware of exceptions like "weird" and "protein."
- **Adding suffixes:** When adding a suffix that begins with a vowel (e.g., -ing, -ed, -able) to a word that ends in a silent "e", drop the "e". For example, "make" becomes "making". However, if the suffix begins with a consonant, keep the "e", as in "hopeful".
- **Doubling consonants:** When adding a suffix to a word that ends with a single vowel followed by a single consonant, and the stress is on the final syllable, double the final consonant. For instance, "run" becomes "running".
- **The silent "e":** A silent "e" at the end of a word often indicates that the vowel in the middle of the word is long (e.g., "ride", "note"). Removing the "e" changes the vowel sound (e.g., "rid", "not").
- **The magic of 'y':** When a word ends in "y" preceded by a consonant, change the "y" to "i" before adding any suffix, except when adding "-ing". For example, "happy" becomes "happier", but "crying" remains unchanged.

Plurales

Pluralizing nouns in English follows several common rules that help determine the correct form. One of the simplest rules involves adding "-s" or "-es" to the end of a singular noun to indicate plurality. For most nouns, adding "-s" suffices. For example, "book" becomes "books," "car" becomes "cars," and "house" becomes "houses." However, certain nouns ending in "-s," "-sh," "-ch," "-x," or "-z" require the addition of "-es" to form the plural, as in "bus" becoming "buses," "dish" becoming "dishes," "bench" becoming "benches," "box" becoming "boxes," and "buzz" becoming "buzzes."

Another rule pertains to nouns ending in "-y." When a noun ends in a consonant followed by "y," the "y" is usually replaced with "-ies" to form the plural. For instance, "baby" becomes "babies," "city" becomes "cities," and "party" becomes "parties." However, if the noun ends in a vowel followed by "y," simply adding "-s" to the end suffices, such as in "toy" becoming "toys."

Irregular plural nouns do not follow these rules and must be memorized individually. Examples include "child" becoming "children," "foot" becoming "feet," "mouse" becoming "mice," and "person" becoming "people."

It's important to note that some nouns have the same singular and plural forms, such as "sheep," "deer," and "fish." Additionally, collective nouns, which refer to groups of individuals or objects, may take singular or plural verbs depending on the context. For example, "the team is winning" versus "the team are practicing."

<u>Here are charts that will help you better understand the concepts.</u>

Adding "-s" or "-es" for Pluralization:

Singular Noun	Plural Noun
book	books
car	cars
house	houses
bus	buses
dish	dishes
bench	benches
box	boxes
buzz	buzzes

Pluralizing Nouns Ending in "-y":

Singular Noun	Plural Noun
baby	babies
city	cities
party	parties
toy	toys

Irregular Plural Nouns:

Singular Noun	Plural Noun
child	children
foot	feet
mouse	mice
person	people

Suffixes

Understanding common rules for suffixes is crucial for improving spelling accuracy and word recognition. Suffixes are letter or group of letters added to the end of a word to change its meaning or function. Here are some common rules for suffixes:

- **Adding "-ing":** When adding the suffix "-ing" to a verb, drop the final "e" if the verb ends in "e." For example, "write" becomes "writing," and "hope" becomes "hoping."
- **Doubling Final Consonant:** When adding a suffix starting with a vowel (such as "-ed" or "-ing") to a word with a single vowel followed by a single consonant, double the final consonant. For instance, "run" becomes "running" and "stop" becomes "stopped."
- **Changing "-y" to "-ies":** When a word ends in a consonant followed by "y," change the "y" to "i" before adding the suffix "-es" to form the plural. For example, "baby" becomes "babies," and "city" becomes "cities."
- **Adding "-s" or "-es":** For nouns, adding "-s" or "-es" forms the plural. Generally, words ending in a consonant or vowel followed by "y" require the suffix "-es" for pluralization, while others simply take "-s."
- **Adding "-ed" for Past Tense:** Adding the suffix "-ed" to a verb forms the past tense. However, irregular verbs may follow different patterns.
- **Adding "-er" and "-est" for Comparison:** Adding "-er" to an adjective forms the comparative degree, while adding "-est" forms the superlative degree.
- **Changing "-fe" to "-ves":** Words ending in "-fe" change the "f" to "v" before adding "-es" to form the plural. For example, "knife" becomes "knives."

Here are charts that will help you better understand the concepts.

Adding "-ing"

Base Word	Word with "-ing" Suffix
run	running
jump	jumping
read	reading

Doubling the Final Consonant

Base Word	Word with "-ed" Suffix	Word with "-ing" Suffix
stop	stopped	stopping
plan	planned	planning
beg	begged	begging

Changing "-y" to "-ies"

Base Word	Word with "-ies" Suffix
baby	babies
city	cities
supply	supplies

Adding "-s" or "-es"

Base Word	Word with "-s" or "-es" Suffix
book	books
box	boxes
watch	watches

Adding "-ed" for the Past

Base Word	Word with "-ed" Suffix
play	played
talk	talked
paint	painted

Adding "-er" and "-est" for Comparison

Base Word	Word with "-er" Suffix	Word with "-est" Suffix
tall	taller	tallest
fast	faster	fastest
big	bigger	biggest

Changing "-fe" to "-ves"

Base Word	Word with "-ves" Suffix
knife	knives
life	lives
wife	wives

ADVERBS AND ADJECTIVES

Adverbs

Adverbs are an essential part of speech in the English language, playing a crucial role in adding depth and detail to sentences. They modify verbs, adjectives, or other adverbs, providing information about how, when, where, and to what extent an action is performed or a quality is exhibited. Understanding the use and placement of adverbs can significantly enhance your writing and speaking skills, making your communication more precise and vivid.

An adverb can change the meaning of a verb, an adjective, another adverb, or even an entire sentence.

For example, the adverb "quickly" in the sentence "She runs quickly" modifies the verb "runs," telling us how she runs. In "She is incredibly fast," the adverb "incredibly" modifies the adjective "fast," intensifying its meaning. Furthermore, in "She runs very quickly," the adverb "very" modifies another adverb "quickly," emphasizing the speed of her running.

The placement of an adverb within a sentence can alter its meaning or emphasis. Generally, adverbs of manner, place, and time follow the verb or verb phrase they modify. However, adverbs of frequency, certainty, and degree usually appear in front of the verb, except when the verb is "to be," in which case the adverb follows it. The flexibility in the placement of adverbs allows for nuanced expression in writing and speech.

Adverbs can be categorized based on the type of information they provide:

- **Adverbs of Manner**: Describe how an action is performed (e.g., "She sings beautifully").
- **Adverbs of Time:** Indicate when an action takes place (e.g., "He arrived early").
- **Adverbs of Place:** Tell us where an action occurs (e.g., "They live nearby").
- **Adverbs of Frequency:** Show how often an action occurs (e.g., "She seldom lies").
- **Adverbs of Degree:** Describe the intensity or degree of an action or adjective (e.g., "The soup is too hot").

Adjectives

Adjectives are the paintbrushes of language, coloring nouns and pronouns with detail and depth, allowing speakers and writers to convey a more vivid picture of the world around them. By describing or modifying nouns and pronouns, adjectives provide essential information that enhances our understanding, adding texture and nuance to our sentences. Whether we're talking about a "beautiful sunset," a "large elephant," or a "colorful painting," adjectives help us to communicate not just what we're discussing, but also how we feel about it, its size, its appearance, and countless other descriptors that bring our language to life.

The primary role of adjectives is to specify the qualities or states of being of nouns, offering a richer description of objects, people, places, and concepts. They can tell us about the size (small, large), color (red, green), age (young, old), shape (circular, square), material (wooden, metallic), origin (American, Chinese), and a multitude of other aspects that can be applied to nouns. This specificity helps listeners and readers form clear, detailed mental images of what is being discussed.

The placement of adjectives is typically before the noun they modify, but can also be after the noun when linked by a verb (e.g., "The sky is blue"). When multiple adjectives modify the same noun, they follow a specific order: opinion, size, age, shape, color, origin, material, and purpose. For example, "a beautiful old Italian marble statue" demonstrates this order.

Adjectives can be categorized into several types, each serving a different purpose in the sentence:

- **Descriptive Adjectives:** Provide detailed information about the noun's qualities (e.g., "happy," "bitter").

- **Quantitative Adjectives:** Indicate the quantity or amount (e.g., "some," "many," "few").
- **Demonstrative Adjectives:** Point out specific items (e.g., "this," "that," "these," "those").
- **Possessive Adjectives:** Show ownership or possession (e.g., "my," "your," "his," "her").
- **Interrogative Adjectives:** Used in questions to ask about nouns (e.g., "which," "what").
- **Comparative and Superlative Adjectives:** Compare two or more nouns (e.g., "bigger," "biggest").

Key Differences Between Adverbs and Adjectives

1. **Modification:** The fundamental difference lies in what they modify. Adjectives modify nouns and pronouns to give more information about them. Adverbs modify verbs, adjectives, and other adverbs to provide more details about actions, states, and qualities.
2. **Question Answered:** Adjectives answer questions like "What kind?", "Which one?", and "How many?" Adverbs answer questions like "How?", "When?", "Where?", and "To what extent?"
3. **Form:** Many adverbs are formed by adding "-ly" to an adjective (e.g., "quick" becomes "quickly"). However, there are exceptions, and not all words ending in "-ly" are adverbs.
4. **Placement:** Adjectives usually come before the noun they modify or after linking verbs. Adverbs can be more flexible in placement, often appearing close to the verb they modify but also capable of modifying an entire sentence or clause.

PUNCTUATION

Punctuation marks, the backbone of written communication, are indispensable tools that provide clarity and structure to sentences. They guide the reader through the text, signaling pauses, indicating the end of sentences, and helping to convey the intended message with precision. Understanding punctuation is crucial for test-takers, as it directly impacts the readability and effectiveness of their writing. Let's explore some of the most important punctuation marks: periods, commas, question marks, and exclamation points.

1. **Periods**: The period (.) is perhaps the simplest yet most powerful punctuation mark. It denotes the end of a sentence, signaling a full stop where the reader should pause before proceeding to the next sentence. This mark of finality is crucial for separating ideas, ensuring that each sentence stands on its own with a clear and distinct message. In the context of the HESI A2 exam, using periods correctly demonstrates your ability to organize thoughts and communicate effectively.
2. **Commas**: Commas (,) introduce nuance and complexity into writing. They indicate a slight pause within a sentence, separating clauses, items in a list, and adjectives that describe the same noun. Commas also prevent confusion, making the text more readable and understandable. For instance, in lists, commas separate items to clarify that each is distinct: "I need to buy eggs, milk, and bread." Misuse of commas can lead to ambiguity, so mastering their use is essential for successful communication on the exam.

3. **Question Marks**: Question marks (?) punctuate inquiries, transforming statements into questions. They invite the reader to think, reflect, or respond, making them crucial for engaging communication. In academic and test-writing contexts, using question marks correctly helps to clearly delineate queries from statements, demonstrating an understanding of sentence structure and intent.

4. **Exclamation Points**: Exclamation points (!) are used sparingly to express strong emotion or emphasize a point. They can convey surprise, urgency, or excitement, adding a dynamic quality to writing. However, due to their intensity, exclamation points should be used judiciously, especially in academic or formal writing contexts like the HESI A2 exam. Overuse can make writing appear unprofessional or overly emotional.

PRONOUNS

Pronouns are words that substitute for nouns, playing a pivotal role in avoiding redundancy and enhancing the fluidity of language. Their use is crucial in constructing clear and coherent sentences, an essential skill for any test-taker. Understanding the different types of pronouns—personal, possessive, and reflexive—will significantly improve your writing and communication skills.

Personal Pronouns: The Basics of Identity

Personal pronouns are used to represent specific people or things without naming them directly. They are categorized according to person (first, second, or third), number (singular or plural), and gender (masculine, feminine, neuter). The pronouns "I, you, he, she, it, we, they" are integral in constructing sentences that are direct and personable. **For example**, instead of repeating a person's name, "John went to John's car to get John's phone," you can use personal pronouns for a smoother sentence: "He went to his car to get his phone."

Possessive Pronouns: Indicating Ownership

Possessive pronouns indicate ownership or possession, referring back to something or someone mentioned previously in the discourse. They are "mine, yours, his, hers, its, ours, theirs." These pronouns help streamline communication by eliminating the need for repetitive language. **For instance**, rather than saying, "The book belongs to Sarah, and the jacket belongs to Sarah," you can say, "The book and the jacket are hers."

Reflexive Pronouns: Reflecting Back

Reflexive pronouns are used when the subject and the object of a sentence are the same, adding clarity or emphasis to a sentence. They include "myself, yourself, himself, herself, itself, ourselves, themselves." These pronouns are often used for emphasis or to indicate that an action is performed by the subject without anyone else's involvement. **For example**, "She prepared herself for the exam."

This table provides clear examples to demonstrate how each type of pronoun functions within a sentence, illustrating their importance in constructing coherent and concise language.

Pronoun Type	Pronouns	Example Sentence
Personal	I, you, he, she, it, we, they	She is going to the market.
Possessive	mine, yours, his, hers, its, ours, theirs	That book is mine.
Reflexive	myself, yourself, himself, herself, itself, ourselves, themselves	He prepared the meal himself.

Understanding and correctly using pronouns can significantly enhance the readability and professionalism of your writing, a crucial aspect of the HESI A2 test. By mastering pronouns, you demonstrate a sophisticated grasp of English grammar, making your sentences clear, concise, and engaging. Moreover, recognizing pronouns' roles and functions will improve your reading comprehension skills, a valuable asset in the exam's reading sections.

CONJUNCTIONS AND PREPOSITIONS

Conjunctions

Conjunctions are the glue of the English language, connecting words, phrases, or clauses to form coherent sentences. They serve various functions, from adding information to contrasting ideas or choosing between alternatives. The most common conjunctions include "and," "but," "or," "so," and "because."

- "And" is used to add information or list items together in a sentence. For example, "She studied biology and chemistry."
- "But" introduces a contrast or exception. For instance, "He wanted to go outside, but it was raining."
- "Or" provides options or alternatives. An example would be, "Would you prefer tea or coffee?"
- "So" indicates a cause or effect relationship. For example, "She was late, so she missed the bus."
- "Because" gives a reason. For instance, "He studied hard because he wanted to pass the test."

Pronoun Type	Pronouns	Example Sentence
and	Adds information or items together.	She studied biology and chemistry.
but	Introduces a contrast or exception.	He wanted to go outside, but it was raining.
or	Offers options or alternatives.	Would you prefer tea or coffee?
so	Indicates a cause and effect relationship.	She was late, so she missed the bus.
because	Provides a reason.	He studied hard because he wanted to pass.

Understanding how to use conjunctions correctly allows you to construct complex, nuanced sentences, a skill that the HESI A2 test assesses.

Prepositions

Prepositions are indispensable in illustrating the relationships between a noun or pronoun and other words in a sentence, often indicating location, time, and direction. These small but mighty words include "in," "on," "at," "from," and "with," among others.

"In" can denote location or time, as in "She lives in New York" or "in the morning."

"On" refers to surfaces or specific days, like "The book is on the table" or "on Monday."

"At" points to more precise locations or times, such as "at the corner" or "at noon."

"From" indicates origin, direction, or distance. For example, "She travels from Boston to New York."

"With" describes accompaniment or possession, like "He came with his friend" or "a girl with blue eyes."

Pronoun Type	Pronouns	Example Sentence
and	Adds information or items together.	She studied biology and chemistry.
but	Introduces a contrast or exception.	He wanted to go outside, but it was raining.
or	Offers options or alternatives.	Would you prefer tea or coffee?
so	Indicates a cause and effect relationship.	She was late, so she missed the bus.
because	Provides a reason.	He studied hard because he wanted to pass.

Prepositions often challenge test-takers due to their varied applications and exceptions. However, understanding their correct use is crucial for accurately conveying meaning and passing the grammar section of the HESI A2.

Integrating Conjunctions and Prepositions

Both conjunctions and prepositions are vital for creating sentences that are not only grammatically correct but also rich in meaning and clarity. Conjunctions allow you to combine ideas effectively, while prepositions help you detail the relationships between those ideas, enhancing the overall coherence of your writing. Through practice and application, mastering these elements will significantly boost your grammar skills, preparing you for the HESI A2 test and beyond.

SECTION 4 - GRAMMAR

PRACTICE QUIZ

1 - Which conjunction best completes the sentence? "I wanted to go to the beach, ___ it was raining.

A. and

B. but

C. or

2 - Choose the correct preposition for the sentence: "He arrived ___ the airport at noon.

A. in

B. on

C. at

D. from

3 - Despite the heavy rain, they continued their picnic." What is "Despite" in this sentence?

A. Conjunction

B. Preposition

C. Adverb

D. Adjective

4 - Which sentence correctly uses a conjunction?

A. She neither likes coffee, nor tea.

B. She likes neither coffee nor tea.

C. She likes coffee neither nor tea.

D. Neither she likes coffee nor tea.

5 - Fill in the blank with the correct preposition: "She is interested ___ learning Spanish."

A. on

B. in

C. at

D. to

6 - Which sentence correctly uses reflexive pronouns?

A. He gave himself a break.

B. She considered herself the best candidate.

C. They bought themselves a new car.

D. All of the above

7 - Choose the correct pronoun to complete the sentence: "This book is ___ (mine/ yours)."

A. mine

B. yours

8 - Identify the type of pronoun in the sentence: "Whose are these keys?"

A. Demonstrative

B. Interrogative

C. Indefinite

D. Possessive

9 - Where should the comma be placed? "Before you leave please close the door."

A. Before you leave, please close the door.

B. Before you leave please, close the door.

10 - Choose the sentence with correct punctuation: "Isn't it beautiful, she exclaimed."

A. Isn't it beautiful she exclaimed.

B. "Isn't it beautiful!" she exclaimed.

11 - What punctuation mark is missing? "Can you believe it We won the game!"

A. Comma

B. Question mark

C. Exclamation point

D. Period

12 - Identify the adverb in the sentence: "She quickly ran to the store."

A. quickly

B. ran

C. to

D. store

13 - Choose the sentence where "fast" is used as an adjective:

A. He runs fast.

B. He drove a fast car.

14 - Which sentence correctly uses an adverb to modify an adjective?

A. The test was surprisingly easy.

B. The surprisingly test was easy.

15 - Identify the adjective in the sentence: "The red apple is mine."

A. apple

B. red

C. mine

D. is

16 - "She spoke in a very soft voice." What is "very" in this sentence?

A. Conjunction
B. Preposition
C. Adverb
D. Adjective

17 - Which word is spelled correctly?

A. Recieve
B. Receive
C. Recieive

18 - What is the correct plural form of "baby"?

A. Babys
B. Babies
C. Babyses
D. Babyes

19 - Choose the word with the correct suffix: "Happiness"

A. Happyness
B. Happiness
C. Happines
D. Happyiness

20 - Which word is spelled correctly?

A. Accomodate
B. Accommodate
C. Acommodate
D. Accomadate

21 - What is the correct plural form of "fox"?

A. Foxs
B. Foxes
C. Foxies
D. Foxxes

SECTION 4 - GRAMMAR
PRACTICE QUIZ - ANSWER KEY

1 - Which conjunction best completes the sentence? "I wanted to go to the beach, ___ it was raining.

B) but

2 - Choose the correct preposition for the sentence: "He arrived ___ the airport at noon."

C) at

3 - "Despite the heavy rain, they continued their picnic." What is "Despite" in this sentence?

B) Preposition

4 - Which sentence correctly uses a conjunction?

B) She likes neither coffee nor tea.

5 - Fill in the blank with the correct preposition: "She is interested ___ learning Spanish."

B) in

6 - Which sentence correctly uses reflexive pronouns?

D) All of the above

7 - Choose the correct pronoun to complete the sentence: "This book is ___ (mine/yours)."

B) yours

8 - Identify the type of pronoun in the sentence: "Whose are these keys?"

B) Interrogative

9 - Where should the comma be placed? "Before you leave please close the door."

A) Before you leave, please close the door.

10 - Choose the sentence with correct punctuation: "Isn't it beautiful, she exclaimed."

B) "Isn't it beautiful!" she exclaimed.

11 - What punctuation mark is missing? "Can you believe it We won the game!"

B) Question mark

12 - Identify the adverb in the sentence: "She quickly ran to the store."

A) quickly

13 - Choose the sentence where "fast" is used as an adjective:

B) He drove a fast car.

14 - Which sentence correctly uses an adverb to modify an adjective?

A) The test was surprisingly easy.

15 - Identify the adjective in the sentence: "The red apple is mine."

B) red

16 - "She spoke in a very soft voice." What is "very" in this sentence?

C) Adverb

17 - Which word is spelled correctly?

B) Receive

18 - What is the correct plural form of "baby"?

B) Babies

19 - Choose the word with the correct suffix: "Happiness"

B) Happiness

20 - Which word is spelled correctly?

B) Accommodate

21 - What is the correct plural form of "fox"?

B) Foxes

Want More?

Download Answer Explanations Now by Framing the QR-Code With Your Phone

SECTION 5 - BIOLOGY

CELL BIOLOGY

Cells are the smallest units of life, capable of performing all life processes, including growth, metabolism, response to environmental stimuli, and reproduction. They are the building blocks from which all living organisms are constructed, ranging from single-celled bacteria to the trillions of specialized cells that make up a human being. The study of cells, known as cell biology, reveals how life is both incredibly diverse and unified by common processes.

There are two main types of cells: prokaryotic and eukaryotic. Prokaryotic cells, typified by bacteria and archaea, are simpler and smaller. They lack a defined nucleus and membrane-bound organelles. Their DNA floats freely within the cell in a region called the nucleoid. Despite their simplicity, prokaryotic cells are incredibly versatile and can inhabit a wide range of environments, from hot springs to the human gut.

Eukaryotic cells, found in plants, animals, fungi, and protists, are more complex. They feature a defined nucleus, where the cell's DNA is enclosed, and various organelles, each enclosed by membranes and performing specific functions vital to the cell's survival and the organism's health. For example, mitochondria generate the cell's energy, chloroplasts (in plant cells) are involved in photosynthesis, and the endoplasmic reticulum synthesizes proteins and lipids.

The cell membrane, a lipid bilayer that encloses every cell, plays a critical role in maintaining the cell's internal environment, allowing selective entry and exit of substances. This selective permeability is essential for nutrient uptake, waste elimination, and communication with other cells. Cells also demonstrate remarkable specialization, particularly evident in multicellular organisms where different types of cells take on unique roles. Muscle cells, for example, are designed for contraction and movement, while nerve cells transmit signals across long distances within an organism.

DIFFERENCES BETWEEN PROKARYOTIC AND EUKARYOTIC CELLS

A pivotal aspect of understanding biology is distinguishing between the two primary cell types: prokaryotic and eukaryotic cells. This distinction is crucial for grasping the broader complexities of biological science and the evolutionary relationships among different life forms.

Prokaryotic

Prokaryotic cells, the most ancient form of life, are characterized by their simplicity. These cells lack a defined nucleus; instead, their genetic material, DNA, is located in a central region known as the nucleoid. Prokaryotes include bacteria and archaea, organisms that are often single-celled but immensely diverse in their energy acquisition methods and environments.

Key features of prokaryotic cells include:

- **Lack of membrane-bound organelles:** Other than the nucleoid, prokaryotic cells do not have compartments enclosed by membranes. Functions like energy production occur across the cell membrane.
- **Size and shape:** Generally smaller than eukaryotic cells, prokaryotes can be spherical (cocci), rod-shaped (bacilli), or spiral.
- **Reproduction:** They typically reproduce asexually through binary fission, a straightforward process of cell division.

Eukaryotic

Eukaryotic cells represent a significant evolutionary advancement, with complex structures that allow for specialized functions. Unlike prokaryotes, eukaryotic cells possess a nucleus, where the cell's genetic material is housed within a double membrane. This category encompasses a wide range of life, including plants, animals, fungi, and protists.

Distinctive traits of eukaryotic cells are:

- **Membrane-bound organelles:** Eukaryotes contain numerous organelles, such as mitochondria (energy production), chloroplasts (photosynthesis in plants), and the Golgi apparatus (protein and lipid processing).
- **Cytoskeleton:** A network of protein filaments provides structural support, enabling cell shape maintenance and intracellular transport.
- **Size and complexity:** Eukaryotic cells are typically larger than prokaryotic cells, with intricate internal structures that support diverse life processes.
- **Reproduction**: Eukaryotes can reproduce asexually and sexually, adding genetic diversity through mechanisms like mitosis and meiosis.

Feature	Prokaryotic Cells	Eukaryotic Cells
Nucleus	Absent; DNA floats freely in the cell	Present; DNA is enclosed within a membrane-bound nucleus
Size	Generally smaller (0.1-5 μm).	Larger (10-100 μm)
Complexity	Simpler structure without compartmentalization	Complex structure with compartmentalization due to membrane-bound organelles
Organelles	No membrane-bound organelles	Contains membrane-bound organelles (e.g., mitochondria, chloroplasts, Golgi apparatus)
Cell Wall	Usually present, made of peptidoglycan in bacteria	Present in plants and fungi, but not in all eukaryotes; when present, composed of cellulose (plants) or chitin (fungi)
DNA Shape	Circular DNA	Linear DNA
Reproduction	Asexual reproduction through binary fission	Both asexual (mitosis) and sexual (meiosis) reproduction

Examples	Bacteria and Archaea	Plants, animals, fungi, and protists
Cytoskeleton	Lacks a complex cytoskeleton	Contains a complex cytoskeleton for structural support and intracellular transport

CELL ORGANELLES AND THEIR FUNCTIONS

- **The Nucleus - The Control Center:** The nucleus, often referred to as the cell's "control center," is responsible for storing the cell's DNA and coordinating activities such as growth, metabolism, protein synthesis, and cell division. Enclosed by a double membrane known as the nuclear envelope, the nucleus contains chromosomes, which are structures made up of DNA that encode the cell's genetic information. The nucleus also houses the nucleolus, where ribosomal RNA is synthesized, playing a critical role in protein production.

- **Mitochondria - The Powerhouse:** Mitochondria are known as the "powerhouses" of the cell because they generate most of the cell's supply of adenosine triphosphate (ATP), used as a source of chemical energy. Through a process called cellular respiration, mitochondria convert glucose and oxygen into ATP, carbon dioxide, and water. This organelle has its own DNA, which suggests an evolutionary origin from free-living prokaryotes that were engulfed by an ancestral eukaryotic cell.

- **Chloroplasts - The Site of Photosynthesis:** Present in plant cells and some protists, chloroplasts are the sites of photosynthesis, the process by which sunlight is converted into chemical energy. Chloroplasts contain the green pigment chlorophyll, which captures light energy to synthesize glucose from carbon dioxide and water, releasing oxygen as a by-product. Like mitochondria, chloroplasts also have their own DNA and are believed to have originated from symbiotic prokaryotes.

- **Endoplasmic Reticulum - The Manufacturing and Packaging System:** The endoplasmic reticulum (ER) is a network of membranous tubules that plays a key role in the synthesis, folding, modification, and transport of proteins. The rough ER is studded with ribosomes, which are sites of protein synthesis. These proteins are then packaged into vesicles and transported to the Golgi apparatus for further processing. The smooth ER, lacking ribosomes, is involved in lipid synthesis and detoxification processes.

- **Golgi Apparatus - The Shipping Department:** The Golgi apparatus functions as the cell's "shipping department," modifying, sorting, and packaging proteins and lipids for secretion or use within the cell. It consists of stacked membrane-bound sacs where proteins received from the ER are processed and sent to their final destinations.

- **Lysosomes and Peroxisomes - The Cleanup Crew:** Lysosomes contain digestive enzymes that break down macromolecules, old cell parts, and foreign invaders, while peroxisomes use oxygen to detoxify harmful substances.

PHOTOSYNTHESIS

Photosynthesis is the remarkable process by which green plants, algae, and certain bacteria convert light energy from the sun into chemical energy stored in glucose, a sugar molecule. This process not only provides food for the organism performing photosynthesis but also generates oxygen, a byproduct essential for the survival of most life forms on Earth.

The process occurs primarily in the chloroplasts of plant cells, where chlorophyll, a green pigment, captures sunlight. Photosynthesis can be broken down into two main stages: the light-dependent reactions and the Calvin cycle (light-independent reactions).

1. **Light-Dependent Reactions:** These occur in the thylakoid membranes of the chloroplasts, where sunlight is absorbed by chlorophyll, generating high-energy electrons. Water molecules are split, releasing oxygen as a byproduct. The high-energy electrons are then used to produce ATP and NADPH, energy carriers that will be used in the next stage of photosynthesis.

2. **The Calvin Cycle:** This stage takes place in the stroma of the chloroplasts and does not require light. Here, ATP and NADPH from the light-dependent reactions are used to convert carbon dioxide from the atmosphere into glucose, which can be used by the plant for energy and growth.

CELLULAR RESPIRATION

Cellular respiration is the process by which organisms break down glucose and other food molecules in the presence of oxygen to produce ATP, the energy currency of the cell. This process occurs in all eukaryotic cells, including those of plants, animals, and fungi, indicating its fundamental importance to life.

Cellular respiration can be divided into three main stages: glycolysis, the Krebs cycle, and oxidative phosphorylation.

1. **Glycolysis:** This anaerobic process (not requiring oxygen) occurs in the cytoplasm and breaks glucose into two molecules of pyruvate, producing a small yield of ATP.

2. **The Krebs Cycle:** Also known as the citric acid cycle, this series of reactions takes place in the mitochondria. Pyruvate from glycolysis is further broken down, releasing carbon dioxide and transferring energy to electron carriers NADH and FADH2.

3. **Oxidative Phosphorylation:** The electron transport chain, located in the inner mitochondrial membrane, uses electrons from NADH and FADH2 to create a proton gradient that drives the synthesis of a large amount of ATP. Oxygen acts as the final electron acceptor, combining with protons to form water.

The Connection Between Photosynthesis and Cellular Respiration

Photosynthesis and cellular respiration are interconnected, forming a cycle that transfers energy from the sun into organisms and then within ecosystems. While photosynthesis captures and stores energy in glucose molecules, cellular respiration releases this stored energy for use by the cell. Oxygen produced during photosynthesis is essential for cellular respiration, and carbon dioxide released during respiration is used in photosynthesis, highlighting the symbiotic relationship between these two processes.

CELLULAR REPRODUCTION

Cellular reproduction encompasses the methods by which cells divide to form new cells, crucial for growth, repair, and reproduction in living organisms. There are two primary modes of cellular reproduction: mitosis and meiosis, each serving distinct functions within the lifecycle of an organism. Cellular reproduction, whether through mitosis or meiosis, is a meticulously regulated process, with numerous checkpoints ensuring accuracy in DNA replication and division. Errors in cellular reproduction can lead to genetic mutations, some of which may cause diseases such as cancer.

Mitosis

Mitosis is a type of cell division that results in two daughter cells, each genetically identical to the parent cell. This process is crucial for growth, tissue repair, and asexual reproduction in single-celled organisms. Mitosis ensures that each new cell receives a complete set of chromosomes, maintaining genetic consistency across generations of cells.

Mitosis can be divided into several stages:

1. **Prophase**: Chromosomes condense and become visible. The nuclear envelope breaks down.
2. **Metaphase**: Chromosomes align in the center of the cell.
3. **Anaphase**: Sister chromatids (each half of a duplicated chromosome) are pulled apart to opposite ends of the cell.
4. **Telophase**: Nuclear envelopes re-form around the separated chromosomes, which begin to de-condense.
5. **Cytokinesis**: The cell divides into two, completing the process.

The significance of mitosis cannot be overstated. It allows multicellular organisms to grow from a single cell to trillions and to replace cells as they become old or damaged. This precision ensures that genetic information remains unchanged with each new cell, providing stability within the organism.

Meiosis

Meiosis, in contrast, is a specialized form of cell division that reduces the chromosome number by half, producing four genetically unique daughter cells. This process is integral to sexual reproduction, occurring in the production of gametes—sperm in males and eggs in females. Meiosis introduces genetic diversity through the recombination of genetic material and independent assortment of chromosomes.

Meiosis involves two consecutive rounds of cell division, meiosis I and meiosis II, but only one round of DNA replication. <u>Key stages include:</u>

1. **Prophase I:** Chromosomes condense, and homologous chromosomes pair up, undergoing crossing over, where genetic material is exchanged.
2. **Metaphase I:** Paired chromosomes align in the cell's center.
3. **Anaphase I:** Homologous chromosomes are separated to opposite ends of the cell.
4. **Telophase I and Cytokinesis:** Cells divide, resulting in two cells with half the original chromosome number.
5. **Meiosis II:** Similar to mitosis, but results in four genetically unique gametes.

The significance of meiosis lies in its ability to generate genetic diversity, a fundamental aspect of evolution and adaptation. By shuffling genetic information, meiosis ensures that offspring are genetically distinct from their parents and each other, contributing to the variation within a species that can drive natural selection.

GENETICS

Genetics is founded on the principles of inheritance first outlined by Gregor Mendel in the 19th century. Mendel's experiments with pea plants revealed that traits are inherited in discrete units, now known as genes. Genes, composed of DNA, are located on chromosomes and serve as the blueprints for proteins, the molecules that perform most life functions. Each organism inherits two copies of each gene, one from each parent, which exist in different versions called alleles. The combination of alleles an organism has for a particular gene determines its traits. Dominant alleles mask the effects of recessive alleles, resulting in the phenotype, or observable traits of an organism.

The structure of DNA, discovered by Watson and Crick, further illuminated the mechanics of inheritance. DNA's double helix structure and the sequence of its nucleotide bases (adenine, thymine, cytosine, and guanine) dictate the synthesis of proteins. Genetic information is copied through DNA replication and distributed to new cells during cell division, ensuring that each cell contains a complete set of genetic instructions.

DNA STRUCTURE AND FUNCTION

The structure of DNA (Deoxyribonucleic Acid) is a marvel of nature, elegantly designed to store and transmit genetic information. Discovered by James Watson and Francis Crick in 1953, DNA is composed of two long strands forming a double helix. These strands are made up of nucleotides, each containing a phosphate group, a sugar molecule (deoxyribose), and one of four nitrogenous bases: adenine (A), thymine (T), cytosine (C), or guanine (G).

The pairing of these bases (A with T and C with G) through hydrogen bonds between the strands allows DNA to store genetic information in the sequence of nucleotides, much like letters forming words in a sentence.

DNA Function

The primary function of DNA is to store the genetic instructions needed for the development and functioning of living organisms. These instructions are encoded in the sequence of the nucleotides. DNA's secondary but equally critical role is in the process of replication and protein synthesis, ensuring that genetic information is accurately passed on to new cells during cell division and to offspring during reproduction.

- **Replication:** DNA replication is the process by which DNA makes a copy of itself during cell division. This ensures that each new cell receives a complete set of genetic instructions. Replication is semi-conservative, meaning each strand of the original DNA molecule serves as a template for a new strand, resulting in two DNA molecules, each with one old and one new strand.

- **Protein Synthesis:** Protein synthesis is the process by which the genetic code in DNA is translated into the amino acid sequence of proteins, the workhorses of the cell. This two-step process involves transcription and translation. During transcription, a segment of DNA is transcribed into messenger RNA (**mRNA**) by RNA polymerase. This mRNA then exits the nucleus and enters the cytoplasm, where it is translated into a protein at the ribosome. The sequence of nucleotides in the mRNA is read in triplets, called codons, each specifying a particular amino acid, leading to the synthesis of proteins based on the information encoded in DNA. In addition to mRNA, there are also:
    - **tRNA**: tRNA stands for transfer RNA, a type of RNA molecule that acts as the physical link between the mRNA (messenger RNA) sequence and the amino acid sequence of proteins. tRNAs are relatively small RNA chains that transport amino acids to the ribosome, the cellular "factory" where proteins are synthesized. Each tRNA molecule is specific to one amino acid but can bind to multiple codons on the mRNA that code for that amino acid, thanks to the wobble base pairing at the third position of the codon. The tRNA has a three-dimensional structure, with one end of the tRNA carrying the specific amino acid and the other end presenting an anticodon loop. The anticodon is a set of three nucleotides that are complementary to the codon on the mRNA. During translation, the anticodon of a tRNA molecule pairs with a codon on the mRNA strand, adding its amino acid to the growing polypeptide chain in the correct sequence dictated by the mRNA.

    - **rRNA** stands for ribosomal RNA, which, together with ribosomal proteins, makes up the ribosome. Ribosomes are the cellular structures responsible for protein synthesis, and they exist in the cell's cytoplasm. rRNA is the most abundant type of RNA in most cells. It plays a structural and catalytic role in ribosomes, helping to form the core of the ribosome's structure and ensuring the proper alignment of mRNA and tRNAs. Additionally, rRNAs are involved in the catalysis of peptide bonds between amino acids, a key reaction in the synthesis of proteins. The rRNA molecules in the ribosome help to create the peptidyl transferase center, where amino acids are joined together to form proteins.

The implications of DNA's structure and function extend far beyond the cell. They are fundamental to understanding genetic diseases, genetic engineering, forensic science, and evolutionary biology. Mutations, or changes in the DNA sequence, can lead to genetic disorders or increase the diversity within a species, driving evolution. Biotechnology exploits our understanding of DNA to develop medical treatments, improve crops, and solve crimes.

CHROMOSOMES

Chromosomes are long, thread-like structures made of DNA and associated proteins called histones, which help package and manage the DNA, making it more compact and allowing for efficient DNA replication and gene expression.

Each chromosome carries thousands of genes, the basic units of heredity, which encode the instructions for making proteins that carry out all cellular functions. Humans typically have 46 chromosomes in each somatic (body) cell, arranged into 23 pairs, including one pair of sex chromosomes (XX for females and XY for males) that determine an individual's sex. This diploid set of chromosomes (2n) is halved during the production of gametes (sperm and eggs) through the process of meiosis, resulting in haploid cells (n) with just one chromosome from each pair.

Chromosomal abnormalities, such as duplications, deletions, inversions, or translocations, can lead to genetic disorders or diseases. For example, Down syndrome is caused by an extra copy of chromosome 21 (trisomy 21), demonstrating the importance of proper chromosome number and structure for normal development and health.

SECTION 5 - BIOLOGY
PRACTICE QUIZ

1 - Which of the following is a feature unique to eukaryotic cells?
A. Ribosomes
B. DNA
C. Nucleus
D. Cell membrane

2 - Prokaryotic cells are characterized by:
A. A membrane-bound nucleus
B. Lack of membrane-bound organelles
C. Presence of chloroplasts
D. Multiple chromosomes

3 - Which organelle is known as the powerhouse of the cell?
A. Nucleus
B. Mitochondria
C. Ribosome
D. Endoplasmic reticulum

4 - The main site of protein synthesis in the cell is the:
A. Nucleus
B. Golgi apparatus
C. Ribosome
D. Mitochondrion

5 - Cell walls are not found in the cells of:
A. Plants
B. Bacteria
C. Animals
D. Fungi

6 - Which pigment is primarily responsible for absorbing light energy in photosynthesis?
A. Hemoglobin
B. Chlorophyll
C. Cytochrome
D. Myoglobin

7 - In which part of the plant cell does photosynthesis take place?

A. Mitochondria

B. Chloroplast

C. Nucleus

D. Ribosome

8 - Cellular respiration typically takes place in the:

A. Nucleus

B. Chloroplast

C. Mitochondria

D. Golgi apparatus

9 - The final electron acceptor in the electron transport chain of cellular respiration is:

A. Carbon dioxide

B. Oxygen

C. Glucose

D. Water

10 - Mitosis results in:

A. Four genetically different haploid cells

B. Two genetically identical diploid cells

C. One diploid cell

D. Four diploid cells

11 - During which phase of mitosis do chromosomes align at the cell's equator?

A. Prophase

B. Metaphase

C. Anaphase

D. Telophase

12 - Crossing over, a process that increases genetic diversity, occurs during:

A. Mitosis

B. Meiosis I

C. Meiosis II

D. Fertilization

13 - The separation of sister chromatids occurs during:

A. Metaphase of mitosis

B. Anaphase of mitosis

C. Prophase of meiosis I

D. Anaphase of meiosis II

14 - An individual's physical appearance is determined by their:

A. Genotype

B. Phenotype

· C. Alleles

D. Chromosomes

15 - Which term describes a segment of DNA that codes for a protein?

A. Chromosome

B. Gene

C. Nucleotide

D. Ribosome

16 - The "rungs" of the DNA ladder are made of:

A. Paired nitrogenous bases

B. Sugar molecules

C. Phosphate groups

D. Amino acids

17 - Which enzyme is responsible for unzipping the DNA double helix during replication?

A. Ligase

B. Helicase

C. Polymerase

D. Ribozyme

18 - The process by which mRNA is synthesized from the DNA template is called:

A. Translation

B. Transcription

C. Replication

D. Translocation

19 - The sequence of _____ in DNA determines the sequence of amino acids in proteins.

A. Phosphates

B. Ribosomes

C. Nucleotides

D. D) Sugars

20 - Which structural feature of DNA is responsible for its ability to store and transmit genetic information effectively?

A. Double helix formation

B. Presence of ribose sugar

C.   Single-stranded nature

D. Uniform size of nucleotides

SECTION 5 - BIOLOGY
PRACTICE QUIZ - ANSWER KEY

1 - Which of the following is a feature unique to eukaryotic cells?

C) Nucleus

2 - Prokaryotic cells are characterized by:

B) Lack of membrane-bound organelles

3 - Which organelle is known as the powerhouse of the cell?

B) Mitochondria

4 - The main site of protein synthesis in the cell is the:

C) Ribosome

5 - Cell walls are not found in the cells of:

C) Animals

6 - Which pigment is primarily responsible for absorbing light energy in photosynthesis?

B) Chlorophyll

7 - In which part of the plant cell does photosynthesis take place?

B) Chloroplast

8 - Cellular respiration typically takes place in the:

C) Mitochondria

9 - The final electron acceptor in the electron transport chain of cellular respiration is:

B) Oxygen

10 - Mitosis results in:

B) Two genetically identical diploid cells

11 - During which phase of mitosis do chromosomes align at the cell's equator?

B) Metaphase

12 - Crossing over, a process that increases genetic diversity, occurs during:

B) Meiosis I

13 - The separation of sister chromatids occurs during:

B) Anaphase of mitosis

14 - An individual's physical appearance is determined by their:

B) Phenotype

15 - Which term describes a segment of DNA that codes for a protein?

B) Gene

16 - The "rungs" of the DNA ladder are made of:

A) Paired nitrogenous bases

17 - Which enzyme is responsible for unzipping the DNA double helix during replication?

B) Helicase

18 - The process by which mRNA is synthesized from the DNA template is called:

B) Transcription

19 - The sequence of _____ in DNA determines the sequence of amino acids in proteins.

C) Nucleotides

20 - Which structural feature of DNA is responsible for its ability to store and transmit genetic information effectively?

A) Double helix formation

Want More?

Download Answer Explanations Now by Framing the QR-Code With Your Phone

SECTION 6 - CHEMISTRY

This chapter is meticulously designed to guide you through the fundamental concepts and principles that form the backbone of chemistry. As an indispensable part of the healthcare field, a strong grasp of chemistry is crucial for understanding how medications interact within the body, the composition of substances, and the biochemical processes that sustain life. From the exploration of matter and its states to the intricate dance of atoms forming bonds, and the transformative power of chemical reactions, this chapter lays down the foundational knowledge necessary for your success on the exam and in your future healthcare career.

MATTER AND ITS STATES

Matter is defined as anything that has mass and occupies space. It is the substance of which all physical objects are made, from the smallest microorganisms to the vast expanse of the universe itself. Matter is composed of atoms and molecules and can exist in one of three primary states: solid, liquid, and gas. Each state has distinct characteristics based on the arrangement and behavior of its particles.

- **Solid** - In the solid state, matter has a definite shape and volume. The particles of a solid are closely packed together in a specific arrangement, which allows solids to maintain a fixed shape that does not change unless acted upon by an external force. The particles vibrate in place but do not move freely. This close packing results in solids being incompressible under normal conditions. Examples of solids include ice, wood, and iron.

- **Liquid** - Liquids have a definite volume but take the shape of their container. The particles in a liquid are still close together but not in a fixed arrangement, allowing them to move and flow around each other. This fluidity is what enables liquids to adapt their shape to the confines of their surroundings. Because the particles are still relatively close, liquids are nearly incompressible but can flow freely, making them distinct from solids. Water, oil, and blood are all examples of liquids.

- **Gas** - Gas has neither a definite shape nor volume. Gas particles are much further apart than in solids or liquids and move freely in all directions, filling any container they are placed in. The distance between particles in a gas means that gases are compressible, a property that distinguishes them from solids and liquids. Gases can expand or compress based on temperature and pressure changes. Examples include oxygen, nitrogen, and carbon dioxide.

These foundational principles not only provide insight into the physical world but also have practical applications in healthcare, from the administration of gases in anesthesia to the formulation of medications in liquid or solid form.

PHASE CHANGE

The transitions known as **phase changes** in matter are an essential concept in chemistry that explains the dynamic nature of substances under varying conditions. These changes occur when matter shifts between its three primary states—solid, liquid, and gas—each distinguished by unique particle arrangements and energy levels.

These changes occur when matter shifts between its three primary states—solid, liquid, and gas—each distinguished by unique particle arrangements and energy levels. Understanding these transformations is vital for aspiring healthcare professionals, as it underpins numerous biological and chemical processes relevant to medicine and patient care.

The process of melting, where a solid becomes a liquid, exemplifies a phase change driven by an increase in temperature and energy, allowing tightly packed particles to move more freely. Conversely, freezing occurs when a liquid loses energy and solidifies, its particles slowing down and adopting a fixed structure. Vaporization, including boiling and evaporation, transforms a liquid into a gas, necessitating energy to overcome intermolecular forces. The reverse, condensation, sees a gas cool down and transition back to a liquid, releasing energy in the process.

Furthermore, sublimation and deposition represent more complex phase changes. Sublimation occurs when a solid directly converts into a gas without passing through the liquid phase, as seen with dry ice. Deposition, its opposite, involves gas transforming directly into a solid, a phenomenon observable in frost formation.

Below is a table summarizing the phase changes of matter, including the transitions between solid, liquid, and gas states:

Phase Change	Description	Energy Change
Melting	Solid to Liquid	Energy is absorbed
Freezing	Liquid to Solid	Energy is released
Vaporization	Liquid to Gas	Energy is absorbed
Condensation	Gas to Liquid	Energy is released
Sublimation	Solid to Gas	Energy is absorbed
Deposition	Gas to Solid	Energy is released

HEATING AND COOLING CURVE

Heating and cooling curves provide a graphical representation of the phase transitions that a substance undergoes as it is gradually heated or cooled. Understanding these curves is crucial for interpreting how energy changes affect matter's state.

A heating curve plots temperature against the amount of heat added to a substance. As heat is applied, the substance's temperature rises until it reaches a phase change point, such as melting or boiling. At these points, the temperature remains constant despite the continued addition of heat, as the energy is used to break the intermolecular forces that hold the substance in its current state. Once the phase change is complete, the temperature rises again until the next phase transition occurs.

Conversely, a cooling curve represents how a substance cools and transitions from gas to liquid to solid. It shows a decrease in temperature over time, with plateaus indicating phase changes where the substance releases energy to the surroundings.

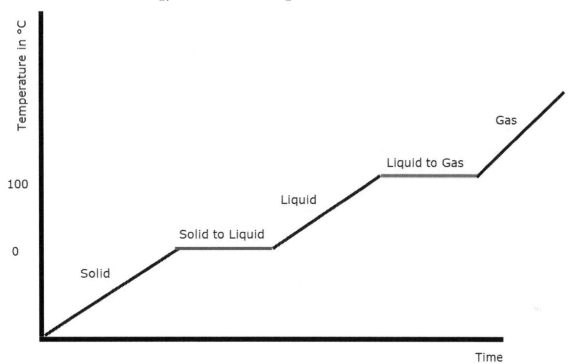

PHYSICAL AND CHEMICAL PROPERTIES

Physical and chemical properties of matter provide insights into how substances interact with each other and with their environment, influencing everything from the formulation of drugs to the diagnosis of diseases.

- **Physical Properties:** Physical properties can be observed or measured without changing the composition or identity of a substance. These properties include color, odor, density, melting point, boiling point, and state of matter (solid, liquid, gas). For instance, the melting point of ice is a physical property that describes the temperature at which it turns to water. Physical changes involve alterations in these properties without affecting the substance's chemical nature. Crushing a tablet into powder changes its form but not its chemical composition; thus, it's a physical change. Understanding physical properties is fundamental in the medical field, where the physical state of substances can affect their application and efficacy.

- **Chemical Properties:** Chemical properties, on the other hand, describe a substance's ability to undergo changes that transform it into different substances. These properties include reactivity with other chemicals, acidity or basicity, stability, and flammability. A chemical property of hydrogen, for example, is that it reacts explosively with oxygen to form water. Chemical changes result in the formation of one or more new substances with new chemical and physical properties. The metabolism of drugs in the body is a chemical change, transforming active drugs into metabolites through biochemical reactions.

The distinction between chemical and physical properties is crucial in healthcare. The solubility of a drug (a physical property) affects its absorption and distribution in the body, determining its effectiveness. The reactivity of a compound (a chemical property) can indicate its potential as a drug or its toxicity. Additionally, the understanding of these properties aids in the development of diagnostic tests, where chemical changes can indicate the presence of disease markers.

THE ATOM

This fundamental unit of chemistry is not just a cornerstone of scientific theory; it's the very essence of the physical universe, including everything from the air we breathe to the cells in our body. Understanding the atom is crucial for anyone entering the healthcare profession, as it underpins the principles of biochemistry, pharmacology, and physiology that are essential in medicine.

An atom is the smallest unit of an element that maintains the chemical properties of that element. At the heart of the atom lies the nucleus, a dense core made up of protons and neutrons. Protons carry a positive charge, while neutrons are neutral, having no charge. The number of protons in the nucleus defines the atomic number of the element, which is a unique identifier for each element in the periodic table. For instance, carbon atoms have six protons, hydrogen atoms have one, and oxygen atoms have eight.

Surrounding the nucleus are electrons, negatively charged particles that orbit the nucleus in electron shells. Despite their much smaller mass compared to protons and neutrons, electrons play a significant role in chemical reactions and bonding due to their charge and distribution around the nucleus. The interactions and arrangements of electrons determine how atoms will bond with each other to form molecules, which are the building blocks of compounds. In detail:

- **Protons** - Protons are positively charged particles found in the nucleus of an atom. The number of protons in an atom's nucleus defines the atomic number of an element, which in turn determines the element's identity. For example, hydrogen has one proton, so its atomic number is 1. The proton's positive charge balances the negative charge of electrons, ensuring that atoms are electrically neutral overall.

- **Neutrons** - Neutrons are neutral particles, possessing no charge, and are also located in the nucleus alongside protons. The number of neutrons in an atom contributes to its atomic mass but does not affect its electrical charge. Neutrons play a critical role in adding mass to an atom and in stabilizing the nucleus. Isotopes of an element differ in their number of neutrons, offering unique properties that have various applications in medicine, such as in diagnostic imaging techniques.

- **Electrons** - Electrons are negatively charged particles that orbit the nucleus in regions known as electron shells. Electrons are much smaller than protons or neutrons and have negligible mass in comparison. However, they play a pivotal role in chemical reactions and bonds, as their arrangement in the outer shells determines an atom's reactivity. The interaction of electrons between atoms forms the basis of chemical bonding, leading to the creation of molecules and compounds essential for life.

The beauty of the atomic structure lies in its simplicity and uniformity across all matter. Yet, this simplicity belies the complexity of interactions that occur at the atomic level, leading to the vast diversity of chemical substances and materials in the world. In healthcare, a deep understanding of atomic theory is applied in diagnosing diseases, developing pharmaceuticals, and even in the technology used for medical imaging and treatments.

ATOMIC NUMBER

The atomic number, denoted as $\mathbf{Z}$, is perhaps the most fundamental characteristic of an element because it defines the element's identity. This number represents the count of protons in an atom's nucleus, and because protons carry a positive charge, the atomic number also indicates the charge of the nucleus. For example, hydrogen, the simplest element, has an atomic number of 1, reflecting its single proton. Oxygen, essential for respiration, has an atomic number of 8, indicating eight protons in its nucleus.

The atomic number is crucial in healthcare for identifying elements and understanding their interactions. For instance, the behavior of electrolytes like sodium ($\mathbf{Na^+}$) and potassium ($\mathbf{K^+}$) in the body is predicated on their atomic numbers, which influence how they participate in nerve conduction and muscle contraction.

MASS NUMBER

The mass number, denoted as $\mathbf{A}$, is the total count of protons and neutrons in an atom's nucleus. Unlike the atomic number, the mass number is not fixed for all atoms of an element due to the presence of isotopes. Neutrons add mass but no charge to the atom, making them essential for understanding an atom's overall weight. The mass number is significant in calculating molecular weights, a fundamental practice in preparing medicinal dosages and solutions in healthcare settings.

ISOTOPES

Isotopes are variants of a particular element that have the same atomic number but different mass numbers due to variations in the number of neutrons. Isotopes retain the chemical properties of the element but differ in physical properties, such as melting point and density. Some isotopes are stable, while others are radioactive, decaying over time and emitting radiation.

Radioactive isotopes, or radioisotopes, have critical applications in medicine. For example, iodine-131 (^{131}I) is used in diagnosing and treating thyroid conditions, leveraging its radioactive properties to target thyroid tissues specifically. Similarly, carbon-14 (^{14}C), a radioactive isotope of carbon, is utilized in radiolabeling to trace biochemical pathways in research and diagnostic tests.

The concept of isotopes underscores the complexity and versatility of elements, illustrating how subtle differences in atomic structure can lead to diverse applications, especially in medical diagnostics and treatment. Understanding isotopes is pivotal for healthcare professionals, as it aids in interpreting laboratory results, understanding drug mechanisms, and applying therapeutic interventions.

PRACTICAL APPLICATIONS IN HEALTHCARE

The knowledge of atomic number, mass number, and isotopes is not merely academic; it has practical applications in various healthcare domains. For instance, pharmacists use the atomic and mass numbers to calculate compound molarities and prepare medication concentrations accurately. In nuclear medicine, understanding isotopes enables professionals to select appropriate radioisotopes for diagnostic imaging and therapeutic purposes, tailoring treatments to specific diseases and patient conditions.

Moreover, the concepts of atomic number and isotopes are crucial in understanding the body's biochemical reactions. For example, the role of calcium Ca^{2+} in bone health and muscle function is deeply rooted in its atomic properties, influencing how it interacts with other elements and molecules within the body.

PERIODIC TABLE OF ELEMENTS

The Periodic Table arranges all known chemical elements in an ordered, tabular format based on their atomic numbers, electron configurations, and recurring chemical properties. The periodic table is structured in rows called periods and columns known as groups or families. Each element on the table is represented by a unique atomic number, which corresponds to the number of protons in its nucleus, serving as the element's identifier.

This atomic number increases sequentially from left to right across the table, organizing the elements according to their increasing number of protons and, consequently, electrons.

Groups and Periods

Elements within the same group share similar properties because they have the same number of electrons in their outermost shell, which determines how they bond with other atoms. For example, the elements in Group 1 (the alkali metals) are highly reactive, especially with water. Meanwhile, the elements in Group 18 are the noble gases, which are known for their lack of reactivity due to having a full valence shell.

The periods represent elements with the same number of atomic orbitals. Moving from left to right across a period, each element has one more proton and is one electron heavier than the element before it. This progression explains the gradual changes in properties observed across a period.

Periodic Table of Elements

																	2 **He** Helium 4.00
4 **Be** Beryllium 9.01												5 **B** Boron 10.81	6 **C** Carbon 12.01	7 **N** Nitrogen 14.01	8 **O** Oxygen 16.00	9 **F** Fluorine 19.00	10 **Ne** Neon 20.18
12 **Mg** Magnesium 24.31												13 **Al** Aluminum 26.98	14 **Si** Silicon 28.09	15 **P** Phosphorus 30.97	16 **S** Sulfur 32.06	17 **Cl** Chlorine 35.45	18 **Ar** Argon 39.95
20 **Ca** Calcium 40.08	21 **Sc** Scandium 44.96	22 **Ti** Titanium 47.87	23 **V** Vanadium 50.94	24 **Cr** Chromium 52.00	25 **Mn** Manganese 54.94	26 **Fe** Iron 55.85	27 **Co** Cobalt 58.93	28 **Ni** Nickel 58.69	29 **Cu** Copper 63.55	30 **Zn** Zinc 65.38	31 **Ga** Gallium 69.72	32 **Ge** Germanium 72.63	33 **As** Arsenic 74.92	34 **Se** Selenium 78.97	35 **Br** Bromine 79.90	36 **Kr** Krypton 83.80
38 **Sr** Strontium 87.62	39 **Y** Yttrium 88.91	40 **Zr** Zirconium 91.22	41 **Nb** Niobium 92.91	42 **Mo** Molybdenum 95.95	43 **Tc** Technetium (98)	44 **Ru** Ruthenium 101.07	45 **Rh** Rhodium 102.91	46 **Pd** Palladium 106.42	47 **Ag** Silver 107.87	48 **Cd** Cadmium 112.41	49 **In** Indium 114.82	50 **Sn** Tin 118.71	51 **Sb** Antimony 121.76	52 **Te** Tellurium 127.60	53 **I** Iodine 126.90	54 **Xe** Xenon 131.29
56 **Ba** Barium 137.33	57 - 71 **Lanthanides**	72 **Hf** Hafnium 178.49	73 **Ta** Tantalum 180.95	74 **W** Tungsten 183.84	75 **Re** Rhenium 186.21	76 **Os** Osmium 190.23	77 **Ir** Iridium 192.22	78 **Pt** Platinum 195.08	79 **Au** Gold 196.97	80 **Hg** Mercury 200.59	81 **Tl** Thallium 204.38	82 **Pb** Lead 207.20	83 **Bi** Bismuth 208.98	84 **Po** Polonium (209)	85 **At** Astatine (210)	86 **Rn** Radon (222)
88 **Ra** Radium (226)	89 - 103 **Actinides**	104 **Rf** Rutherfordium (265)	105 **Db** Dubnium (268)	106 **Sg** Seaborgium (271)	107 **Bh** Bohrium (270)	108 **Hs** Hassium (277)	109 **Mt** Meitnerium (276)	110 **Ds** Darmstadtium (281)	111 **Rg** Roentgenium (280)	112 **Cn** Copernicium (285)	113 **Nh** Nihonium (284)	114 **Fl** Flerovium 289	115 **Mc** Moscovium (288)	116 **Lv** Livermorium (293)	117 **Ts** Tennessine (294)	118 **Og** Oganesson (294)

57 **La** Lanthanum 138.91	58 **Ce** Cerium 140.12	59 **Pr** Praseodymium 140.91	60 **Nd** Neodymium 144.24	61 **Pm** Promethium (145)	62 **Sm** Samarium 150.36	63 **Eu** Europium 151.96	64 **Gd** Gadolinium 157.25	65 **Tb** Terbium 158.93	66 **Dy** Dysprosium 182.50	67 **Ho** Holmium 164.93	68 **Er** Erbium 167.26	69 **Tm** Thulium 168.93	70 **Yb** Ytterbium 173.05	71 **Lu** Lutetium 174.97
89 **Ac** Actinium (227)	90 **Th** Thorium 232.04	91 **Pa** Protactinium 231.04	92 **U** Uranium 238.03	93 **Np** Neptunium (237)	94 **Pu** Plutonium (244)	95 **Am** Americium (243)	96 **Cm** Curium (247)	97 **Bk** Berkelium (247)	98 **Cf** Californium (251)	99 **Es** Einsteinium (252)	100 **Fm** Fermium (257)	101 **Md** Mendelevium (258)	102 **No** Nobelium (259)	103 **Lr** Lawrencium (262)

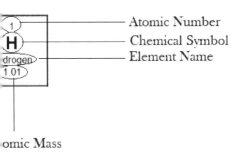

Atomic Number
Chemical Symbol
Element Name

omic Mass

CHEMICAL REACTIONS

A chemical reaction is a process that leads to the transformation of one set of chemical substances to another. Classically, it involves changes that only affect the arrangement of electrons in the formation of chemical bonds but do not change the nuclei of atoms. Chemical reactions are represented by chemical equations, which list the reactants (starting materials) on the left and the products (newly formed substances) on the right, with an arrow indicating the direction of the reaction.

There are several types of chemical reactions, each with unique characteristics and implications:

1. **Synthesis Reactions:** Two or more simple substances combine to form a more complex product. For instance, the synthesis of water from hydrogen and oxygen gases is fundamental to understanding cellular respiration.

2. **Decomposition Reactions:** A compound breaks down into simpler substances, often requiring energy input. This type is crucial in understanding how the body breaks down complex molecules for energy.

3. **Single Replacement Reactions:** One element replaces another in a compound, a reaction type that is vital in the metabolism of various minerals in the body.

4. **Double Replacement Reactions:** The ions of two compounds exchange places in an aqueous solution to form two new compounds. This process can be seen in the neutralization reactions between acids and bases.

5. **Combustion Reactions:** A substance combines with oxygen to release energy, as seen in the cellular process of producing ATP.

CHEMICAL BONDS

Chemical bonds are the forces of attraction that hold atoms together in molecules and compounds, dictating the structure and properties of substances. A solid grasp of chemical bonding is crucial for future healthcare professionals, as it informs everything from the pharmacodynamics of drugs to the biochemical pathways essential for life.

Types of Chemical Bonds

There are three primary types of chemical bonds: ionic, covalent, and metallic.

- **Ionic Bonds** form between atoms when one atom donates an electron to another, creating ions: positively charged cations and negatively charged anions. This transfer of electrons results in a force of attraction between the oppositely charged ions. Ionic bonds are typically formed between metals and nonmetals. For example, sodium chloride (table salt) consists of sodium ions ($Na+$) and chloride ions ($Cl-$) bonded together through ionic bonds. In healthcare, ionic bonds play a role in the structure of many drugs and in the electrolyte balance critical for bodily functions.

- **Covalent Bonds** occur when two atoms share one or more pairs of electrons, allowing each atom to achieve a stable electron configuration. Covalent bonding is common between non-metal atoms. Molecules like oxygen (O2) and water (H2O) are classic examples, where atoms share electrons to form strong bonds. Understanding covalent bonds is vital in biochemistry, where they determine the structure and function of biomolecules, from the DNA double helix to proteins and enzymes.

- **Metallic Bonds** are found in metals, where electrons are shared among a lattice of metal atoms, allowing electrons to flow freely. This unique bonding gives metals their characteristic properties, such as conductivity and malleability. While less directly related to healthcare than ionic and covalent bonds, metallic bonds are important in the context of medical devices and implants.

While ionic and covalent bonds involve the interactions of specific atoms through either the transfer or sharing of electrons, metallic bonds involve a collective sharing of electrons across a network of atoms. Ionic bonds result in the formation of crystalline solids that are brittle and conduct electricity in solution, whereas covalent compounds form molecules with varying physical properties. Metallic bonds confer unique properties to metals that are exploited in technology and medicine.

Chemical bonds are fundamental to the structure and function of the myriad compounds involved in bodily processes and medical treatments. The strength and type of bonds influence the physical and chemical properties of molecules, including their reactivity, boiling and melting points, and how they interact with the human body.
For example, the breaking and forming of chemical bonds underlie the mechanisms of many drugs, affecting how they are absorbed, distributed, metabolized, and excreted by the body.

ENERGY IN CHEMICAL REACTIONS

Energy is the driving force behind the transformation of substances, and understanding its involvement is essential for aspiring healthcare professionals. This knowledge underpins everything from metabolic processes in the body to the mechanism of action of medications.

Chemical reactions involve the breaking and forming of bonds between atoms, processes that require or release energy.

Energy in the context of chemical reactions can be broadly classified into two types: endothermic and exothermic:

- **Endothermic Reactions:** absorb energy from the surrounding environment. This absorption is necessary to break the bonds in the reactants, allowing them to form new bonds and thus new products. An example of an endothermic reaction is photosynthesis, wherein plants absorb sunlight to convert carbon dioxide and water into glucose and oxygen. In healthcare, understanding endothermic reactions is crucial when considering how certain drugs are metabolized, as some reactions require energy input to proceed.

- **Exothermic Reactions:** release energy into the surrounding environment. This release occurs when the energy needed to break the bonds in the reactants is less than the energy released when the products form. Combustion is a classic example of an exothermic reaction, where substances like glucose oxidize rapidly with oxygen to release energy. Exothermic reactions are fundamental to understanding how the body generates heat and energy from food.

The concept of activation energy, the minimum energy required to initiate a chemical reaction, further illustrates the role of energy in chemical processes. Enzymes, which are biological catalysts, lower the activation energy of biochemical reactions in the body, facilitating vital processes like digestion and respiration.

REACTION RATES AND EQUILIBRIUM

- **Reaction Rates:** The reaction rate refers to the speed at which reactants are converted into products in a chemical reaction. It's influenced by several factors, including the concentration of reactants, temperature, presence of a catalyst, and surface area of the reactants. In the human body, enzymes act as biological catalysts, significantly increasing the reaction rates of biochemical processes essential for life. Understanding how these factors affect reaction rates is crucial for healthcare professionals, as it aids in predicting how quickly a drug will be metabolized or how fast a patient can respond to treatment.

- **Chemical Equilibrium:** Chemical equilibrium occurs when the rates of the forward and reverse reactions in a system become equal, leading to a constant ratio of product and reactant concentrations. It's important to note that reaching equilibrium does not mean the reactants and products are equal in concentration, but rather that their rates of formation are balanced. In healthcare, the concept of equilibrium is essential for understanding many physiological processes, such as the oxygenation of blood in the lungs and the regulation of pH in bodily fluids.

CHEMICAL SOLUTIONS

A solution consists of a solute and a solvent. The solute is the substance that is dissolved, and the solvent is the medium in which the solute is dissolved. Typically, in a solution, the solvent is present in a greater amount than the solute.

Water, due to its capability to dissolve a wide range of substances, is the most common solvent in biological systems, earning it the title of "**universal solvent**."

Solutions can exist in various phases: gaseous, liquid, or solid. In healthcare, liquid solutions, such as saline solution or dextrose in water, are commonly used for patient hydration, medication delivery, and as a medium for various diagnostic tests. The concentration of a solution—often expressed in molarity (moles of solute per liter of solution) or molality (moles of solute per kilogram of solvent)—is crucial in preparing medications and intravenous fluids to ensure they are safe and effective for patient treatment.

Solubility and Saturation

Solubility, the maximum amount of solute that can dissolve in a solvent at a given temperature and pressure, is key to understanding how drugs are absorbed into the body and how they can be efficiently delivered to their target sites. Factors affecting solubility, such as temperature, pressure, and the nature of the solute and solvent, are essential considerations in pharmaceutical formulation. A saturated solution has reached its maximum solute concentration under specific conditions, while unsaturated solutions can dissolve more solute.

Electrolytes and Nonelectrolytes

In healthcare, the distinction between electrolyte and nonelectrolyte solutions is vital. Electrolytes are solutes that dissociate into ions in solution, conducting electricity, essential for maintaining cellular function and nerve impulse transmission. Nonelectrolytes do not dissociate into ions and therefore do not conduct electricity. Understanding the behavior of electrolytes in solution is critical for managing electrolyte imbalances in patients, a common concern in medical care.

MOLES AND AVOGADRO'S NUMBER

The mole is a standard unit of measurement in chemistry used to express amounts of a chemical substance. It allows chemists and healthcare professionals to quantify the number of particles, such as atoms, molecules, or ions, in a given sample. One mole of any substance contains the same number of particles as there are atoms in exactly 12 grams of carbon-12. This number is astonishingly large, highlighting the need for such a unit to measure the vast numbers of particles involved in chemical reactions.

The mole also plays a critical role in understanding and balancing chemical equations. It provides a basis for quantifying the reactants and products, ensuring that the principle of conservation of mass is maintained in chemical reactions. This is vital for accurately predicting the outcomes of chemical reactions, including those that occur in pharmaceutical formulations and metabolic processes.

Avogadro's Number

Avogadro's number, named after the Italian scientist Amedeo Avogadro, is the number of particles in one mole of a substance. It is a constant, defined as **6.022×10^{23}** particles per mole. This incredibly large number allows chemists to work with the atomic and molecular levels in a manageable way, providing a concrete figure to calculate and compare the amounts of substances involved in chemical reactions.

Applications in Healthcare

In healthcare, the concept of the mole and Avogadro's number is applied in various ways, from the pharmacological development of drugs to the clinical diagnostics of diseases. For example:

- **Drug Formulation and Dosage:** Understanding the mole concept allows pharmacists to accurately formulate drugs and determine dosages, ensuring that patients receive the correct amount of active ingredients.
- **Diagnostic Tests:** Laboratory tests often involve measuring the concentration of substances in blood or urine samples. The mole concept is used to express these concentrations in terms such as molarity, the number of moles of solute per liter of solution, providing a standardized method for interpreting test results.
- **Metabolic Pathways:** The body's biochemical reactions, such as those involved in metabolism, are quantified using the mole concept. This helps in understanding how substances are broken down or synthesized within the body, crucial for diagnosing metabolic disorders.

CONVERTING BETWEEN MOLES, MASS, AND THE NUMBER OF PARTICLES

This ability is not just academic; it is foundational for various applications in healthcare, including pharmacology, laboratory diagnostics, and nutritional science. Understanding these conversions enables healthcare professionals to quantify and manipulate chemical substances accurately, ensuring precise formulations, correct dosages, and accurate interpretations of laboratory results. At the heart of these conversions is the mole, a unit that links the microscopic world of atoms and molecules to the macroscopic world we measure and observe. One mole of any substance contains Avogadro's number (6.022×10^{23}) of particles (atoms, molecules, or ions), providing a bridge between an element's atomic mass on the molecular scale and its mass in grams on the tangible scale.

From Moles to Mass

Converting moles to mass (and vice versa) is a fundamental process in chemistry. The molar mass, which is the mass of one mole of a substance, directly relates the amount of substance in moles to its mass in grams. The molar mass of an element (in grams per mole) is numerically equal to its atomic mass (in atomic mass units, amu) listed on the periodic table. For compounds, the molar mass is the sum of the atomic masses of all atoms in the molecule.

$$\text{Mass(g)} = \text{Moles} \times \text{Molar Mass (g/mol)}$$

From Moles to Number of Particles

To convert moles to the number of particles or vice versa, Avogadro's number is used. This conversion is crucial for understanding the quantity of molecules involved in chemical reactions, which directly impacts reaction stoichiometry and the preparation of solutions in healthcare settings.

$$\text{Number of Particles} = \text{Moles} \times \text{Avogadro's Number}$$

From Mass to Number of Particles

Combining the two conversions, we can directly relate the mass of a substance to the number of its constituent particles. This is particularly useful in healthcare for calculating drug dosages based on molecular quantities or determining the number of ions in electrolyte solutions.

$$\text{Number of Particles} = \left(\frac{\text{Mass (g)}}{\text{Molar Mass (g/mol)}} \right) \times \text{Avogadro's Number}$$

STOICHIOMETRY

Stoichiometry is the quantitative relationship between reactants and products in a chemical reaction. It allows us to predict the amounts of substances consumed and produced in reactions, providing a mathematical framework for understanding chemical processes.

At the heart of stoichiometry lies the balanced chemical equation, which provides the mole ratios of reactants and products. These ratios are the key to calculating how much of one substance is required to react with another and what quantity of products will be formed. Understanding stoichiometry is essential for accurately interpreting and conducting chemical reactions, from synthesizing pharmaceuticals to diagnosing and treating diseases.

Stoichiometric calculations often involve several steps, including:

* Converting masses of reactants or products to moles using molar mass.
* Using the mole ratios from the balanced equation to calculate the moles of other substances involved.
* Converting moles back to masses if required, using molar mass again.
* Considering the limiting reactant, which determines the maximum amount of product that can be formed.

ACIDS AND BASES

Acids and bases are crucial components of chemical theory with significant implications in healthcare. Understanding the nature of acids and bases, their properties, and how they interact with one another is essential for students entering the healthcare field, as these interactions underlie many physiological processes and treatment methodologies.

Acids

Acids are substances that donate protons (H^+ ions) in a chemical reaction. In aqueous solutions, acids have a sour taste, can turn blue litmus paper red, and react with metals to produce hydrogen gas. The strength of an acid is determined by its ability to donate protons; strong acids, such as hydrochloric acid (HCl), dissociate completely in water, releasing a high concentration of H^+ ions, while weak acids, like acetic acid (CH_3COOH), only partially dissociate.

In the body, acids play a critical role in maintaining the pH balance of various fluids, such as gastric acid in the stomach, which aids in digestion. In healthcare, acids are used in various treatments, from aspirin (acetylsalicylic acid) for pain relief to topical salicylic acid for treating skin conditions.

Bases

Bases, in contrast, are substances that accept protons. They can also be defined as substances that donate hydroxide ions (OH^-) in aqueous solutions. Bases feel slippery, taste bitter, and turn red litmus paper blue. Strong bases, like sodium hydroxide (NaOH), dissociate completely in water to release a high concentration of OH^- ions, while weak bases, such as ammonia (NH_3), dissociate partially.

Bases are fundamental to many bodily functions, including the buffering of blood to maintain its pH. In healthcare, bases are used in medications such as antacids to neutralize stomach acid and in the formulation of various drugs and medical products.

PH SCALE

The pH scale quantitatively measures the acidity or basicity of a solution. It ranges from 0 to 14, with 7 being neutral. pH values less than 7 indicate acidic solutions, while values greater than 7 denote basic solutions. The pH scale is logarithmic, meaning each unit change represents a tenfold change in H^+ ion concentration.

pH Value	Description	Examples
0-1	Extremely Acidic	Battery Acid
2-3	Highly Acidic	Lemon Juice, Vinegar

4-5	Acidic	Tomato Juice, Black Coffee
6	Slightly Acidic	Urine, Milk
7	Neutral	Pure Water
8-9	Slightly Basic	Sea Water, Baking Soda
10-11	Basic	Ammonia Solution
12-13	Highly Basic	Soapy Water
14	Extremely Basic	Liquid Drain Cleaner

This table categorizes the pH scale into various levels of acidity and basicity, providing examples of common substances at different pH levels. A pH of 7 is considered neutral, neither acidic nor basic, exemplified by pure water. Values below 7 represent acidic solutions, with lower numbers indicating higher acidity. Conversely, values above 7 represent basic (alkaline) solutions, with higher numbers indicating greater basicity. The pH scale is logarithmic, meaning each whole pH value below 7 is ten times more acidic than the next higher value, and each whole pH value above 7 is ten times more basic than the next lower value.

ACID-BASE REACTIONS

Acid-base reactions involve the transfer of protons (H^+ ions) from acids to bases, leading to the formation of water and a salt. This process, known as neutralization, is central to many biological systems and medical treatments.

Acids are substances that can donate protons, characterized by their sour taste and ability to turn blue litmus paper red. Bases, on the other hand, are proton acceptors, often slippery to the touch, bitter in taste, and turn red litmus paper blue. The strength of an acid or base depends on its ability to donate or accept protons; strong acids and bases dissociate completely in water, releasing a large number of ions, while weak acids and bases only partially dissociate.

The neutralization reaction between an acid and a base can be represented by the general equation:

$$\text{Acid} + \text{Base} \rightarrow \text{Salt} + \text{Water}$$

For example, when hydrochloric acid (HCl) reacts with sodium hydroxide (NaOH), they form sodium chloride (NaCl), commonly known as table salt, and water (H_2O):

$$HCl + NaOH \rightarrow NaCl + H_2O$$

106 SECTION 6 - CHEMISTRY

SECTION 6 - CHEMISTRY
PRACTICE QUIZ

1 - Which state of matter has a definite shape and definite volume?
A. Liquid
B. Gas
C. Solid
D. Plasma

2 - Which is not a characteristic of a gas?
A. Fills the shape of its container
B. Has a definite volume
C. Compressible
D. Expands to fill its container

3 - In which state of matter do particles have the highest kinetic energy?
A. Solid
B. Liquid
C. Gas
D. Plasma

4 - What is the process of a gas turning into a liquid?
A. Freezing
B. Condensation
C. Melting
D. Sublimation

5 - Melting point is the temperature at which:
A. A solid becomes a liquid
B. A liquid becomes a gas
C. A gas becomes a liquid
D. A liquid becomes a solid

6 - Sublimation refers to the transition of:
A. Liquid to gas
B. Solid to gas
C. Gas to solid
D. Solid to liquid

Hesi A2 Study Guide

7 - Boiling and evaporation are processes that describe the transition from:

A. Solid to liquid

B. Liquid to gas

C. Gas to liquid

D. Solid to gas

8 - On a heating curve, what does a plateau indicate?

A. Phase change

B. Temperature increase

C. Increase in kinetic energy

D. Decrease in potential energy

9 - In a cooling curve, during which part does the substance change from gas to liquid?

A. Initial decrease in temperature

B. Plateau

C. Final part of the curve

10 - Boiling point is an example of a:

A. Physical property

B. Chemical property

C. Biological property

11 - The ability of iron to rust is an example of a:

A. Physical property

B. Chemical property

C. Biological property

12 - Which of the following is a chemical property?

A. Density

B. Flammability

C. Melting point

D. Solubility

13 - The nucleus of an atom contains:

A. Electrons and protons

B. Protons and neutrons

C. Only protons

D. Only neutrons

14 - Electrons

A. Have a negative charge

B. Are found in the nucleus

C. Have the largest mass

D. Do not participate in chemical reactions

15 - Which part of the atom participates in chemical bonds?

A. Electrons

B. Protons

C. Neutrons

D. Nucleus

16 - The atomic number of an element indicates:

A. The number of protons in the nucleus

B. The number of neutrons in the nucleus

C. The total number of protons and neutrons

D. The number of electrons in the outer shell

17 - The mass number of an atom is calculated by adding the number of:

A. Protons and neutrons

B. Protons and electrons

C. Electrons and neutrons

D. Neutrons only

18 - Isotopes of an element have different:

A. Numbers of neutrons

B. Numbers of protons

C. Atomic numbers

D. Chemical properties

19 - Which statement about isotopes is true?

A. They have different atomic numbers.

B. They have the same number of protons but different numbers of neutrons.

C. They have different numbers of electrons.

D. They are always radioactive.

20 - Avogadro's number is significant in chemistry because:

A. It represents the number of atoms or molecules in one mole of a substance.

B. It determines the atomic mass of elements.

C. It is the number of protons in hydrogen.

D. It indicates the number of electrons needed for an atom to be stable.

21 - Elements in the same group on the periodic table:

A. Have similar chemical properties

B. Have the same atomic mass

C. Are all gases at room temperature

D. Have the same number of neutrons

22 - The periodic table is arranged by:

A. Increasing atomic number

B. Decreasing atomic mass

C. Alphabetical order

D. Increasing melting points

23 - A covalent bond is formed by:

A. The sharing of electron pairs between atoms

B. The transfer of electrons from one atom to another

C. The attraction between a proton and a neutron

D. The attraction between two nuclei

24 - An ionic bond is characterized by:

A. The transfer of electrons from one atom to another

B. The sharing of electrons between atoms

C. The equal distribution of electrons

D. The formation of a metallic lattice

25 - Which type of bond involves the delocalization of electrons across a lattice of metal atoms?

A. Covalent

B. Ionic

C. Metallic

26 - In a chemical reaction, the substances that are consumed are called:

A. Reactants

B. Products

C. Catalysts

D. Inhibitors

27 - A reaction that absorbs energy from its surroundings is called:

A. Endothermic

B. Exothermic

C. Catalytic

D. Reversible

28 - The law of conservation of mass states that:

A. Mass is neither created nor destroyed in a chemical reaction

B. Mass increases in a chemical reaction

C. Mass decreases in a chemical reaction

D. Only energy is conserved in a chemical reaction

29 - Which type of reaction absorbs energy from its surroundings?

A. Exothermic

B. Endothermic

C. Neutralization

D. Catalytic

30 - What is the term used to describe the minimum energy required for a chemical reaction to proceed?

A. Activation energy

B. Kinetic energy

C. Potential energy

D. Thermal energy

31 - An exothermic reaction releases energy primarily in the form of:

A. Light

B. Heat

C. Electricity

D. Sound

32 - How many atoms are in one mole of any element?

A. 3.01×10^{22}

B. 6.022×10^{23}

C. 6.022×10^{22}

D. 3.01×10^{23}

33 - In an exothermic chemical reaction:

A. Energy is absorbed from the surroundings, increasing the temperature of the system.

B. Energy is released into the surroundings, decreasing the temperature of the system.

C. Energy is released into the surroundings, increasing the temperature of the surroundings.

D. No energy exchange occurs between the system and the surroundings.

34 - The stoichiometric coefficient in a balanced chemical equation indicates:

A. The phase of the substance

B. The temperature at which the reaction occurs

C. The relative number of moles of reactants and products

D. The concentration of the solution

35 - Which substance has a pH level of 7?

A. Vinegar

B. Stomach acid

C. Pure water

D. Soap

36 - A solution with a pH of 8 is:

A. Strongly acidic

B. Slightly basic

C. Neutral

D. Strongly basic

37 - What is the pH of a solution that is neither acidic nor basic?

A. 4

B. 7

C. 12

D. 14

38 - An acid reacts with a base to form:

A. Another acid

B. Water and a salt

C. Oxygen

D. A precipitate

39 - Which of the following is a strong base?

A. NH_3 (Ammonia)

B. NaOH (Sodium Hydroxide)

C. HF (Hydrofluoric Acid)

D. CH_3COOH (Acetic Acid)

Want More?

Download Answer Explanations Now by Framing the QR-Code With Your Phone

SECTION 6 - CHEMISTRY
PRACTICE QUIZ - ANSWER KEY

1 - Which state of matter has a definite shape and definite volume?

C) Solid

2 - Which is not a characteristic of a gas?

B) Has a definite volume

3 - In which state of matter do particles have the highest kinetic energy?

C) Gas

4 - What is the process of a gas turning into a liquid?

B) Condensation

5 - Melting point is the temperature at which:

A) A solid becomes a liquid

6 - Sublimation refers to the transition of:

B) Solid to gas

7 - Boiling and evaporation are processes that describe the transition from:

B) Liquid to gas

8 - On a heating curve, what does a plateau indicate?

A) Phase change

9 - In a cooling curve, during which part does the substance change from gas to liquid?

B) Plateau

10 - Boiling point is an example of a:

A) Physical property

11 - The ability of iron to rust is an example of a:

B) Chemical property

12 - Which of the following is a chemical property?

B) Flammability

13 - The nucleus of an atom contains:

B) Protons and neutrons

14 - Electrons:

A) Have a negative charge

15 - Which part of the atom participates in chemical bonds?

A) Electrons

16 - The atomic number of an element indicates:

A) The number of protons in the nucleus

17 - The mass number of an atom is calculated by adding the number of:

A) Protons and neutrons

18 - Isotopes of an element have different:

A) Numbers of neutrons

19 - Which statement about isotopes is true?

B) They have the same number of protons but different numbers of neutrons.

20 - Avogadro's number is significant in chemistry because:

A) It represents the number of atoms or molecules in one mole of a substance.

21 - Elements in the same group on the periodic table:

A) Have similar chemical properties

22 - The periodic table is arranged by:

A) Increasing atomic number

23 - A covalent bond is formed by:

A) The sharing of electron pairs between atoms

24 - An ionic bond is characterized by:

A) The transfer of electrons from one atom to another

25 - Which type of bond involves the delocalization of electrons across a lattice of metal atoms?

C) Metallic

26 - In a chemical reaction, the substances that are consumed are called:

A) Reactants

27 - A reaction that absorbs energy from its surroundings is called:

A) Endothermic

28 - The law of conservation of mass states that:

A) Mass is neither created nor destroyed in a chemical reaction

29 - Which type of reaction absorbs energy from its surroundings?

B) Endothermic

30 - What is the term used to describe the minimum energy required for a chemical reaction to proceed?

A) Activation energy

31 - An exothermic reaction releases energy primarily in the form of:

B) Heat

32 - How many atoms are in one mole of any element?

B) 6.022×10^{23}

33 - In an exothermic chemical reaction:

C) Energy is released into the surroundings, increasing the temperature of the surroundings.

34 - The stoichiometric coefficient in a balanced chemical equation indicates:

C) The relative number of moles of reactants and products.

35 - Which substance has a pH level of 7?

C) Pure water

36 - A solution with a pH of 8 is:

B) Slightly basic

37 - What is the pH of a solution that is neither acidic nor basic?

B) 7

38 - An acid reacts with a base to form:

B) Water and a salt

39 - Which of the following is a strong base?

B) NaOH (Sodium Hydroxide)

SECTION 7 - HUMAN ANATOMY AND PHYSIOLOGY

Human anatomy is the scientific study of the body's structure. It delves into the intricate details of how the body is organized, from the smallest cellular level to the complex systems that carry out life-sustaining functions. Anatomy is often divided into two main categories: gross (or macroscopic) anatomy, which involves structures that can be seen with the naked eye, and microscopic anatomy, which requires magnification to view cell and tissue structures. This detailed exploration allows healthcare professionals to understand where organs and systems are located, how they are constructed, and their spatial relationships to one another, which is essential for diagnosis, surgery, and treatment.

Physiology complements the study of anatomy by focusing on the functions and processes of the various body parts. It seeks to understand how bodily structures work and respond to challenges. Physiology covers a broad range of scales from the molecular mechanisms within cells to the overall functions of major body systems. This discipline is dynamic, considering how the body operates under normal circumstances, how it adjusts in adverse conditions, and how imbalances in one part of the body can affect the system as a whole.

Anatomy and physiology are inherently interconnected, offering a comprehensive picture of the human body's form and function. For healthcare practitioners, understanding this relationship is paramount. For instance, knowing the anatomical structure of the heart helps in understanding how blood is pumped and circulated (physiology), which is crucial for diagnosing and treating cardiovascular diseases.

HUMAN TISSUES

Tissues are groups of cells that work together to perform specific functions. Understanding the four primary types of tissues—epithelial, connective, muscle, and nervous—is crucial for anyone entering the healthcare profession, as it forms the basis for understanding organ structure, disease processes, and treatment modalities.

- **Epithelial Tissue:** Epithelial tissue forms the lining of internal organs, the skin's outer layer, and the structures of many glands. Characterized by its closely packed cells, epithelial tissue serves as a barrier against microorganisms, physical injuries, and fluid loss. It is involved in functions such as absorption (as in the intestines), secretion (as in glands), and sensation (as in the skin). Epithelial tissue is classified by the shape of its cells (squamous, cuboidal, columnar) and the number of cell layers (simple, stratified, pseudostratified).

- **Connective Tissue:** Connective tissue is the most abundant and diverse tissue type, providing support, protection, and insulation for the body. It consists of cells embedded in an extracellular matrix composed of protein fibers and ground substance. This tissue type ranges from soft (e.g., adipose tissue) to hard (e.g., bone), including loose connective tissue, dense connective tissue, cartilage, bone, and blood. Connective tissue functions to bind organs together, store energy reserves as fat, and participate in immune responses.

- **Muscle Tissue:** Muscle tissue is specialized for contraction and movement. It is categorized into three types: skeletal, cardiac, and smooth muscle tissue. Skeletal muscle is attached to bones, facilitating voluntary movements and posture control. Cardiac muscle, found only in the heart, pumps blood through involuntary, rhythmic contractions. Smooth muscle, located in the walls of internal organs, controls involuntary movements such as the passage of food through the digestive system and the regulation of blood vessel diameter.

- **Nervous Tissue:** Nervous tissue is the main component of the nervous system, including the brain, spinal cord, and peripheral nerves. It consists of neurons, which transmit electrical signals throughout the body, and glial cells, which provide support and protection for neurons. Nervous tissue is involved in receiving sensory information, processing it, and eliciting responses, playing a critical role in controlling and coordinating body functions.

Tissue Type	Main Functions	Characteristics	Locations
Epithelial	Protection, absorption, secretion, sensation	Closely packed cells; layers can be simple or stratified	Skin surface, lining of organs and ducts
Connective	Support, bind, protect, store energy, transport	Cells embedded in an extracellular matrix of protein fibers	Bones, tendons, adipose tissue, blood
Muscle	Movement, stability, heat production	Cells can contract; types include skeletal, cardiac, and smooth	Attached to bones, heart, walls of organs
Nervous	Transmit impulses, process information	Composed of neurons (nerve cells) and neuroglia (supporting cells)	Brain, spinal cord, peripheral nerves

THE SKELETAL SYSTEM

The skeletal system is not just the framework that supports the body; it is a complex structure that plays crucial roles in protection, movement, and homeostasis.

The human skeletal system comprises **206 bones** at adulthood, classified into two main categories: **the axial skeleton**, which includes the skull, vertebral column, and rib cage, and **the**

appendicular skeleton, consisting of the limbs and girdles.

The skeletal system performs several key functions:

- **Support:** Bones provide a rigid framework that supports the body and cradles soft organs.
- **Protection:** Bones protect internal organs from injury, with the skull encasing the brain and the rib cage shielding the heart and lungs.
- **Movement:** Muscles are attached to bones; when muscles contract, they move the bones, facilitating movement.
- **Mineral Storage:** Bones serve as a reservoir for minerals, especially calcium and phosphate, crucial for various cellular processes.
- **Blood Cell Production:** The bone marrow, found within the hollow centers of many bones, is the site of red blood cell production, a process known as hematopoiesis.
- **Energy Storage:** Yellow marrow, stored in the bones, contains adipocytes that can serve as an energy reserve.

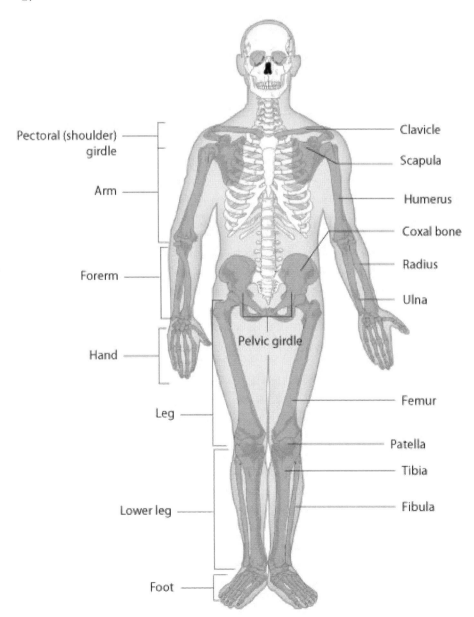

BONE STRUCTURE AND GROWTH

Bones come in various shapes and sizes, tailored to their specific functions within the body. The classification of bone shapes includes:

1. **Long Bones:** Characterized by a length greater than their width, such as the femur. They are crucial for large movements and act as levers.

2. **Short Bones:** Approximately equal in length, width, and thickness, providing stability with little movement, as seen in the carpal bones of the wrist.

3. **Flat Bones:** Thin and often curved, like the ribs and skull bones, providing protection for vital organs and surfaces for muscle attachment.

4. **Irregular Bones:** Complex shapes that do not fit into other categories, such as the vertebrae, supporting structural integrity and protecting the spinal cord.

Ossification

Ossification is the process by which bone tissue is formed, a crucial aspect of both prenatal development and the growth of children and adolescents. There are two primary types of ossification:

1. **Intramembranous Ossification:** This process forms the flat bones of the skull, facial bones, and the clavicles. It involves the direct conversion of mesenchymal tissue into bone without a prior cartilage template.

2. **Endochondral Ossification:** Responsible for the formation of long bones, endochondral ossification proceeds through a cartilage model that gradually is replaced by bone tissue. This process is critical for the lengthening of bones during growth and involves a growth plate (epiphyseal plate), where new bone is added as the cartilage is replaced.

Bone Remodeling

Bone remodeling is a lifelong process involving the resorption of old or damaged bone and the deposition of new bone. This process is essential for bone health, allowing the skeleton to adapt to stress, repair microdamage, and regulate calcium levels in the body. Bone remodeling is coordinated by two main types of cells:

1. **Osteoclasts:** These cells break down and resorb bone, releasing calcium into the bloodstream. They are crucial for removing damaged or unnecessary bone tissue.

2. **Osteoblasts:** Following the osteoclasts, osteoblasts deposit new bone tissue, utilizing calcium from the blood. They play a key role in bone formation and repair.

3. **Osteocytes**: Osteocytes are mature bone cells that have become embedded in the bone ma-

trix. They originate from osteoblasts, the cells responsible for bone formation. Once osteoblasts have secreted the bone matrix around themselves, they become trapped within it, transitioning into osteocytes. These cells reside in small cavities called lacunae, which are interconnected by tiny channels called canaliculi. Through the canaliculi, osteocytes are able to communicate and exchange nutrients and waste products with each other and with blood vessels in the bone.

This dynamic balance between bone resorption and formation allows the skeleton to maintain its strength and density. Factors influencing bone remodeling include mechanical stress, hormones (such as parathyroid hormone and calcitonin), and dietary nutrients (including calcium and vitamin D).

MUSCULAR SYSTEM

The muscular system comprises over 600 muscles that work in harmony to execute a wide range of movements and functions. Muscles are categorized into three main types based on structure and function: **Skeletal, Cardiac, and Smooth Muscles**.

SKELETAL MUSCLES

Skeletal muscles are under voluntary control, meaning we can consciously command them to contract and produce movement, a feature that distinguishes them from cardiac and smooth muscles.

Skeletal muscle is composed of individual muscle fibers, which are long, cylindrical cells that can be several centimeters in length. Each fiber is encased in a plasma membrane known as the sarcolemma, which contains the cytoplasm (sarcoplasm) and a specialized endoplasmic reticulum (sarcoplasmic reticulum). Muscle fibers are packed with myofibrils, the components that give muscle its striated appearance and are responsible for contraction. Myofibrils contain repeating units called sarcomeres, which are the basic functional units of muscle contraction and are composed of thin (actin) and thick (myosin) filaments.

Function and Contraction

Skeletal muscle contraction is a highly regulated process initiated by a motor neuron impulse that triggers the release of calcium ions from the sarcoplasmic reticulum. Calcium ions bind to troponin, a regulatory protein on the actin filaments, causing a shift that allows myosin heads to bind to actin and form cross-bridges. Through the ATP-dependent "power stroke" process, myosin heads pivot, pulling the actin filaments toward the center of the sarcomere, resulting in muscle contraction.

The force of a muscle contraction can vary based on the number of motor units (a motor neuron and the muscle fibers it innervates) activated, a principle known as the size principle. This allows for precise control of muscle force, from delicate movements to powerful contractions.

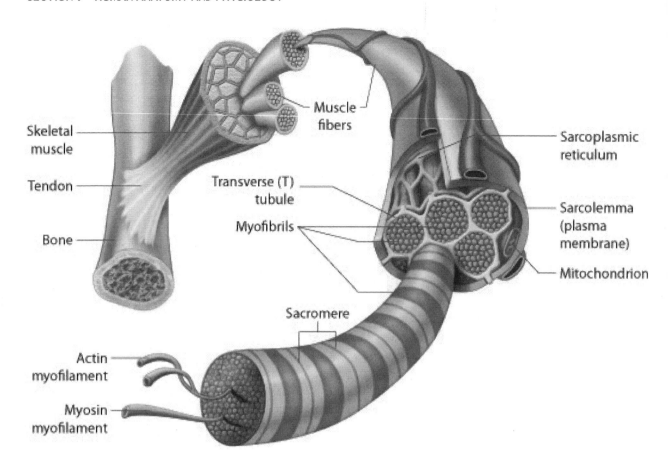

CARDIAC MUSCLE

Cardiac muscle tissue is unique to the heart, where it performs the indispensable task of pumping blood throughout the body, supplying oxygen and nutrients to tissues while removing waste products. Unlike skeletal muscle, cardiac muscle operates involuntarily, under the control of the body's autonomic nervous system, showcasing its crucial role in sustaining life.

Cardiac muscle cells, or cardiomyocytes, are striated like skeletal muscle cells, due to their organized arrangement of actin and myosin filaments. However, cardiac muscle fibers are shorter, branched, and interconnected by specialized junctions known as intercalated discs. These discs are critical for cardiac muscle function, as they facilitate the rapid transmission of electrical impulses across the heart muscle, ensuring coordinated, rhythmic contractions that constitute the heartbeat.

Each cardiomyocyte contains a single nucleus, and the cells are surrounded by a rich supply of capillaries, reflecting the high energy demand of continuous heart contractions. The presence of abundant mitochondria within cardiomyocytes meets this demand, generating the ATP necessary for sustained cardiac function.

Function and Contraction

The contraction of cardiac muscle is initiated by electrical impulses that originate in the sinoatrial (SA) node, the heart's natural pacemaker. These impulses spread rapidly through the atria, to the atrioventricular (AV) node, and then through the ventricles via the conduction system, resulting in a coordinated heart contraction.

The unique feature of cardiac muscle contraction is its reliance on calcium ions from both the sarcoplasmic reticulum and the extracellular fluid, a process that allows for longer contractions compared to skeletal muscle. This prolonged contraction period is essential for a more effective heart pump, ensuring adequate blood ejection with each heartbeat.

Regulation of Cardiac Muscle Activity

The activity of cardiac muscle is finely regulated by the autonomic nervous system, with the sympathetic nervous system increasing heart rate and force of contraction during times of stress or physical activity, and the parasympathetic nervous system reducing heart rate during rest and recovery periods. Additionally, hormones such as adrenaline can increase heart rate, showcasing the heart's responsive nature to the body's needs.

Cardiac Muscle in Health and Disease

The health of cardiac muscle is paramount for overall well-being. Diseases affecting cardiac muscle, such as myocardial infarction (heart attack), cardiomyopathy, or heart failure, can have severe consequences on the body's ability to function effectively. These conditions highlight the importance of maintaining cardiovascular health through lifestyle choices and, when necessary, medical intervention.

SMOOTH MUSCLE

Unlike skeletal muscles, which are under voluntary control, smooth muscles operate involuntarily, governed by the autonomic nervous system, making their actions automatic and essential for life. Smooth muscles are named for their uniform, non-striated appearance under the microscope, distinguishing them from the striated skeletal and cardiac muscles. These muscles are composed of spindle-shaped cells, each with a single nucleus, and are found primarily in the walls of hollow organs, including the stomach, intestines, blood vessels, and the urinary bladder.

Function of Smooth Muscle

The primary function of smooth muscle is to contract and relax in response to stimuli, thus facilitating various bodily functions such as the movement of food through the digestive tract (peristalsis), regulation of blood flow and pressure via the contraction of blood vessels, and the expulsion of urine from the bladder. The unique ability of smooth muscle to maintain tension for extended periods without fatigue is essential for the continuous operation of these organs.

Regulation of Smooth Muscle Activity

Smooth muscles, characterized by their ability to operate involuntarily, are found throughout the body in various systems, including the digestive, respiratory, cardiovascular, and urinary systems. The regulation of their activity is complex, integrating signals from the autonomic nervous system, hormonal influences, and local environmental factors, ensuring that smooth muscle function is precisely coordinated with the body's needs.

- **Autonomic Nervous System Control:** Smooth muscle activity is largely governed by the autonomic nervous system (ANS), which comprises the sympathetic and parasympathetic divisions. These divisions have opposing effects; the sympathetic nervous system generally stimulates smooth muscle contraction, preparing the body for 'fight or flight' responses, while the parasympathetic nervous system often induces relaxation or 'rest and digest' states. Neurotransmitters released from autonomic nerve endings, such as norepinephrine for the sympathetic and acetylcholine for the parasympathetic, bind to receptors on smooth muscle cells, modulating their activity.

- **Hormonal Influences:** Hormones play a crucial role in the regulation of smooth muscle activity. Various hormones, including epinephrine, angiotensin II, and vasopressin, can influence smooth muscle contraction, affecting blood pressure, gastrointestinal motility, and more. Hormones may act directly on smooth muscle cells or indirectly by altering neural control mechanisms.

- **Local Factors:** Local environmental factors such as changes in pH, oxygen, and carbon dioxide levels, as well as the presence of certain ions and metabolites, can directly affect smooth muscle activity. For example, low oxygen levels can trigger vasodilation in blood vessels to improve blood flow and oxygen delivery.

Contraction Mechanism

Smooth muscle contraction is primarily controlled by the autonomic nervous system and is modulated by various hormones and local chemical signals. The process begins with a rise in intracellular calcium levels, which can be triggered by electrical impulses, mechanical stretch, or chemical stimuli. Unlike skeletal muscle, where calcium directly facilitates the interaction of actin and myosin filaments, smooth muscle contraction involves a more complex pathway.

Calcium ions entering the smooth muscle cell bind to calmodulin, a calcium-binding protein. The calcium-calmodulin complex then activates myosin light-chain kinase (MLCK), an enzyme that phosphorylates the light chains of myosin heads, enabling them to attach to actin filaments. This phosphorylation changes the conformation of the myosin heads, allowing them to pull on the actin filaments and generate muscle contraction through a cyclic process of attachment, pivoting, and detachment.

The contraction of smooth muscle can be sustained for extended periods with minimal energy expenditure, a feature crucial for maintaining functions such as blood pressure and organ constriction. The relaxation of smooth muscle occurs when calcium levels decrease, myosin phosphatase removes the phosphate groups from myosin, and the cell's calcium pumps restore low intracellular calcium levels.

NERVOUS SYSTEM

The nervous system is an intricate collection of tissues that facilitates communication between the brain, spinal cord, and the rest of the body, coordinating voluntary and involuntary actions and transmitting signals between different parts of the body. It's divided into two main parts: the central nervous system (CNS) and the peripheral nervous system (PNS). The CNS comprises the brain and spinal cord, serving as the control center for processing and interpreting sensory information and sending out instructions. The PNS consists of all the nerves that branch out from the brain and spinal cord to the rest of the body, connecting the CNS to limbs, organs, and tissues.

More specifically:

- **Central Nervous System (CNS):** The CNS is the integration and command center of the body. The brain processes and interprets sensory information sent from the spinal cord and issues commands for responses. The spinal cord acts as a conduit for signals between the brain and the rest of the body and is also responsible for reflex actions.

- **Peripheral Nervous System (PNS):** The PNS is divided into the somatic nervous system, which controls voluntary movements and reflexes, and the autonomic nervous system, which regulates involuntary functions like heart rate and digestion. The autonomic nervous system is further subdivided into the sympathetic and parasympathetic nervous systems, which work in opposition to maintain homeostasis in response to changing internal and external conditions.

The primary functions of the nervous system include:

1. **Sensory Input:** Collecting information from sensory receptors that monitor the body's internal and external environments.

2. **Integration:** Processing and interpreting sensory input, and deciding what action, if any, should be taken.

3. **Motor Output:** Activating effector organs—muscles and glands—to produce a response.

Communication within the nervous system is achieved through electrical impulses and chemical signals. Neurotransmitters are chemical messengers that transmit signals across synapses (the junctions between neurons) or from neurons to muscles or glands. These substances are crucial for the proper functioning of the nervous system, influencing mood, thought processes, and bodily functions.

NEURONS

Neurons, or nerve cells, are specialized cells designed to transmit information throughout the body in the form of electrical and chemical signals.

This unique ability makes them pivotal in controlling bodily functions, from basic muscle contractions to complex cognitive processes such as thinking, learning, and memory. The structure of a neuron is uniquely suited to its function. A typical neuron consists of three main parts: the cell body (soma), dendrites, and an axon.

- **Cell Body (Soma):** The cell body is the neuron's metabolic center, containing the nucleus and organelles that maintain cell health. It integrates incoming signals from dendrites and generates outgoing signals to the axon.

- **Dendrites:** These are tree-like structures that extend from the cell body, receiving signals from other neurons or sensory receptors. Dendrites funnel these signals to the soma for processing.

- **Axon:** The axon is a long, slender projection that transmits electrical impulses away from the cell body toward other neurons or muscles. Most axons are covered with a myelin sheath, an insulating layer that speeds up signal transmission.

Neuronal communication involves both electrical signals, known as action potentials, and chemical signals, through neurotransmitters. An action potential is generated when a neuron's membrane potential becomes more positive, leading to a rapid rise and fall in voltage. This electrical impulse travels along the axon to the axon terminals, where it triggers the release of neurotransmitters into the synaptic cleft, the gap between neurons. These chemical messengers bind to receptors on the postsynaptic neuron, initiating a response. Neurotransmitters are crucial for neuronal communication. Different neurotransmitters have varied effects on the postsynaptic neuron, which can be excitatory, increasing the chance of firing an action potential, or inhibitory, decreasing its likelihood. The balance between these effects is essential for proper nervous system function.

Types of Neurons

Neurons can be classified based on their function or structure:

1. **Sensory Neurons:** Carry information from sensory receptors to the central nervous system (CNS).

2. **Motor Neurons:** Transmit commands from the CNS to muscles and glands.

3. **Interneurons**: Found only in the CNS, they process information and facilitate communication between sensory and motor neurons.

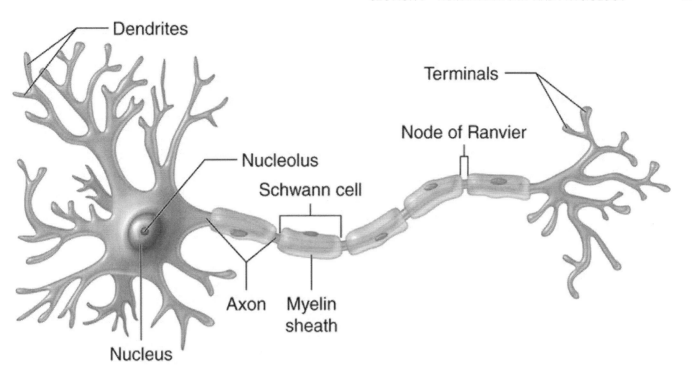

BRAIN ANATOMY

The brain is the control center of the nervous system, housed within the skull, and is responsible for processing sensory information, regulating bodily functions, and facilitating cognition and emotions.

The human brain can be divided into three main parts: the cerebrum, the cerebellum, and the brainstem, each playing unique roles in the body's functioning.

1. **The Cerebrum:** The largest part of the brain, the cerebrum, is divided into two hemispheres (left and right) and is responsible for higher cognitive functions such as reasoning, problem-solving, emotions, and language. It is further divided into four lobes:
   - **Frontal Lobe:** Involved in decision-making, problem-solving, and controlling behavior and emotions.
   - **Parietal Lobe:** Processes sensory information like touch, temperature, and pain.
   - **Temporal Lobe:** Important for memory, language, and auditory processing.
   - **Occipital Lobe:** Dedicated to visual processing.

2. **The Cerebellum:** Located under the cerebrum, the cerebellum is involved in coordinating voluntary movements, balance, and posture, ensuring that movements are smooth and precise.

3. **The Brainstem:** Connecting the brain to the spinal cord, the brainstem controls essential life-sustaining functions, including breathing, heart rate, and blood pressure. It comprises the midbrain, pons, and medulla oblongata.

The brain receives blood through the carotid and vertebral arteries, ensuring a constant supply of oxygen and nutrients. The blood-brain barrier protects the brain by preventing harmful substances in the blood from entering brain tissue.

Neuroplasticity

The brain exhibits neuroplasticity, its ability to reorganize itself by forming new neural connections throughout life. This adaptability allows for learning, memory formation, and recovery from brain injury.

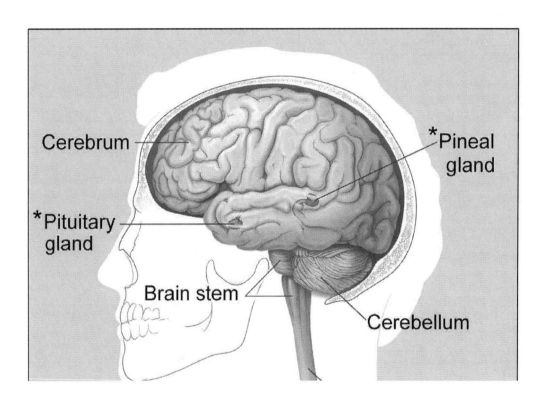

THE LIMBIC SYSTEM

The limbic system, often referred to as the "emotional brain," is a complex set of structures located deep within the brain, encircling the upper part of the brainstem and beneath the cerebral cortex. This system is pivotal in regulating emotions, memory, and motivation, influencing our survival instincts, mood regulation, and attachment behaviors.

Key components of the limbic system include:

- **Hippocampus:** Essential for memory formation and retrieval, the hippocampus plays a crucial role in converting short-term memory into long-term memory and spatial navigation.

- **Amygdala:** Involved in processing emotions, the amygdala is critical for fear responses, emotional memories, and decision-making influenced by emotions.

- **Hypothalamus:** Although part of the endocrine system, the hypothalamus links the nervous system to the hormonal system via the pituitary gland and is key in regulating physiological homeostasis, including hunger, thirst, sleep, and sexual response.

THE THALAMUS

The thalamus, located above the brainstem between the cerebral cortex and the midbrain, functions primarily as a relay station for sensory and motor signals to the cerebral cortex. Nearly all sensory information (with the exception of smell) passes through the thalamus before being processed and interpreted by the brain. The thalamus also plays a significant role in regulating sleep and wakefulness.

Key functions include:

- **Sensory Processing:** The thalamus receives sensory signals from the optic nerve, ears, and skin and relays this information to the appropriate areas of the cerebral cortex for processing.

- **Motor Control:** It receives information from the cerebellum and the basal ganglia and relays it to motor areas in the cortex, influencing voluntary motor control.

- **Consciousness and Alertness:** The thalamus contributes to consciousness, sleep, and alertness levels, acting as a critical component in the brain's arousal system.

The limbic system and the thalamus are interconnected, with the thalamus acting as a gateway for sensory information that can trigger emotional responses in the limbic system. For example, sensory experiences that are perceived as threats can activate the amygdala through pathways involving the thalamus, initiating fear or stress responses. Similarly, the hippocampus and thalamus work together in memory formation and retrieval, linking sensory experiences to emotional contexts.

THE RESPIRATORY SYSTEM

The respiratory system not only facilitates breathing but also plays a significant role in maintaining homeostasis of blood pH, producing speech sounds, and defending against microbes. It can be divided into two main parts: the upper respiratory tract and the lower respiratory tract.

1. **Upper Respiratory Tract:** Includes the nasal cavity, pharynx, and larynx. The nasal cavity filters, warms, and humidifies inhaled air. The pharynx serves as a passageway for air, leading to the larynx, which houses the vocal cords.

2. **Lower Respiratory Tract:** Comprises the trachea, bronchi, bronchioles, and lungs. The trachea bifurcates into two main bronchi, each leading to a lung. These bronchi branch into smaller bronchioles, ending in alveoli, the tiny air sacs where gas exchange occurs.

The primary function of the respiratory system is to facilitate gas exchange—oxygen is absorbed from the atmosphere into the bloodstream, and carbon dioxide is expelled from the bloodstream to the atmosphere. This exchange occurs in the alveoli, where oxygen diffuses across the alveolar and capillary walls into the blood, and carbon dioxide diffuses from the blood into the alveoli to be exhaled.

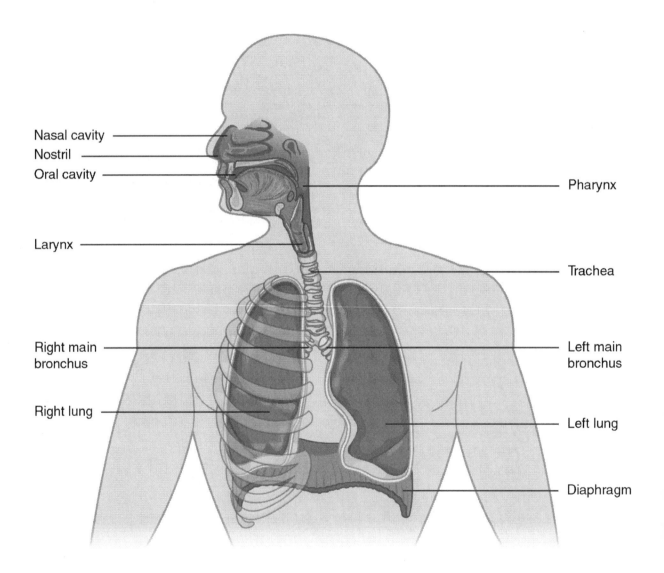

BREATHING MECHANISMS

Breathing, or ventilation, is the process by which air moves in and out of the lungs, facilitating the essential exchange of oxygen and carbon dioxide between the atmosphere and the bloodstream.

Breathing involves two primary phases: inhalation (inspiration) and exhalation (expiration), each driven by changes in thoracic cavity volume and pressure.

- **Inhalation:** This active phase begins with the contraction of the diaphragm, a dome-shaped muscle that separates the thoracic and abdominal cavities. As the diaphragm contracts, it flattens downward, enlarging the thoracic cavity and reducing the pressure inside the lungs below atmospheric pressure. The external intercostal muscles between the ribs also contract, raising the rib cage and further increasing thoracic volume. This decrease in pressure allows air to flow into the lungs.

- **Exhalation:** Typically a passive process during normal, restful breathing, exhalation occurs when the diaphragm and external intercostal muscles relax, reverting the thoracic cavity to its original volume and increasing the pressure inside the lungs above atmospheric pressure, thereby pushing air out of the lungs. Forced exhalation, which occurs during vigorous breathing, involves the contraction of abdominal muscles and the internal intercostal muscles, further decreasing thoracic volume and expelling air more forcefully.

Regulation of Breathing

The breathing rate and depth are finely tuned by the respiratory centers located in the medulla oblongata and the pons of the brainstem. These centers receive input from central and peripheral chemoreceptors that monitor levels of carbon dioxide, oxygen, and blood pH:

- **Central Chemoreceptors:** Located in the medulla, these receptors primarily respond to changes in the concentration of carbon dioxide in the blood by adjusting the rate and depth of breathing.
- **Peripheral Chemoreceptors:** Found in the carotid bodies and aortic bodies, they are sensitive to the levels of oxygen and carbon dioxide in the blood, as well as to pH changes.

Additionally, higher brain centers, including those involved in emotional and pain responses, can influence the respiratory centers, altering breathing patterns.

CARDIOVASCULAR SYSTEM

The cardiovascular system is composed of the heart, blood vessels, and blood. The heart acts as the pump, circulating blood throughout the body. Blood vessels, including arteries, veins, and capillaries, form an extensive network that transports blood to all body parts.

Blood itself carries the essential components required for the functioning of various organs.

The cardiovascular system is regulated by neural and hormonal signals that adjust heart rate, blood pressure, and the distribution of blood to meet the body's changing demands. The autonomic nervous system, through the sympathetic and parasympathetic branches, plays a key role in this regulation.

THE CIRCULATORY ROUTES

The circulatory system comprises two main routes: the systemic circulation and the pulmonary circulation. Each plays a pivotal role in sustaining life, facilitating the exchange of gases, delivering nutrients to body tissues, and removing waste products.

- **Pulmonary Circulation**: is the path that blood takes through the heart to the lungs and back. This route begins with the right ventricle pumping deoxygenated blood into the pulmonary arteries, which transport it to the lungs. In the lungs, carbon dioxide is exchanged for oxygen during the process of respiration. Oxygenated blood then returns to the heart via the pulmonary veins, entering the left atrium. This circuit is critical for gas exchange, ensuring that blood is reoxygenated before it is pumped back out to the systemic circulation.

- **Systemic Circulation**: distributes oxygen-rich blood from the heart to all body tissues and returns deoxygenated blood back to the heart. Starting from the left ventricle, oxygenated blood is pumped into the aorta, the body's main artery, which branches into a network of arteries and arterioles that reach every organ and tissue. Oxygen and nutrients diffuse from the blood through capillary walls to body tissues, while carbon dioxide and metabolic waste products are collected for removal. Veins and venules collect the deoxygenated blood and transport it back to the right atrium of the heart, completing the circuit.

- Coronary Circulation: An essential sub-component of systemic circulation is coronary circulation, which supplies blood to the heart muscle itself. Given the heart's constant activity, it requires a continuous supply of oxygen and nutrients. Coronary arteries branch off the aorta to supply the heart muscle (myocardium) with oxygenated blood. Veins within the heart muscle collect deoxygenated blood, which is then returned to the right atrium via the coronary sinus.

BLOOD

Blood is a specialized bodily fluid that circulates through the heart, arteries, veins, and capillaries. It comprises two main components: plasma and formed elements.

- **Plasma:** Making up about 55% of the blood's volume, plasma is a straw-colored liquid that is mostly water (90%) but also contains proteins, glucose, ions, hormones, and waste products.

Plasma proteins, including albumins, globulins, and fibrinogen, play roles in maintaining osmotic pressure, immune responses, and blood clotting.

- **Formed Elements:** Constituting about 45% of blood, the formed elements include red blood cells (erythrocytes), white blood cells (leukocytes), and platelets (thrombocytes).
    1. **Red Blood Cells (Erythrocytes):** These cells are responsible for carrying oxygen from the lungs to the body's tissues and returning carbon dioxide to the lungs for exhalation. Their biconcave shape increases surface area for gas exchange, and the protein hemoglobin within these cells binds oxygen.
    2. **White Blood Cells (Leukocytes):** Leukocytes are involved in defending the body against infections and other diseases. They are classified into granulocytes (neutrophils, eosinophils, basophils) and agranulocytes (lymphocytes and monocytes), each with specific functions in the immune response.
    3. **Platelets (Thrombocytes):** These cell fragments are crucial for blood clotting. When bleeding occurs, platelets aggregate to form a plug at the injury site, and they release chemicals that activate clotting factors.

The primary functions of blood underscore its importance in maintaining homeostasis:

- **Transportation:** Blood transports oxygen from the lungs to tissues and carbon dioxide from tissues to the lungs. It also carries nutrients from the digestive system to cells, waste products to the kidneys and liver for excretion, and hormones to target organs.

- **Regulation:** Blood helps regulate body temperature by distributing heat throughout the body and maintaining fluid and pH balance in bodily tissues.

- **Protection:** The immune components of blood, including white blood cells and antibodies, protect the body against pathogens. Blood clotting mechanisms prevent excessive blood loss after injuries.

BLOOD TYPES

Blood typing is based on the presence or absence of specific antigens on the surface of red blood cells and antibodies in the plasma, leading to the classification into various groups.

The ABO blood group system is the primary blood type classification and is determined by the presence or absence of two antigens, A and B, on the surface of red blood cells:

- **Type A:** Has A antigens on the red cells and anti-B antibodies in the plasma.
- **Type B:** Has B antigens on the red cells and anti-A antibodies in the plasma.
- **Type AB:** Has both A and B antigens on the red cells but neither anti-A nor anti-B antibodies in the plasma. This type is known as the universal recipient.

- **Type O:** Has neither A nor B antigens on the red cells but both anti-A and anti-B antibodies in the plasma. This type is known as the universal donor.

In addition to the ABO system, the **Rh factor** (named after the Rhesus monkey in which it was first discovered) plays a significant role in blood typing. It is determined by the presence or absence of the Rh antigen (specifically, the D antigen) on the surface of red blood cells:

- **Rh-positive (Rh+):** Individuals have the D antigen on their red blood cells.
- **Rh-negative (Rh-):** Individuals lack the D antigen on their red blood cells.

The combination of the ABO system and the Rh factor leads to eight main blood types: A+, A-, B+, B-, AB+, AB-, O+, and O-.

Below is a table summarizing the ABO and Rh blood group systems, illustrating from whom individuals of each blood type can receive blood and to whom they can donate blood.

Blood Type	Can Receive From	Can Donate To
A+	A+, A-, O+, O-	A+, AB+
A-	A-, O-	A+, A-, AB+, AB-
B+	B+, B-, O+, O-	B+, AB+
B-	B-, O-	B+, B-, AB+, AB-
AB+	Everyone (Universal Recipient)	AB+
AB-	AB-, A-, B-, O-	AB+, AB-
O+	O+, O-	O+, A+, B+, AB+
O-	O- (Universal Donor)	Everyone

BLOOD VESSELS

The blood vessels are the essential components of the cardiovascular system that create a vast network for transporting blood throughout the body. Blood vessels are not merely passive conduits but dynamic structures that play a crucial role in regulating blood flow, pressure, and distribution according to the body's needs.

Blood vessels can be broadly classified into three main types: arteries, veins, and capillaries, each serving distinct but interrelated functions in the circulatory system.

1. **Arteries:** Arteries carry oxygen-rich blood away from the heart to the body's tissues and organs. The largest artery, the aorta, branches into smaller arteries, arterioles, and ultimately capillaries. Arteries have thick, elastic walls that allow them to withstand and regulate the pressure of the blood pumped by the heart. This elasticity also facilitates the arteries' role in maintaining a steady flow of blood despite the heart's intermittent pumping action.

2. **Veins:** Veins return deoxygenated blood from the body back to the heart. They have thinner walls than arteries and contain valves that prevent the backflow of blood, ensuring its unidirectional flow toward the heart. Veins rely on the contraction of skeletal muscles and changes in thoracic pressure during breathing to help push blood through the venous system.

3. **Capillaries:** Capillaries are the smallest and most numerous blood vessels, forming a dense network that penetrates nearly all tissues in the body. Their thin walls consist of a single layer of endothelial cells, facilitating the exchange of gases, nutrients, and waste products between the blood and tissues. This exchange occurs through diffusion, filtration, and osmosis, processes that are essential for cellular function and homeostasis.

The walls of blood vessels consist of three layers: the tunica intima, tunica media, and tunica externa, each contributing to the vessels' strength, flexibility, and functionality. The tunica intima, the innermost layer, includes the endothelium, which provides a smooth surface for blood flow and plays a role in regulating vessel diameter and blood pressure. The tunica media, the middle layer, contains smooth muscle and elastic fibers that allow vessels to contract or dilate. The tunica externa, the outer layer, provides structural support and protection.

HEART

The heart is a muscular organ located in the thoracic cavity, between the lungs, and slightly left of the midline. It consists of four chambers: two atria (upper chambers) and two ventricles (lower chambers). The right side of the heart (right atrium and right ventricle) pumps deoxygenated blood to the lungs for oxygenation, while the left side (left atrium and left ventricle) pumps oxygenated blood to the rest of the body.

The heart's chambers are separated by valves to ensure unidirectional blood flow: the tricuspid valve between the right atrium and ventricle, the pulmonary valve leading to the lungs, the mitral valve between the left atrium and ventricle, and the aortic valve leading to the body. The heart's muscle layer, or myocardium, is encased in a double-layered membrane called the pericardium, which provides support and protection.

Function of the Heart
The heart's pumping action is divided into two phases: systole (contraction phase) and diastole (relaxation phase). During systole, the ventricles contract, propelling blood into the pulmonary artery and aorta. During diastole, the heart relaxes, allowing the chambers to fill with blood from the veins. This cycle is meticulously regulated by electrical impulses that originate from the sinoatrial (SA) node, travel to the atrioventricular (AV) node, and then spread through the Purkinje fibers, ensuring synchronized heart contractions.

Blood Supply to the Heart

The heart itself requires a constant supply of oxygen-rich blood, provided by the coronary arteries. These arteries branch off the aorta and envelop the heart's surface. Veins collect deoxygenated blood from the myocardium, draining into the coronary sinus and then into the right atrium, completing the circulation.

Heart Rate and Cardiac Output

The heart rate, the number of beats per minute, and cardiac output, the volume of blood pumped by each ventricle per minute, are critical indicators of heart function. These parameters can vary based on the body's demands, influenced by factors such as physical activity, stress, and pathological conditions.

THE DIGESTIVE SYSTEM

The digestive system can be segmented into two main groups: the alimentary canal (gastrointestinal tract) and the accessory digestive organs. The alimentary canal is a continuous, coiled, hollow tube that starts from the mouth and ends at the anus, comprising the mouth, pharynx, esophagus, stomach, small intestine, large intestine, and anus. The accessory organs, including the salivary glands, liver, gallbladder, and pancreas, play crucial roles in digestion though they are not part of the direct alimentary pathway.

- **The Alimentary Canal:** The alimentary canal, or the gastrointestinal (GI) tract, is a continuous muscular tube that extends from the mouth to the anus, through which food is ingested, broken down, and absorbed, leaving waste to be eliminated. Its primary components include:
  1. **Mouth (Oral Cavity):** The entrance to the digestive tract where mechanical digestion begins with chewing and chemical digestion starts with saliva mixing with food to initiate the breakdown of carbohydrates.
  2. **Pharynx:** A muscular passage for food and air, the pharynx plays a key role in swallowing, moving food from the mouth to the esophagus.
  3. **Esophagus:** A muscular tube that transports food from the pharynx to the stomach using rhythmic contractions known as peristalsis.
  4. **Stomach**: A muscular organ that further mixes food with gastric juices, including acid and enzymes, turning it into a semi-liquid substance called chyme. The stomach's sections include the fundus, body, and pylorus, each playing a role in digestion.
  5. **Small Intestine:** Divided into the duodenum, jejunum, and ileum, the small intestine is the primary site for chemical digestion and nutrient absorption. The inner surface is highly folded, featuring villi and microvilli, to maximize nutrient absorption.
  6. **Large Intestine:** Comprising the cecum, colon, rectum, and anal canal, the large intestine absorbs water and electrolytes, forming and storing feces for eventual elimination.

- **Accessory Digestive Organs:** These organs, while not part of the alimentary canal, secrete essential enzymes and substances that aid in digestion:

1. **Salivary Glands:** Including the parotid, submandibular, and sublingual glands, they produce saliva, which contains enzymes that initiate the breakdown of starches.
2. **Liver:** The body's largest gland, it performs numerous functions, most notably producing bile, which helps emulsify fats, enhancing their digestion and absorption.
3. **Gallbladder:** Situated beneath the liver, it stores and concentrates bile, releasing it into the small intestine as needed.
4. **Pancreas:** Produces a broad spectrum of digestive enzymes and bicarbonate, which neutralize stomach acid in the small intestine, creating an optimal environment for enzyme action.

- **Layers of the GI Tract:** The walls of the GI tract from the esophagus to the anal canal share a common structure, made up of four layers:
  1. **Mucosa:** The innermost layer, which secretes mucus and digestive enzymes. It also absorbs nutrients through its surface.
  2. **Submucosa:** Contains blood and lymph vessels that transport absorbed nutrients.
  3. **Muscularis Externa:** Consists of two layers of muscle that produce movements of the tract, including peristalsis.
  4. **Serosa:** The outermost layer, a protective membrane secreting serous fluid to reduce friction from muscle movements.

THE PROCESS OF DIGESTION

Digestion begins the moment food enters the mouth and continues through a meticulously coordinated path along the gastrointestinal (GI) tract until waste is excreted. This multifaceted process can be categorized into two main types: mechanical digestion, which physically breaks down food into smaller pieces, and chemical digestion, which breaks down food into its molecular components.

Mechanical Digestion
- **Oral Cavity:** Digestion starts in the mouth, where chewing (mastication) reduces food to smaller particles, increasing its surface area. Saliva, produced by the salivary glands, moistens food, forming a bolus that can be easily swallowed.
- **Stomach:** The stomach's muscular walls churn the food, mixing it with gastric juices to produce a semi-liquid mixture called chyme.

Chemical Digestion
- **Saliva:** Contains the enzyme amylase, which initiates the breakdown of carbohydrates into simpler sugars.
- **Stomach:** Gastric glands secrete hydrochloric acid, which kills bacteria and provides the acidic environment for the enzyme pepsin to begin protein digestion.
- **Small Intestine:** The primary site for chemical digestion and nutrient absorption. The pancreas produces digestive enzymes and bicarbonate, which are released into the duodenum. Bile, produced by the liver and stored in the gallbladder, emulsifies fats, aiding in their digestion and absorption.
- **Digestive Enzymes:** Different enzymes, each specific to proteins, carbohydrates, or fats, continue the breakdown process, resulting in molecules small enough to be absorbed (amino acids, simple sugars, and fatty acids, respectively).

Absorption
The small intestine, with its extensive surface area provided by villi and microvilli, is where most nutrient absorption occurs. Nutrients pass through the intestinal wall into the bloodstream or lymphatic system, to be distributed throughout the body. Water and electrolytes are primarily absorbed in the colon.

The Role of the Large Intestine
The large intestine absorbs remaining water and salts, transforming the undigested food material into feces. Bacteria in the colon help break down remaining nutrients and synthesize certain vitamins. Feces are stored in the rectum until they are expelled through the anus, completing the digestive process.

Regulation of Digestive Processes
The digestive system's activities are regulated by neural and hormonal signals, ensuring that digestive processes are initiated in response to the presence of food. For example, the sight, smell, or thought of food can trigger the secretion of saliva. Similarly, the stretching of the stomach wall stimulates the secretion of gastric juices.

Hormones like gastrin, cholecystokinin (CCK), and secretin play crucial roles in stimulating or inhibiting various parts of the digestive process, optimizing digestion and nutrient absorption.

METABOLISM

Metabolism is the engine that drives our bodies, converting food into energy, building and repairing tissues, and regulating bodily functions.

Metabolism comprises two interconnected categories of processes: catabolism and anabolism:

1. **Catabolism** refers to the breakdown of molecules into smaller units, releasing energy. This process is exemplified by the digestion of food to produce energy in the form of adenosine triphosphate (ATP).

*   **Anabolism**, on the other hand, is the synthesis of all compounds needed by the cells, using energy. It includes processes that build complex molecules from simpler ones, such as the synthesis of proteins from amino acids.

Cellular Respiration

Cellular respiration is a key metabolic process that cells use to extract energy from nutrients. It can be divided into three main stages: glycolysis, the citric acid cycle (Krebs cycle), and oxidative phosphorylation.

*   **Glycolysis:** Occurs in the cytoplasm and breaks glucose into two molecules of pyruvate, producing a small yield of ATP and reducing equivalents (NADH).

*   **Citric Acid Cycle:** Occurs in the mitochondria, where acetyl-CoA (derived from pyruvate) is oxidized, producing reducing equivalents (NADH and FADH2), a small amount of ATP, and carbon dioxide as a waste product.

*   **Oxidative Phosphorylation:** Also in the mitochondria, this process involves the electron transport chain and chemiosmosis, utilizing the reducing equivalents to generate a significant amount of ATP and water.

Metabolic Rate and Energy Balance

The metabolic rate is the rate at which the body consumes energy. It is influenced by several factors, including age, sex, muscle mass, and physical activity. The basal metabolic rate (BMR) is the amount of energy expended while at rest in a neutrally temperate environment, in the post-absorptive state. Energy balance, the relationship between energy intake and energy expenditure, is crucial for maintaining healthy body weight and overall well-being.

Hormonal Regulation of Metabolism

Metabolism is tightly regulated by hormones, ensuring that energy production matches the body's varying demands. Key hormones include:

- **Insulin:** Promotes glucose uptake and storage, and fat synthesis.

- **Glucagon:** Stimulates the breakdown of glycogen and fat, raising blood glucose levels.

- **Thyroid Hormones:** Increase the overall metabolic rate.

ENDOCRINE SYSTEM

Unlike the nervous system, which sends rapid electrical signals, the endocrine system works through the slower but enduring method of hormonal release into the bloodstream.
These hormones act as messengers, influencing metabolism, growth, reproduction, and mood among other functions. Understanding the endocrine system's components and their roles is pivotal for healthcare professionals, as it underlies the mechanisms of numerous diseases and conditions.

The endocrine system comprises several glands, each producing specific hormones with targeted effects on various organs and tissues. Key glands include:

- **Hypothalamus:** Often considered the system's command center, it regulates the pituitary gland through releasing and inhibiting hormones, thus controlling many endocrine functions.

- **Pituitary Gland:** Located at the base of the brain, it's known as the "master gland" because its hormones regulate other endocrine glands. It has two parts: the anterior pituitary, which releases hormones like growth hormone (GH), and the posterior pituitary, which stores and releases oxytocin and vasopressin.

- **Thyroid Gland:** Produces thyroid hormones (thyroxine and triiodothyronine), which regulate metabolism, energy generation, and growth. The gland also secretes calcitonin, involved in calcium homeostasis.

- **Parathyroid Glands:** These small glands on the thyroid's posterior surface produce parathyroid hormone (PTH), crucial for calcium and phosphate balance.

- **Adrenal Glands:** Located atop the kidneys, they produce cortisol, aldosterone, adrenaline, and noradrenaline, which help manage stress, blood pressure, and metabolic activities.

- **Pancreas:** Functions as both an endocrine and exocrine gland. Its endocrine role involves producing insulin and glucagon, key regulators of blood glucose levels.

- **Gonads:** The ovaries in females produce estrogen and progesterone, regulating menstrual cycles, pregnancy, and secondary sexual characteristics. The testes in males produce testosterone, responsible for sperm production and male secondary sexual characteristics.

NATURE AND FUNCTION OF RECEPTORS

Receptors in the endocrine system are dynamic entities that bind to specific hormones, triggering a cascade of cellular responses that alter physiological states. These receptors can be broadly categorized based on their location and the type of hormone they bind:

- **Cell Surface Receptors:** Located on the cell membrane, these receptors bind to water-soluble hormones, such as peptides and catecholamines. Binding typically triggers a secondary messenger system within the cell, amplifying the hormone's signal and leading to rapid cellular responses.

- **Intracellular Receptors:** Found within the cell cytoplasm or nucleus, these receptors bind to lipid-soluble hormones, such as steroid hormones and thyroid hormones. The hormone-receptor complex then directly influences gene expression, resulting in longer-term cellular changes.

Specificity and Sensitivity
Hormone receptors exhibit a high degree of specificity, meaning they bind only to their target hormone or a closely related structure. This specificity ensures that each hormone elicits the appropriate physiological response. Receptors also display remarkable sensitivity, capable of responding to minute concentrations of hormones, which underscores the potency and efficiency of the endocrine system in regulating bodily functions.

Regulation of Receptor Activity
The activity of hormone receptors is finely tuned by mechanisms that ensure responsiveness to hormonal signals is adapted to the body's needs. This includes:

- **Upregulation:** An increase in the number of receptors on the cell surface in response to low hormone levels, enhancing the cell's sensitivity to the hormone.

- **Downregulation:** A decrease in receptor numbers in response to high levels of hormone, protecting the cell from overstimulation and maintaining homeostasis.

Receptor Signaling Pathways
Upon hormone binding, receptors initiate signaling pathways that translate the extracellular hormone signal into a specific intracellular response. These pathways can involve:

- Activation of G-protein coupled receptors (GPCRs), leading to the production of secondary messengers like cyclic AMP (cAMP).

- Activation of enzyme-linked receptors, such as receptor tyrosine kinases, leading to phosphorylation cascades that alter enzyme activity and gene expression.
- Direct regulation of gene transcription by hormone-receptor complexes in the case of intracellular receptors.

Hormonal Regulation and Actions

Hormones, the chemical messengers of the endocrine system, are released into the bloodstream and travel to target tissues or organs, where they bind to specific receptors, eliciting responses that maintain homeostasis and regulate physiological functions. Hormonal actions can be broad, affecting many tissues, or targeted, affecting a specific organ.

The endocrine system's activity is tightly regulated through feedback mechanisms, primarily negative feedback loops, which maintain hormone levels within narrow ranges. For example, the hypothalamus and pituitary gland regulate thyroid function through a feedback system involving thyroid-releasing hormone (TRH), thyroid-stimulating hormone (TSH), and thyroid hormones.

IMMUNE SYSTEM

The immune system is our body's defense mechanism against pathogens such as bacteria, viruses, fungi, and parasites. It not only protects us from infectious diseases but also plays a role in wound healing, cancer surveillance, and the rejection of foreign transplants. It's composed of various cells, tissues, and organs that work in concert to protect the body:

- **White Blood Cells (Leukocytes):** Serve as the primary operatives of the immune response. They are produced in the bone marrow and include lymphocytes (B cells and T cells), neutrophils, eosinophils, basophils, and monocytes.

- **Lymphatic System:** Comprises lymph nodes, lymphatic vessels, the spleen, the thymus, and tonsils. It transports lymph, a fluid containing infection-fighting white blood cells, throughout the body.

- **Skin and Mucous Membranes:** Act as physical barriers preventing the entry of pathogens into the body.

The immune system operates on two levels: innate (or nonspecific) immunity and adaptive (or specific) immunity.

1. **Innate Immunity:** The first line of defense, providing immediate but generalized protection. Components include physical barriers (skin and mucosa), phagocytic cells (neutrophils and macrophages), natural killer cells, and the complement system, which enhances the ability of antibodies and phagocytic cells to clear pathogens.

2. **Adaptive Immunity:** Develops as a response to exposure to pathogens. It is characterized by specificity (the ability to target specific pathogens) and memory (the ability to remember and more effectively respond to pathogens previously encountered). Adaptive immunity involves lymphocytes: B cells, which produce antibodies, and T cells, which can kill infected cells or help activate other immune cells.

When a pathogen breaches the body's physical barriers, the innate immune response is the first to act. If pathogens are not cleared, the adaptive immune response is activated. Antigens, unique molecules found on pathogens, are recognized by B cells and T cells, initiating a cascade of events that leads to the production of specific antibodies by B cells or the direct attack on infected cells by T cells.

LYMPHATIC SYSTEM

The lymphatic system's primary components include lymph, lymphatic vessels, lymph nodes, and lymphoid organs. Lymph is a clear fluid that circulates throughout the lymphatic vessels, containing white blood cells, especially lymphocytes, which are crucial for immune responses. Lymphatic vessels, resembling veins but with thinner walls and more valves, transport lymph from peripheral tissues to the venous system. Lymph nodes, small, bean-shaped structures found along the lymphatic vessels, filter lymph, trapping pathogens and foreign particles, which are then destroyed by immune cells housed within the nodes. Lymphoid organs, such as the spleen, thymus, and tonsils, play specialized roles in immune surveillance and response.

The lymphatic system's primary functions include maintaining fluid balance in the body's tissues, absorbing and transporting dietary fats from the gastrointestinal tract to the blood, and facilitating immune responses. By returning excess interstitial fluid to the bloodstream, the lymphatic system prevents edema, a condition characterized by swelling due to fluid accumulation in tissues.

The absorption of fats and fat-soluble vitamins in the small intestine occurs via specialized lymphatic vessels known as lacteals, which transport dietary lipids to the bloodstream, where they become available to body cells. Moreover, the lymphatic system is integral to the body's defense mechanisms; it filters pathogens from the lymph and blood, houses and activates lymphocytes, and serves as a conduit for the distribution of immune cells throughout the body.

A key function of the lymphatic system is its role in immune surveillance and response. Lymph nodes, strategically located throughout the body, act as filtration points where immune cells can encounter and respond to pathogens. The spleen monitors blood for foreign invaders, destroying old or damaged red blood cells and mounting immune responses when necessary. The thymus, active primarily during childhood, is where T lymphocytes mature and differentiate, becoming key players in the adaptive immune response.

Disase of the Lymphatic System

- **Lymphedema** - Lymphedema is a condition characterized by swelling due to the accumulation of lymph fluid in body tissues, commonly affecting the arms and legs. It can result from congenital malformations of the lymphatic system (primary lymphedema) or damage to lymphatic vessels or nodes due to surgery, radiation therapy, or infection (secondary lymphedema). Lymphedema impairs quality of life, leading to pain, decreased mobility, and increased risk of infections.

- **Lymphangitis** - Lymphangitis is an inflammation of the lymphatic vessels, usually resulting from a bacterial infection, often streptococcus or staphylococcus, that has entered the lymphatic system from a wound. Symptoms include red streaks extending from the infection site, fever, chills, and malaise. Lymphangitis indicates a rapid spread of infection, requiring prompt antibiotic treatment.

- **Lymphadenitis** - Lymphadenitis, the inflammation of lymph nodes, is typically caused by an infection that has spread to the nodes from a nearby site. Nodes become swollen, tender, and warm, and the condition may be accompanied by fever. The underlying infection, bacterial or viral, dictates the treatment, which often involves antibiotics.

- **Lymphadenopathy** - Lymphadenopathy refers to enlarged lymph nodes, a symptom rather than a disease itself, which can result from infections, autoimmune diseases, or cancers like lymphoma and leukemia. The cause of lymphadenopathy determines the approach to treatment, ranging from observation for minor infections to chemotherapy or radiation for cancer.

- **Lymphoma** - Lymphoma is a type of cancer that originates in the lymphocytes, a kind of white blood cell. It is categorized into two main types: Hodgkin lymphoma, characterized by the presence of Reed-Sternberg cells, and non-Hodgkin lymphoma, which is more common and diverse. Symptoms include swollen, painless lymph nodes, fatigue, fever, and weight loss. Treatment may involve chemotherapy, radiation therapy, immunotherapy, or stem cell transplant, depending on the type and stage of lymphoma.

- **Filariasis** - Filariasis is a parasitic disease caused by infection with filarial worms, transmitted through mosquito bites. These worms invade the lymphatic system, leading to lymphedema and, in severe cases, elephantiasis — extreme swelling of the limbs and genitals. Prevention and treatment involve medication to kill the parasites and care to manage symptoms.

- **Autoimmune Lymphoproliferative Syndrome (ALPS)** - ALPS is a rare genetic disorder affecting the lymphatic system, characterized by an abnormal proliferation of lymphocytes, leading to lymphadenopathy, splenomegaly, and increased risk of autoimmune disorders and lymphoma. Management includes immunosuppressive drugs and, in some cases, biological therapy targeting specific immune pathways.

THE URINARY SYSTEM

The urinary system consists of the kidneys, ureters, bladder, and urethra, each with specific functions in urine production and excretion.

- **Kidneys:** Paired organs located on either side of the vertebral column, just below the rib cage. The kidneys filter the blood, removing waste products and excess substances to form urine. They are made up of approximately a million nephrons, the functional units where blood filtration and urine formation occur. Each nephron consists of a glomerulus for filtration and a tubular component for reabsorption and secretion. The kidneys also play a critical role in regulating blood pressure, red blood cell production (via erythropoietin), and the metabolism of calcium and phosphate.

- **Ureters:** Muscular tubes that transport urine from the kidneys to the bladder. Peristaltic waves along the ureters facilitate the movement of urine, preventing backflow and ensuring its one-way passage toward the bladder.

- **Bladder:** A hollow, muscular organ situated in the pelvic cavity that stores urine until excretion. The bladder's wall is lined with transitional epithelium, allowing it to expand as it fills and contract during urination. The internal urethral sphincter, controlled involuntarily, and the external urethral sphincter, controlled voluntarily, regulate the passage of urine into the urethra.

- **Urethra:** The conduit through which urine is expelled from the body. The length and function of the urethra differ between males and females, with the male urethra also serving as part of the reproductive system by transporting semen.

FUNCTION OF THE URINARY SYSTEM

The functioning of the urinary system can be summarized in five points:

1. **Waste Excretion:** The kidneys filter blood to remove waste products, such as urea, creatinine, and uric acid, produced by the metabolism of proteins and nucleic acids. These waste products, along with excess water and other substances, are excreted as urine, helping to prevent the buildup of toxins in the body.

2. **Regulation of Blood Volume and Blood Pressure:** The urinary system controls blood volume by adjusting the amount of water excreted in urine. It also regulates blood pressure through the renin-angiotensin-aldosterone system (RAAS), which adjusts arterial constriction and sodium and water retention.

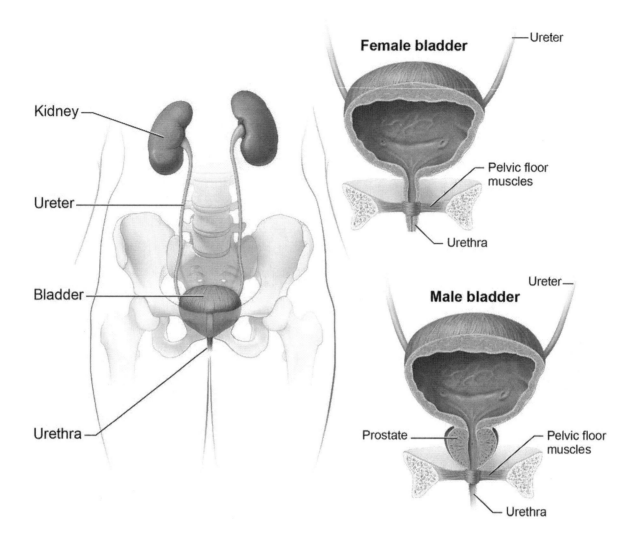

3. **Regulation of Electrolyte Levels:** The kidneys maintain electrolyte balance (e.g., sodium, potassium, and calcium) by filtering electrolytes from the blood, reabsorbing what is needed, and excreting the rest in urine. This balance is vital for many bodily functions, including nerve signaling and muscle contraction.

4. **Regulation of pH:** The urinary system helps maintain the acid-base balance of the body by excreting hydrogen ions and reabsorbing bicarbonate from urine, thus regulating plasma pH and preventing acidosis or alkalosis.

5. **Production of Hormones:** The kidneys produce several important hormones, including erythropoietin (EPO), which stimulates red blood cell production in the bone marrow, and renin, which is involved in blood pressure regulation. The kidneys also convert vitamin D into its active form, calcitriol, essential for calcium absorption and bone health.

URINE FORMATION

Urine formation involves three primary processes: glomerular filtration, tubular reabsorption, and tubular secretion. These processes ensure that waste products are excreted, and vital substances are retained or regulated.

1. **Glomerular Filtration:** This first step occurs in the glomerulus, a tiny ball of capillaries within the nephron. Blood pressure forces water, salts, glucose, amino acids, and urea from the blood in the glomerulus into the Bowman's capsule, forming the glomerular filtrate. Large proteins and blood cells are too big to pass through the glomerular membrane and remain in the bloodstream.

2. **Tubular Reabsorption:** As the filtrate moves along the nephron's tubule, essential nutrients and a significant amount of water are reabsorbed back into the bloodstream through the walls of the tubules. This reabsorption is selective and occurs primarily in the proximal convoluted tubule, loop of Henle, and distal convoluted tubule. Sodium ions ($Na+$) are actively transported out of the filtrate, with water following passively due to osmosis, along with glucose and amino acids through active or facilitated transport. This process significantly reduces the volume of the filtrate, concentrating the waste products.

3. **Tubular Secretion:** The final adjustment of the filtrate involves the secretion of additional waste products and excess ions from the blood into the tubule. This occurs mainly in the distal convoluted tubule and collecting duct. It includes the active transport of hydrogen ions ($H+$), potassium ions ($K+$), creatinine, and drugs into the filtrate, thereby removing substances that were not filtered initially at the glomerulus. Tubular secretion is crucial for controlling blood pH and eliminating toxins.

The kidneys' ability to concentrate or dilute urine is tightly regulated to maintain the body's fluid and electrolyte balance. This regulation is influenced by several factors, including:

- **Antidiuretic Hormone (ADH):** Released by the posterior pituitary gland, ADH increases the permeability of the nephron's collecting ducts to water, promoting water reabsorption and concentrating the urine.

- **Aldosterone:** Secreted by the adrenal cortex, aldosterone stimulates the reabsorption of sodium and water in the distal convoluted tubule and collecting duct, indirectly affecting urine concentration.

- **Atrial Natriuretic Peptide (ANP):** Produced by the heart, ANP inhibits sodium and water reabsorption, leading to increased urine output and decreased blood volume and pressure.

THE REPRODUCTIVE SYSTEM

The reproductive system, an intricate assembly of organs and structures, plays a pivotal role in perpetuating species through the process of reproduction. Comprising two distinct yet interdependent components—the male and female reproductive systems—this elaborate network is tailored to perform specific functions.

While each system boasts unique elements and capabilities, they unite in a harmonious collaboration aimed at achieving fertilization, nurturing fetal development, and ultimately facilitating childbirth.

The Male Reproductive System

The male reproductive system consists of both external and internal organs that work in concert to produce, mature, and transport spermatozoa, as well as secrete male sex hormones.

- **Testes (Testicles):** The cornerstone of the male reproductive system, the testes are paired oval glands housed within the scrotum, a sac of skin below the penis. The primary function of the testes is to produce sperm and testosterone, the principal male sex hormone. Within the testes, seminiferous tubules harbor the germ cells where spermatogenesis, or sperm production, occurs.

- **Epididymis:** Positioned atop the testes, the epididymis is a tightly coiled tube where sperm mature and gain motility. This maturation process is crucial for the sperm's fertilizing capability.

- **Vas Deferens:** Extending from the epididymis, the vas deferens is a muscular tube that transports mature sperm to the urethra in preparation for ejaculation. It also stores sperm, contributing to their viability.

- **Seminal Vesicles:** These glands produce a significant portion of the semen, a fluid that nourishes and facilitates sperm movement. The seminal fluid contains sugars, enzymes, and prostaglandins, which contribute to the viability and motility of sperm.

- **Prostate Gland:** The prostate encircles the urethra just below the bladder and secretes a milky fluid that forms part of semen. This fluid plays a key role in sperm motility and longevity, and its alkaline nature helps neutralize the acidic environment of the female reproductive tract.

- **Bulbourethral Glands (Cowper's Glands):** Situated below the prostate, these glands secrete a clear fluid during sexual arousal that lubricates the urethra and neutralizes any acidity, facilitating the passage of sperm.

- **Penis:** The external organ through which urine and semen are expelled from the body. It contains the urethra and is composed of erectile tissue that enables erection, an essential function for sexual intercourse and the delivery of sperm into the female reproductive tract.

Hormonal Regulation and Spermatogenesis

The production and function of the male reproductive system are tightly regulated by hormones. The hypothalamus releases gonadotropin-releasing hormone (GnRH), stimulating the pituitary gland to secrete follicle-stimulating hormone (FSH) and luteinizing hormone (LH). FSH is crucial for spermatogenesis, while LH stimulates testosterone production, necessary for the development of male secondary sexual characteristics and the maintenance of reproductive tissues.

The Female Reproductive System

The female reproductive system comprises both internal and external organs that work in synergy to support reproduction.

- **Ovaries:** Small, almond-shaped glands located on either side of the uterus. They produce eggs (ova) and secrete female sex hormones, estrogen, and progesterone, which regulate the menstrual cycle and support pregnancy.

- **Fallopian Tubes (Uterine Tubes):** Narrow tubes extending from the upper uterus to the ovaries. Following ovulation, the fallopian tubes facilitate the passage of the egg, where it may meet sperm for fertilization. Cilia within the tubes gently propel the fertilized egg (zygote) towards the uterus.

- **Uterus (Womb):** A pear-shaped muscular organ where a fertilized egg implants and develops into a fetus. The uterus is lined with the endometrium, a tissue layer that thickens in preparation for pregnancy or sheds during menstruation if fertilization does not occur.

- **Cervix:** The lower, narrow part of the uterus that opens into the vagina. It serves as the passage through which sperm enter the uterus and, eventually, the pathway for childbirth.

- **Vagina:** A muscular, tubular canal that extends from the cervix to the external genitalia. It serves as the site for sexual intercourse, the menstrual flow exit, and the birth canal during childbirth.

- **External Genitalia (Vulva):** Includes the mons pubis, labia majora, labia minora, clitoris, and the openings of the vagina and urethra. The vulva protects the internal reproductive organs and plays a significant role in sexual arousal.

The Menstrual Cycle

The menstrual cycle, averaging 28 days, is a series of hormonal changes that prepare the female body for pregnancy each month. It consists of three phases:

- **Follicular Phase:** Stimulated by follicle-stimulating hormone (FSH), several ovarian follicles develop, with one becoming dominant and maturing into an ovum.

- **Ovulation:** Triggered by a surge in luteinizing hormone (LH), the mature egg is released from the ovary into the fallopian tube.

- **Luteal Phase:** The ruptured follicle transforms into the corpus luteum, which secretes progesterone to maintain the endometrial lining for potential pregnancy. If fertilization does not occur, the corpus luteum degenerates, leading to menstruation.

Hormonal Regulation

The hypothalamus and pituitary gland regulate the menstrual cycle through the release of hormones such as GnRH, FSH, and LH. Estrogen and progesterone from the ovaries further influence the cycle's phases, affecting the uterine lining's preparation for pregnancy.

Clinical Significance

Disorders of the female reproductive system include menstrual irregularities, polycystic ovary syndrome (PCOS), endometriosis, and reproductive cancers. Fertility issues and complications during pregnancy also fall within this system's purview. Advances in medical science, including hormonal therapies, surgical interventions, and assisted reproductive technologies (ART), offer solutions to many of these conditions, highlighting the importance of comprehensive knowledge in this area.

SECTION 7 - HUMAN ANATOMY AND PHYSIOLOGY

PRACTICE QUIZ

1 - Which type of tissue is responsible for movement in the body?

A. Nervous

B. Epithelial

C. Muscle

D. Connective

2 - Which tissue type forms the lining of the respiratory tract?

A. Connective

B. Muscle

C. Epithelial

D. Nervous

3 - What is the primary function of connective tissue?

A. Conduction of electrical impulses

B. Movement

C. Support and protection

D. Secretion of hormones

4 - Which of the following is NOT a characteristic of nervous tissue?

A. Ability to generate electrical signals

B. High capacity for regeneration

C. Presence of neurons and glial cells

D. Conductivity

5 - What process describes the replacement of cartilage with bone?

A. Ossification

B. Calcification

C. Deposition

D. Resorption

6 - Which cell type is responsible for bone resorption?

A. Osteoblasts

B. Osteocytes

C. Osteoclasts

D. Chondrocytes

7 - Where does longitudinal bone growth occur?

A. Periosteum

B. Epiphyseal plate

C. Haversian canal

D. Endosteum

8 - What is the fundamental unit of contraction in a skeletal muscle?

A. Myofibril

B. Sarcomere

C. Muscle fiber

D. Myofilament

9 - Which feature is unique to cardiac muscle cells?

A. Voluntary control

B. Presence of multiple nuclei

C. Intercalated discs

D. Ability to regenerate

10 - Cardiac muscle tissue is characterized by:

A. Striations and involuntary control

B. Smooth texture and voluntary control

C. Lack of striations and involuntary control

D. Multiple nuclei per cell

11 - What allows cardiac muscle cells to contract as a unit?

A. Sarcomeres

B. Gap junctions within intercalated discs

C. The presence of multiple nuclei

D. Voluntary nervous stimulation

12 - What type of neuron transmits signals from the central nervous system to muscles?

A. Sensory neuron

B. Interneuron

C. Motor neuron

D. Pyramidal neuron

13 - The brain and spinal cord comprise which part of the nervous system?

A. Peripheral nervous system

B. Central nervous system

C. Autonomic nervous system

D. Somatic nervous system

14 - Which part of the neuron receives signals from other neurons?

A. Axon

B. Dendrites

C. Soma

D. Synapse

15 - What is the primary function of the myelin sheath?

A. To transmit nerve impulses

B. To protect and insulate axons

C. To produce neurotransmitters

D. To receive signals from other neurons

16 - Which structure forms the blood-brain barrier?

A. Neurons

B. Astrocytes

C. Oligodendrocytes

D. Microglia

17 - What is the primary muscle involved in inhalation?

A. External intercostals

B. Internal intercostals

C. Diaphragm

D. Abdominal muscles

18 - Where does gas exchange occur in the lungs?

A. Trachea

B. Bronchi

C. Alveoli

D. Bronchioles

19 - What mechanism ensures that air is moistened, warmed, and filtered before reaching the lungs?

A. The action of the diaphragm

B. The mucous membrane in the nasal cavity

C. The contraction of intercostal muscles

D. The presence of surfactant in the alveoli

20 - What is the role of surfactant in the respiratory system?

A. Filtering the air

B. Warming the air

C. Preventing alveolar collapse

D. Facilitating oxygen transport

21 - Which circulatory route carries oxygen-poor blood from the heart to the lungs and back?

A. Systemic circulation

B. Pulmonary circulation

C. Coronary circulation

D. Portal circulation

22 - What is the primary function of systemic circulation?

A. To supply blood to the heart muscle itself

B. To transport nutrients from the gastrointestinal tract to the liver

C. To deliver oxygen-rich blood to the body and return oxygen-poor blood to the heart

D. To circulate blood through the lungs for gas exchange

23 - What component of blood is primarily responsible for transporting oxygen?

A. White blood cells

B. Platelets

C. Red blood cells

D. Plasma

24 - Which type of blood cell plays a crucial role in the immune system?

A. Red blood cells

B. Platelets

C. Plasma cells

D. White blood cells

25 - What is the function of platelets in blood?

A. Oxygen transport

B. Immune defense

C. Blood clotting

D. Nutrient transport

26 - Which plasma protein is primarily involved in maintaining osmotic pressure and fluid balance in the bloodstream?

A. Albumin

B. Globulin

C. Fibrinogen

D. Hemoglobin

27 - What type of blood vessel carries blood away from the heart?

A. Veins

B. Capillaries

C. Arteries

D. Venules

28 - Which vessels are primarily responsible for the exchange of nutrients and waste between blood and tissues?

A. Arteries

B. Veins

C. Capillaries

D. Arterioles

29 - Where does the majority of nutrient absorption occur in the digestive system?

A. Stomach

B. Large intestine

C. Small intestine

D. Mouth

30 - What is the role of the liver in digestion?

A. It produces insulin

B. It absorbs nutrients

C. It produces bile

D. It stores undigested food

31 - Which digestive organ is responsible for water absorption and the formation of feces?

A. Stomach

B. Small intestine

C. Liver

D. Large intestine

32 - What is the main purpose of cellular respiration in metabolism?

A. To synthesize new proteins

B. To generate adenosine triphosphate (ATP)

C. To produce carbon dioxide

D. To increase oxygen in cells

33 - Which hormone is primarily involved in lowering blood glucose levels?

A. Glucagon

B. Insulin

C. Cortisol

D. Epinephrine

34 - Which gland is known as the "master gland" of the endocrine system?

A. Thyroid gland

B. Adrenal gland

C. Pituitary gland

D. Pineal gland

35 - What role does the thyroid gland play in the body?

A. Regulates calcium levels

B. Controls blood pressure

C. Regulates metabolism and energy use

D. Manages blood sugar levels

36 - Where are steroid hormone receptors typically located?

A. On the cell membrane

B. Within the cytoplasm or nucleus

C. On the mitochondria

D. Within the endoplasmic reticulum

37 - What is the primary function of cell surface receptors?

A. To facilitate cell-to-cell communication

B. To synthesize DNA

C. To produce cellular energy

D. To detoxify harmful substances

38 - Which type of immune cell is primarily responsible for antibody production?

A. T lymphocytes

B. B lymphocytes

C. Natural killer cells

D. Macrophages

39 - What is the role of the complement system in the immune response?

A. To produce antibodies

B. To regulate body temperature

C. To enhance the ability of antibodies and phagocytic cells to clear microbes

D. To generate memory immune cells

40 - Which type of immunity is produced by vaccination?

A. Innate immunity

B. Passive immunity

C. Active immunity

D. Cellular immunity

41 - What is the primary function of T lymphocytes?

A. To produce antibodies

B. To directly kill infected host cells or help other immune cells

C. To capture antigens

D. To produce complement proteins

42 - What is the primary function of the lymphatic system?

A. To transport oxygen to tissues

B. To regulate body temperature

C. To maintain fluid balance and participate in immune defense

D. To digest fats

43 - Where are lymphocytes primarily produced and matured?

A. In the liver and spleen

B. In the bone marrow and thymus

C. In the kidneys and liver

D. In the heart and lungs

44 - What is the primary function of the kidneys?

A. To regulate blood glucose levels

B. To produce hormones

C. To filter waste products from the blood

D. To absorb nutrients

45 - How does the urinary system contribute to blood pressure regulation?

A. By regulating the volume of blood plasma

B. By producing red blood cells

C. By secreting digestive enzymes

D. By absorbing vitamins

46 - In males, where does spermatogenesis primarily occur?

A. Prostate gland

B. Seminal vesicles

C. Testes

D. Epididymis

47 - What is the role of the fallopian tubes in the female reproductive system?

A. To produce oocytes

B. To serve as the site for fertilization

C. To secrete female sex hormones

D. To support the development of the fetus

49 - Which hormone triggers ovulation in the female reproductive cycle?

A. Estrogen

B. Progesterone

C. Luteinizing hormone (LH)

D. Follicle-stimulating hormone (FSH)

SECTION 7 - HUMAN ANATOMY AND PHYSIOLOGY

PRACTICE QUIZ - ANSWER KEY

1 - Which type of tissue is responsible for movement in the body?

C) Muscle

2 - Which tissue type forms the lining of the respiratory tract?

C) Epithelial

3 - What is the primary function of connective tissue?

C) Support and protection

4 - Which of the following is NOT a characteristic of nervous tissue?

B) High capacity for regeneration

5 - What process describes the replacement of cartilage with bone?

A) Ossification

6 - Which cell type is responsible for bone resorption?

C) Osteoclasts

7 - Where does longitudinal bone growth occur?

B) Epiphyseal plate

8 - What is the fundamental unit of contraction in a skeletal muscle?

B) Sarcomere

9 - Which feature is unique to cardiac muscle cells?

C) Intercalated discs

10 - Cardiac muscle tissue is characterized by:

A) Striations and involuntary control

11 - What allows cardiac muscle cells to contract as a unit?

B) Gap junctions within intercalated discs

12 - What type of neuron transmits signals from the central nervous system to muscles?

C) Motor neuron

13 - The brain and spinal cord comprise which part of the nervous system?

B) Central nervous system

14 - Which part of the neuron receives signals from other neurons?

B) Dendrites

15 - What is the primary function of the myelin sheath?

B) To protect and insulate axons

16 - Which structure forms the blood-brain barrier?

B) Astrocytes

17 - What is the primary muscle involved in inhalation?

C) Diaphragm

18 - Where does gas exchange occur in the lungs?

C) Alveoli

19 - What mechanism ensures that air is moistened, warmed, and filtered before reaching the lungs?

B) The mucous membrane in the nasal cavity

20 - What is the role of surfactant in the respiratory system?

C) Preventing alveolar collapse

21 - Which circulatory route carries oxygen-poor blood from the heart to the lungs and back?

B) Pulmonary circulation

22 - What is the primary function of systemic circulation?

C) To deliver oxygen-rich blood to the body and return oxygen-poor blood to the heart

23 - What component of blood is primarily responsible for transporting oxygen?

C) Red blood cells

24 - Which type of blood cell plays a crucial role in the immune system?

D) White blood cells

25 - What is the function of platelets in blood?

C) Blood clotting

26 - Which plasma protein is primarily involved in maintaining osmotic pressure and fluid balance in the bloodstream?

A) Albumin

27 - What type of blood vessel carries blood away from the heart?

C) Arteries

28 - Which vessels are primarily responsible for the exchange of nutrients and waste between blood and tissues?

C) Capillaries

29 - Where does the majority of nutrient absorption occur in the digestive system?

C) Small intestine

30 - What is the role of the liver in digestion?

C) It produces bile

31 - Which digestive organ is responsible for water absorption and the formation of feces?

D) Large intestine

32 - What is the main purpose of cellular respiration in metabolism?

B) To generate adenosine triphosphate (ATP)

33 - Which hormone is primarily involved in lowering blood glucose levels?

B) Insulin

34 - Which gland is known as the "master gland" of the endocrine system?

C) Pituitary gland

35 - What role does the thyroid gland play in the body?

C) Regulates metabolism and energy use

36 - Where are steroid hormone receptors typically located?

B) Within the cytoplasm or nucleus

37 - What is the primary function of cell surface receptors?

A) To facilitate cell-to-cell communication

38 - Which type of immune cell is primarily responsible for antibody production?

B) B lymphocytes

39 - What is the role of the complement system in the immune response?

C) To enhance the ability of antibodies and phagocytic cells to clear microbes

40 - Which type of immunity is produced by vaccination?

C) Active immunity

41 - What is the primary function of T lymphocytes?

B) To directly kill infected host cells or help other immune cells

42 - What is the primary function of the lymphatic system?

C) To maintain fluid balance and participate in immune defense

43 - Where are lymphocytes primarily produced and matured?

B) In the bone marrow and thymus

44 - What is the primary function of the kidneys?

C) To filter waste products from the blood

45 - How does the urinary system contribute to blood pressure regulation?

A) By regulating the volume of blood plasma

46 - In males, where does spermatogenesis primarily occur?

C) Testes

47 - What is the role of the fallopian tubes in the female reproductive system?

B) To serve as the site for fertilization

49 - Which hormone triggers ovulation in the female reproductive cycle?

C) Luteinizing hormone (LH)

Want More?

Download Answer Explanations Now by Framing the QR-Code With Your Phone

SECTION 8 - PHYSICS

Physics, the discipline that reveals the laws governing the universe and all within it, is fundamentally anchored in the scientific method. This method, a systematic approach for exploring observations, answering questions, and testing hypotheses, stands as the cornerstone of all scientific inquiry. It offers a structured pathway to not only understanding complex phenomena but also solving the intricate puzzles posed by the natural world. Through this method, Physics progresses, weaving a clearer understanding of the cosmos from the fabric of experimentation and evidence.

THE SCIENTIFIC METHOD

The scientific method is a cyclical process that begins with **observation**—the careful noting and detailed description of natural phenomena. This could range from the simple act of noticing how objects fall to the ground to the complex observation of particle behavior in a collider. Observations often lead to questions, setting the stage for deeper investigation.

Hypothesis formulation follows observation. A hypothesis is a reasoned assumption made to explain the observed phenomenon. It is predictive, testable, and falsifiable, meaning it can be proven wrong through experimentation. The strength of a hypothesis lies in its ability to propose a cause-and-effect relationship that can be empirically tested.

Experimentation is the critical phase where hypotheses are rigorously tested. This involves designing and conducting experiments under controlled conditions to validate or refute the proposed hypothesis. Experiments must be replicable, allowing other scientists to verify results and ensure reliability. In Physics, experimentation can range from controlled laboratory experiments to observations made with sophisticated instruments like telescopes and particle accelerators.

Following experimentation, scientists analyze the data to draw conclusions. If the experimental results consistently support the hypothesis, it gains credibility; if not, the hypothesis may be revised or discarded. This iterative process is crucial for refining our understanding and ensuring that conclusions are based on empirical evidence.

A well-supported hypothesis, confirmed through repeated experimentation and observation, may contribute to the development of a theory. In Physics, theories are comprehensive explanations of aspects of the natural world, grounded in a body of evidence gathered from multiple observations and experiments. They unify a broad set of observations and provide frameworks for making predictions about the universe. Notable theories in Physics include Newton's laws of motion, the theory of relativity, and quantum mechanics.

The scientific method is dynamic, allowing for the continual evolution of scientific understanding as new evidence comes to light.

In Physics, this means that theories and laws are not static but are subject to revision and refinement. This adaptability is a strength, ensuring that Physics remains at the forefront of exploring the universe's most profound mysteries.

Observation, Experimentation, and Theory

The interplay of observation, experimentation, and theory is exemplified in the discovery and understanding of gravitational waves. Initially predicted by Einstein's theory of general relativity, gravitational waves were observed nearly a century later through meticulous experimentation involving laser interferometers capable of detecting the minuscule ripples in spacetime caused by massive astronomical events. This observation confirmed a fundamental prediction of general relativity, showcasing the power of the scientific method in Physics.

MECHANICS

Mechanics is traditionally divided into two main branches: **classical mechanics**, which deals with the motion of bodies under the influence of forces, and **quantum mechanics**, which describes the motion of particles at the atomic and subatomic levels.

KINEMATICS

Kinematics is a crucial field of study that delves into the motion of points, objects, and entire systems without delving into the forces behind their movements. Focused solely on the geometry of motion, including aspects such as distance, displacement, speed, velocity, and acceleration, kinematics lays the groundwork for a deeper understanding of physics. It provides the essential foundation needed to navigate and comprehend more complex physical principles, making it an indispensable area of study for anyone seeking to grasp the fundamentals of mechanics.

At the core of kinematics is the study of motion, which is universally observable in the natural world. Motion is described through parameters that include:

- **Distance and Displacement:** Distance refers to the total length of the path traveled by an object, a scalar quantity that does not involve direction. Displacement, on the other hand, is a vector quantity that represents the change in position of an object, considering only the initial and final positions, and the direction of movement.

- **Speed and Velocity:** Speed is a scalar quantity that measures how fast an object is moving, calculated as the distance traveled divided by the time it takes. Velocity adds direction to speed, making it a vector quantity that defines the rate of change of displacement over time. Average velocity and instantaneous velocity provide insights into an object's motion over a period and at a specific moment, respectively.

- **Acceleration:** Acceleration is a vector quantity that describes the rate of change of velocity over time. It indicates how quickly an object speeds up, slows down, or changes direction. Like velocity, acceleration can be average or instantaneous, offering a comprehensive view of how an object's motion evolves.

The Equations of Kinematics

Kinematics is characterized by a set of equations that allow for the calculation of an object's motion when certain values are known. These equations elegantly link displacement, initial and final velocities, acceleration, and time, enabling predictions about an object's position and velocity at any given point in its trajectory.

The four key kinematic equations for constant acceleration are:

1. $v = v_0 + at$

2. $\Delta x = v0t + \frac{1}{2} at^2$

3. $v^2 = v_0^2 + 2a\Delta x$

4. $\Delta x = \frac{1}{2}(v+v_0)t$

Where:

- v is the final velocity
- v_0 is the initial velocity
- a is the acceleration
- Δx is the displacement
- t is the time

DYNAMICS

Dynamics stands as a fascinating segment of mechanics, dedicated to unraveling how forces influence the movement of objects and systems. Diverging from Kinematics, which merely outlines motion without considering its origins, Dynamics ventures deeper, probing into the reasons behind motion. It sheds light on the forces that initiate, stop, and guide movement, providing a comprehensive understanding of not only the motion itself but also the underlying interactions and principles steering it. This exploration is vital for grasping the full scope of motion and the rules that govern it.

Dynamics is anchored in Newton's three laws of motion, which collectively form the bedrock upon which modern physics is built.

These laws explain the relationship between an object's motion and the forces acting upon it, providing a framework that applies to a wide range of physical phenomena, from celestial mechanics to the minutiae of subatomic particles.

- **Newton's First Law (Law of Inertia)** posits that an object will remain at rest or in uniform motion in a straight line unless acted upon by an external force. This principle introduces the concept of inertia, illustrating the natural tendency of objects to resist changes in their state of motion.

- **Newton's Second Law** establishes the equation F=ma, indicating that the force applied to an object is equal to the mass of the object multiplied by its acceleration. This law quantifies the impact of forces, showing that an object's acceleration is directly proportional to the net force acting on it and inversely proportional to its mass.

- **Newton's Third Law** states that for every action, there is an equal and opposite reaction. This law highlights the reciprocal nature of forces, emphasizing that interactions between two objects involve forces of equal magnitude but opposite direction, influencing both objects involved.

Beyond Newton's laws, Dynamics also encompasses the study of specific forces, such as gravitational force, which governs the motion of planets and objects on Earth; frictional force, which opposes motion between surfaces in contact; and centripetal force, required for circular motion. The understanding of these and other forces is critical for predicting and manipulating the physical world.

RELATIONSHIP BETWEEN FORCE MASS AND ACCELERATION

The relationship between force, mass, and acceleration is foundational, captured eloquently by Newton's Second Law of Motion. This law serves as a cornerstone in understanding the dynamics of objects, explaining how and why motion occurs. The interplay between force, mass, and acceleration is not just a topic of academic interest but a principle that underpins much of the physical world, from the design of vehicles and buildings to the trajectory of celestial bodies.

Newton's Second Law of Motion

Newton's Second Law provides the mathematical framework to describe the relationship between force, mass, and acceleration, stating that the force acting on an object is equal to the mass of that object multiplied by its acceleration (F=ma). This law implies that for a given force, the acceleration of an object is inversely proportional to its mass. In other words, the more massive an object, the less it will accelerate under the same force.

Force

Force, in physics, is a vector quantity that represents an interaction that changes the motion of an object. A force can cause an object with mass to change its velocity, which includes to begin moving from a state of rest, to stop, to accelerate, or to change direction. Measured in newtons (N) in the International System of Units (SI), force encapsulates the push or pull acting upon any object.

Mass

Mass is a fundamental property of physical objects and is a measure of an object's resistance to acceleration when a force is applied. It is an intrinsic characteristic of the object, independent of its environment or the method of measurement. Mass is often confused with weight, but while weight is the force exerted by gravity on an object, mass is the amount of matter in the object, providing it with inertia—the resistance to change in motion.

Acceleration

Acceleration is a vector quantity that measures the rate at which an object changes its velocity. An object accelerates if it speeds up, slows down, or changes direction. Acceleration is directly proportional to the net force acting on the object and inversely proportional to its mass.

The Interconnection

The relationship between force, mass, and acceleration is a dynamic interplay where each element influences the others. Applying a force to an object will cause it to accelerate, with the magnitude of that acceleration directly proportional to the magnitude of the force and inversely proportional to the object's mass. This principle allows us to predict the behavior of objects under various forces, making it essential for both theoretical and practical applications in physics and engineering.

For example, when a car accelerates down the road, the engine generates a force that propels the car forward. The acceleration of the car depends on both the force applied by the engine and the mass of the car. A more massive car will require a greater force to achieve the same acceleration as a lighter car.

VECTOR AND SCALAR

Scalars are quantities that are fully described by a magnitude (or numerical value) alone. They do not have direction. Common examples of scalar quantities include temperature, mass, speed, energy, and time. For instance, when we say the temperature is 30 degrees Celsius, the mass of an object is 2 kilograms, or a car is moving at a speed of 60 kilometers per hour, we are referring to scalar quantities. These values tell us the "how much" aspect but nothing about the "which way" direction. Scalar quantities are straightforward in their mathematical treatment because they align with our basic understanding of arithmetic—addition, subtraction, multiplication, and division are applied just as they are with ordinary numbers.

In contrast, **vectors** are quantities that possess both magnitude and direction. This dual characteristic makes them more complex but also more informative. Examples of vector quantities include displacement, velocity, acceleration, and force.

For instance, stating that a plane is flying at a velocity of 500 kilometers per hour north provides a complete description of its motion, unlike speed, which would only tell us how fast the plane is going.

A vector is graphically represented as an arrow. The length of the arrow corresponds to the vector's magnitude, which quantifies how much or how large the quantity is, while the arrow's direction indicates the vector's orientation in space. Mathematically, vectors in a two-dimensional space can be expressed in terms of their components along the x and y axes, often written as $v = (v_x, v_y)$, where v_x and v_y are the magnitudes of the vector along the x and y axes, respectively.

For example, the representation of point (6,5) is shown in the figure:

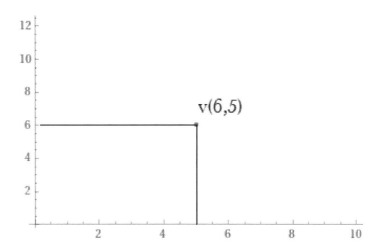

Calculating the length (or magnitude) of a vector utilizes the principles of Pythagorean theorem, a fundamental concept in geometry that relates the lengths of the sides of a right-angled triangle. For a two-dimensional vector **v** with components V_x and V_y along the x and y axes, respectively, the vector can be visualized as a diagonal in a right-angled triangle, with V_x and V_y forming the adjacent and opposite sides.

The Pythagorean theorem states that in a right-angled triangle, the square of the length of the hypotenuse (the side opposite the right angle) is equal to the sum of the squares of the lengths of the other two sides. Mathematically, this is expressed as:

$$c^2 = a^2 + b^2$$

where c is the length of the hypotenuse, a and b are the lengths of the other two sides.

Applying the Pythagorean theorem to vector calculations, the length (or magnitude) of the vector v, denoted as $|v|$ or simply v, can be found using the formula:

$$v = \sqrt{V_x^2 + V_y^2}$$

Here, V_x and V_y are the horizontal and vertical components of the vector, respectively. This formula directly follows from treating V_x and V_y as the sides of a right-angled triangle and the vector v as the hypotenuse.

VECTOR OPERATIONS

Vectors are subject to several mathematical operations that allow for the analysis of physical systems:

- **Addition:** Vector addition follows the principle of the parallelogram or the tip-to-tail method. When adding two vectors, they are placed so that the tail of the second vector meets the tip of the first. The resultant vector, or sum, extends from the tail of the first vector to the tip of the second. This operation is essential in physics for combining multiple forces acting on an object.

- **Subtraction:** Vector subtraction can be viewed as adding a negative vector. It involves reversing the direction of the vector to be subtracted and then adding it to the first vector following the tip-to-tail method. This process is useful for determining the net displacement or the difference in velocity between two states of motion.

- **Scalar Multiplication:** Multiplying a vector by a scalar changes the magnitude of the vector but not its direction. If the scalar is negative, the vector's direction is reversed. Scalar multiplication is used in physics to scale physical quantities up or down, such as when calculating the force of gravity on an object of different masses.

- **Dot Product:** The dot product (or scalar product) of two vectors results in a scalar quantity. It is calculated as the product of the magnitudes of the two vectors and the cosine of the angle between them. The dot product is significant in determining the work done when a force is applied to an object along a displacement.

- **Cross Product:** The cross product (or vector product) of two vectors results in another vector that is perpendicular to the plane containing the original vectors. The magnitude of the cross product vector is proportional to the area of the parallelogram formed by the original vectors. The cross product is used in physics to calculate torques and angular momenta.

VELOCITY AND ACCELERATION

Velocity and acceleration, both crucial vector quantities, play a pivotal role in kinematics—the branch of mechanics focused on describing object motion. By detailing not just how objects move but also how their motion changes over time, these quantities are indispensable for a comprehensive understanding of motion, all without delving into the forces behind these movements.

Velocity

Velocity is a vector quantity that describes both the speed and direction of an object's motion. It tells us how fast an object is moving and in which direction. Mathematically, velocity (v) is defined as the rate of change of displacement (Δx) over time (Δt), expressed as:

$$v = \Delta x / \Delta t$$

Where:

- v is velocity,
- Δx is the change in position (displacement),
- Δt is the change in time.

Velocity provides a more comprehensive description of motion than speed, a scalar quantity that only measures how fast an object is moving regardless of its direction. For instance, saying a car is traveling at 60 kilometers per hour northward conveys both the magnitude (60 km/h) and direction (northward) of the car's motion, offering a complete picture of its velocity.

Acceleration

Acceleration is another vector quantity that describes the rate at which an object's velocity changes over time. It indicates how quickly an object speeds up, slows down, or changes direction. Mathematically, acceleration (a) is defined as the rate of change of velocity (Δv) over time (Δt), expressed as:

$$a = \Delta v / \Delta t$$

Where:

- a is acceleration,
- Δv is the change in velocity,
- Δt is the change in time.

Acceleration is present whenever there is a change in the speed or direction of motion, making it a critical concept for understanding dynamic situations. For example, when a car increases its speed from 50 km/h to 70 km/h in 5 seconds, it is accelerating. Similarly, a planet orbiting the sun experiences acceleration due to its constantly changing direction, even if its speed remains constant.

Velocity and acceleration are intimately connected in the study of motion. Acceleration is the driving factor behind changes in velocity. An object moving with constant velocity is said to have zero acceleration, while an object with changing velocity is undergoing acceleration. This relationship is the essence of Newton's Second Law of Motion, which states that the acceleration of an object is directly proportional to the net force acting upon it and inversely proportional to its mass.

FORCE OF GRAVITY

Gravity is a natural phenomenon by which all things with mass or energy are brought toward one another. On Earth, it gives weight to physical objects, and the Moon's gravity causes the ocean tides. The force of gravity is an attraction that exists between any two masses, any two bodies, any two particles. It is one of the four fundamental forces of nature, alongside the electromagnetic force, the strong nuclear force, and the weak nuclear force.

Sir Isaac Newton was the first to develop a comprehensive mathematical theory for gravity with his law of universal gravitation in the late 17th century. Newton's law posits that every point mass attracts every other point mass in the universe with a force that is directly proportional to the product of their masses and inversely proportional to the square of the distance between their centers. The formula for this force is:

$$F = G \frac{m_1 m_2}{r^2}$$

where:

- F is the force of gravity,
- G is the gravitational constant,
- m_1 and m_2 are the masses of the two objects,
- r is the distance between the centers of the two masses.

On Earth, gravity gives weight to physical objects and causes the ocean tides. The force of gravity near the Earth's surface accelerates objects at approximately $9.8 m/s^2$ downward. This acceleration is what we commonly refer to as "**g**"

WAVES AND SOUND

This section offers an in-depth analysis of how waves serve as carriers of energy, highlighting their defining characteristics and diving into the unique aspects of sound waves. By shedding light on these principles, we uncover their critical roles across a spectrum of scientific discoveries, technological advancements, and everyday phenomena, enhancing our understanding of the world around us.

WAVES

Waves are disturbances that transfer energy from one point to another without the physical transfer of matter. They are characterized by several key properties:

- **Wavelength (λ):** The distance between successive crests or troughs in a wave.
- **Frequency (f):** The number of waves that pass a given point per unit of time, typically measured in hertz (Hz).
- **Amplitude:** The height of the wave from its midpoint to its crest, representing the wave's energy.
- **Speed (v):** The rate at which a wave travels through a medium. The relationship between wave speed, frequency, and wavelength is given by $v=f\lambda$
- **Peak:** It's the point where the wave exhibits its maximum amplitude, which is the measure of the wave's strength or intensity.

Waves can be classified into two main types: transverse and longitudinal. In transverse waves, the disturbance is perpendicular to the direction of the wave's travel, typical of light and water waves. In longitudinal waves, the disturbance occurs in the same direction as the wave's propagation, as in the case of sound waves.

REFLECTION, REFRACTION, AND DIFFRACTION

The phenomena of reflection, refraction, and diffraction are three foundational principles critical to the study of wave behavior, encompassing both light and sound waves. Grasping these concepts is crucial for understanding the intricate ways in which waves interact with different materials and their surroundings. This knowledge forms the backbone of countless applications and technologies that permeate our daily lives and fuel advances across a broad spectrum of scientific disciplines.

Reflection

Reflection occurs when a wave encounters a surface or boundary that does not absorb the wave's energy but instead bounces it back into the medium from which it originated. The most familiar example of reflection is the mirroring effect observed on smooth surfaces, such as a calm body of water or a flat mirror. Reflection is governed by the law of reflection, which states that the angle of incidence (the angle at which the incoming wave strikes the surface) is equal to the angle of reflection (the angle at which the wave departs from the surface). This principle applies to all types of waves, including light, sound, and water waves.

Reflection enables the formation of images by mirrors, the echo of sound, and the transmission of radio waves. It is also a key concept in the design of optical devices, such as telescopes and binoculars, as well as in architectural acoustics to control sound distribution within spaces.

Refraction

Refraction is the bending of a wave as it passes from one medium into another in which its speed is different. This bending is caused by the change in wave speed, which results in a change in the wave's direction at the boundary between the two media. Refraction is most commonly observed with light waves; for example, when light passes through water or a glass lens, it bends in a manner that can cause objects to appear shifted or distorted.

The law of refraction, also known as Snell's law, quantitatively describes the relationship between the angles of incidence and refraction and the indices of refraction of the two media. Refraction is responsible for a range of phenomena, from the focusing of light by lenses in eyeglasses and cameras to the formation of rainbows and the apparent bending of objects partially submerged in water.

Diffraction

Diffraction is the spreading out of waves as they pass through an opening or around obstacles. It occurs when the size of the opening or obstacle is comparable to the wavelength of the wave. Diffraction is responsible for the ability of sound waves to bend around corners and spread into regions behind barriers, a property not shared by light waves under normal circumstances due to their much shorter wavelengths.

Diffraction plays a crucial role in the design of various optical and acoustic systems. It limits the resolving power of microscopes and telescopes—devices that rely on the manipulation of waves to magnify images. Understanding diffraction is also vital in engineering, especially in designing structures to minimize or utilize the diffraction of sound and electromagnetic waves.

ELECTROMAGNETIC WAVES

Electromagnetic waves are generated by the vibration or oscillation of electric charges, which create oscillating electric and magnetic fields perpendicular to each other and to the direction of the wave's propagation. This unique characteristic allows electromagnetic waves to carry energy and momentum without the need for a physical medium, distinguishing them from other types of waves. Electromagnetic waves exhibit both wave-like and particle-like properties, a duality that is a cornerstone of quantum mechanics. They can be reflected, refracted, and diffracted like wave phenomena, but they can also be thought of as streams of particles, called photons, particularly when interacting with matter.

The Electromagnetic Spectrum

The electromagnetic spectrum encompasses a wide range of electromagnetic waves, categorized based on their wavelength and frequency. The spectrum is typically divided into several regions, including, from longest wavelength to shortest: radio waves, microwaves, infrared radiation, visible light, ultraviolet radiation, X-rays, and gamma rays. Each category has its unique properties and applications:

- **Radio Waves:** Used in communication technologies, such as television, radio broadcasts, and cell phones.
- **Microwaves:** Employed in radar technology and microwave ovens.
- **Infrared Radiation:** Used in thermal imaging cameras, remote controls, and to study the heat of objects in astronomy.
- **Visible Light:** The only part of the spectrum visible to the human eye, crucial for vision and photography.
- **Ultraviolet Radiation:** Has applications in sterilization, fluorescent lighting, and can cause sunburn.
- **X-rays:** Used in medical imaging to view the inside of the body.
- **Gamma Rays:** Emitted by radioactive materials and certain astronomical events, used in cancer treatment and to study the universe.

BASICS OF ELECTROSTATICS

Electric Charge

Electric charge is a fundamental property of matter that causes it to experience a force when placed in an electromagnetic field. There are two types of electric charges: positive and negative. Like charges repel each other, while unlike charges attract. The smallest unit of charge is carried by subatomic particles: protons (positive charge) and electrons (negative charge). The neutrality of an atom comes from the balance of these charges, but when an imbalance occurs, either through gaining or losing electrons, the atom becomes a charged particle or ion, leading to electrostatic phenomena.

Electric Force: Coulomb's Law

The force between two charged particles is described by Coulomb's law, named after Charles-Augustin de Coulomb, who formulated the law in the 18th century. Coulomb's law states that the magnitude of the electrostatic force between two point charges is directly proportional to the product of the magnitudes of the charges and inversely proportional to the square of the distance between them. The law is mathematically expressed as:

$$F = k \frac{|q_1 q_2|}{r^2}$$

where:

- F is the magnitude of the force
- q_1 and q_2 are the charges
- r is the distance between the charges
- k is Coulomb's constant ($8.987 \times 10^9 \, \mathrm{Nm^2/C^2}$)

Coulomb's law is a cornerstone of electrostatics, allowing us to calculate the electric force between any two charged particles, revealing the fundamental principles that govern electric interactions.

Electric Field

The concept of the electric field is pivotal in understanding how charges interact with their surroundings. An electric field is a region around a charged object where other charges experience a force. The strength and direction of the electric field are represented by electric field lines, which emanate from positive charges and terminate on negative charges. The electric field (E) at any point in space is defined as the electric force (F) experienced by a small positive test charge (q) placed at that point, divided by the magnitude of the test charge:

$$E = \frac{F}{q} = k\frac{Q}{r^2}$$

The electric field is measured in units of volts per meter (V/m) or newtons per coulomb (N/C). It provides a way to quantify the influence a charge exerts on its environment, extending Coulomb's law to a broader context.

Electric Current

At its core, electric current represents the movement of electric charge along a conductor, quantified in amperes (A). This movement is initiated when electrons transition between atoms, propelled by the potential difference, or voltage, across the conductor. Although we conventionally describe current as flowing from the positive to the negative terminal of a power source, it's actually the electrons that migrate from the negative to the positive end in conductive materials.

Voltage

Voltage—or electric potential difference—acts as the driving force that propels electric charge through a circuit. Expressed in volts (V), voltage signifies the amount of energy per unit of charge that's available to push the charge through a conductor. In essence, voltage serves as the electrical "pressure" that propels the current along its path.

Resistance

Resistance measures how much a material opposes the flow of electric current, with its value in ohms (Ω) influenced by the material's characteristics, temperature, and dimensions. While materials exhibiting low resistance, like metals, efficiently conduct electricity, those with higher resistance, such as rubber or glass, act as insulators, obstructing the current's flow.

Ohm's Law

Named after the German physicist Georg Simon Ohm, who formulated this fundamental relationship in 1827, Ohm's Law is essential for understanding how electric circuits operate. It provides a simple yet powerful equation that relates voltage, current, and resistance — three core elements that dictate the behavior of electric circuits.

Ohm's Law states that the current flowing through a conductor between two points is directly proportional to the voltage across the two points and inversely proportional to the resistance between them.

This relationship can be succinctly expressed by the equation:

$$V = IR$$

where

- V represents the voltage across the conductor (in volts, V),
- I is the current flowing through the conductor (in amperes, A), and
- R is the resistance of the conductor (in ohms, Ω). This equation lays the groundwork for analyzing and designing electrical and electronic circuits.

Components of Ohm's Law

1. **Voltage (V)**: Often described as electrical pressure, voltage is the potential difference that drives electric charge through a circuit. It's the energy per unit charge that pushes the current from one point to another.

2. **Current (I)**: Current is the rate at which charge is flowing through a conductor. It's a measure of the flow of electric charge, with its direction conventionally considered from the positive to the negative terminal of a power source.

3. **Resistance (R)**: Resistance quantifies how much a material opposes the flow of electric current. Factors such as the material's type, temperature, length, and cross-sectional area affect its resistance. Materials with low resistance (like copper) are excellent conductors of electricity, whereas those with high resistance (such as rubber) serve as insulators.

MAGNETIC FIELDS

A magnetic field is a vector field surrounding magnets, electric currents, and changing electric fields. It represents the region where magnetic forces are observable and can influence other magnetic objects or charged particles in motion. The strength and direction of the magnetic field are described by magnetic field lines, which emanate from the north pole of a magnet and loop around to its south pole. The density of these lines indicates the field's strength—closer lines suggest a stronger field.

Magnetic fields are generated through several methods:

- **Permanent Magnets:** Materials like iron, nickel, and cobalt possess domains of aligned atoms that produce a stable magnetic field.
- **Electric Currents:** According to Ampère's law, an electric current flowing through a wire generates a circular magnetic field around the wire. The right-hand rule helps visualize the direction of this field.
- **Electromagnetic Induction:** Changing electric fields can induce magnetic fields, a prin-

ciple discovered by Michael Faraday, which forms the basis of many electrical generators and transformers.

The strength of a magnetic field is measured in teslas (T) in the International System of Units (SI), or in gauss (G) in the centimeter-gram-second (CGS) system. Earth's magnetic field, for example, has an average strength of about 50 microteslas (µT), which is equivalent to 0.5 gauss.

The Relationship Between Electricity and Magnetism

The connection between electricity and magnetism, known as electromagnetism, was first comprehensively described by James Clerk Maxwell in the 19th century. One of the most striking revelations of electromagnetism is that electric currents produce magnetic fields. Conversely, changing magnetic fields can induce electric currents in conductors, a principle known as electromagnetic induction.

This interplay can be observed in electromagnets, devices that utilize electric current to generate a magnetic field. When current flows through a coiled wire wrapped around a ferromagnetic core, a strong magnetic field is produced, the strength of which can be adjusted by varying the current. Conversely, moving a magnet inside a coil can induce a current in the coil, illustrating the principle of induction.

SECTION 8 - PHYSICS

PRACTICE QUIZ

1 - What is the first step of the scientific method?
A. Forming a hypothesis
B. Conducting an experiment
C. Making an observation
D. Analyzing the results

2 - Which of the following best describes a hypothesis?
A. A guess with no basis in observation
B. A proven conclusion
C. An educated guess that can be tested
D. A detailed record of experimental observations

3 - If a car accelerates from 0 to 60 km/h in 5 seconds, what is its average acceleration?
A. 12 km/h^2
B. 12 m/s^2
C. 3.33 m/s^2
D. 3.33 km/h^2

4 - A ball is thrown vertically upwards with a velocity of 20 m/s. Ignoring air resistance, what is its velocity at the top of its path?
A. 20 m/s
B. 0 m/s
C. 9.8 m/s
D. -9.8 m/s

5 - Which of Newton's laws explains why a book at rest on a table stays at rest?
A. Newton's First Law
B. Newton's Second Law
C. Newton's Third Law
D. Newton's Law of Gravitation

6 - According to Newton's third law, if you push on a wall with a force of 5 N, how much force does the wall exert on you?
A. 0 N
B. 5 N in the same direction
C. 5 N in the opposite direction
D. 10 N in the opposite direction

7 - If a force of 10 N is applied to a mass of 2 kg, what is the acceleration?

A. 20 m/s^2

B. 5 m/s^2

C. 10 m/s^2

D. 2 m/s^2

8 - A 4 kg object experiences an acceleration of 2 m/s^2. What is the net force acting on it?

A. 2 N

B. 6 N

C. 8 N

D. 4 N

9 - If two objects with different masses experience the same force, which one will have a greater acceleration?

A. The object with the greater mass

B. The object with the lesser mass

C. Both will have the same acceleration

D. It depends on the surface

10 - Which of the following is a vector quantity?

A. Temperature

B. Mass

C. Velocity

D. Energy

11 - What scalar quantity is equivalent to the magnitude of a velocity vector?

A. Acceleration

B. Speed

C. Force

D. Momentum

12 - If two vectors of equal magnitude are pointed in opposite directions, what is their sum?

A. A vector of zero magnitude

B. A vector of double the magnitude

C. A scalar quantity

D. Impossible to determine

13 - How do you calculate the resultant magnitude of two perpendicular vectors, A and B?

A. $A^2 + B^2$

B. $A + B$

C. $\sqrt{A^2 + B^2}$

D. $A - B$

14 - What differentiates a vector from a scalar?

A. Only vectors have units

B. Vectors have direction, and scalars do not

C. Scalars can only be positive numbers

D. Vectors can only represent physical quantities

15 - Which operation can you perform with scalar quantities but not with vector quantities?

A. Addition

B. Subtraction

C. Multiplication

D. Division

16 - What is the acceleration due to gravity on Earth's surface?

A. $6.67 \times 10^{-11} \text{ m/s}^2$

B. 9.8 m/s^2

C. 9.8 N/Kg

D. Both B and C are correct.

17 - If the mass of Earth were to double while its radius remained the same, how would the acceleration due to gravity at its surface change?

A. It would halve

B. It would remain the same

C. It would double

D. It would quadruple

18 - What is the frequency of a wave that has a wavelength of 2 meters and travels at 300 meters per second?

A. 150 Hz

B. 600 Hz

C. 150 m/s

D. 300 Hz

19 - Which principle explains why you can hear sounds around a corner?

A. Reflection

B. Refraction

C. Diffraction

D. Dispersion

20 - What happens when light passes from air into water at an angle?

A. It speeds up and bends away from the normal

B. It speeds up and bends towards the normal

C. It slows down and bends away from the normal

D. It slows down and bends towards the normal

21 - Which phenomenon occurs when light waves encounter a small slit and spread out?

A. Reflection

B. Refraction

C. Diffraction

D. Polarization

22 - What is the speed of electromagnetic waves in a vacuum?

A. $3 \times 10^8 \, \text{m/s}$

B. $3 \times 10^6 \, \text{m/s}$

C. $2.5 \times 10^8 \, \text{m/s}$

D. $1.5 \times 10^8 \, \text{m/s}$

23 - Which of the following is NOT a characteristic of electromagnetic waves?

A. They require a medium to travel through

B. They can travel through a vacuum

C. They are transverse waves

D. They include visible light, X-rays, and radio waves

24 - What type of charge does an electron have?

A. Positive

B. Negative

C. Neutral

D. Variable

25 - Which law calculates the force between two charged particles?

A. Newton's Second Law

B. Coulomb's Law

C. Ohm's Law

D. Faraday's Law

26 - What unit is electric charge measured in?

A. Joules

B. Watts

C. Coulombs

D. Ohms

27 - A material that allows electrons to move freely within it is called a:

A. Conductor

B. Semiconductor

C. Insulator

D. Resistor

SECTION 8 - PHYSICS
PRACTICE QUIZ - ANSWER KEY

1 - What is the first step of the scientific method?
C) Making an observation

2 - Which of the following best describes a hypothesis?
C) An educated guess that can be tested

3 - If a car accelerates from 0 to 60 km/h in 5 seconds, what is its average acceleration?
C) 3.33 m/s^2

4 - A ball is thrown vertically upwards with a velocity of 20 m/s. Ignoring air resistance, what is its velocity at the top of its path?
B) 0 m/s

5 - Which of Newton's laws explains why a book at rest on a table stays at rest?
A) Newton's First Law

6 - According to Newton's third law, if you push on a wall with a force of 5 N, how much force does the wall exert on you?
C) 5 N in the opposite direction

7 - If a force of 10 N is applied to a mass of 2 kg, what is the acceleration?
B) 5 m/s^2

8 - A 4 kg object experiences an acceleration of 2 m/s². What is the net force acting on it?
C) 8N

9 - If two objects with different masses experience the same force, which one will have a greater acceleration?
B) The object with the lesser mass

10 - Which of the following is a vector quantity?
C) Velocity

11 - What scalar quantity is equivalent to the magnitude of a velocity vector?
B) Speed

12 - If two vectors of equal magnitude are pointed in opposite directions, what is their sum?

A) A vector of zero magnitude

13 - How do you calculate the resultant magnitude of two perpendicular vectors, A and B?

C) $\sqrt{A^2 + B^2}$

14 - What differentiates a vector from a scalar?

B) Vectors have direction, and scalars do not

15 - Which operation can you perform with scalar quantities but not with vector quantities?

D) Division

16 - What is the acceleration due to gravity on Earth's surface?

D) Both B and C are correct

17 - If the mass of Earth were to double while its radius remained the same, how would the acceleration due to gravity at its surface change?

C) It would double

18 - What is the frequency of a wave that has a wavelength of 2 meters and travels at 300 meters per second?

A) 150 Hz

19 - Which principle explains why you can hear sounds around a corner?

C) Diffraction

20 - What happens when light passes from air into water at an angle?

D) It slows down and bends towards the normal

21 - Which phenomenon occurs when light waves encounter a small slit and spread out?

C) Diffraction

22 - What is the speed of electromagnetic waves in a vacuum?

A) 3×10^8 m/s

23 - Which of the following is NOT a characteristic of electromagnetic waves?

A. They require a medium to travel through.

24 - What type of charge does an electron have?

B) Negative

25 - Which law calculates the force between two charged particles?

B) Coulomb's Law

26 - What unit is electric charge measured in?

C) Coulombs

27 - A material that allows electrons to move freely within it is called a:

A) Conductor

Want More?

Download Answer Explanations Now by Framing the QR-Code With Your Phone

FULL-LENGTH TESTS

THE MOST UP-TO-DATE COMPREHENSIVE TESTS OF THE HESI A2 EXAM

SECTION 1 - MATHEMATICS

FULL-LENGTH PRACTICE TESTS
SECTION 1 - MATHEMATICS

Start Time ....

End Time ....

1 - What is the sum of 243 and 567?
A. 800
B. 810
C. 900

2 - What is the result of adding $\frac{1}{4}$ and $\frac{1}{2}$?

A. $\frac{1}{6}$

B. $\frac{3}{4}$

C. $\frac{2}{3}$

3 - Simplify the fraction $\frac{10}{25}$

A. $\frac{1}{3}$

B. $\frac{2}{5}$

C. $\frac{2}{3}$

4 - Convert the decimal 0.75 to a fraction.

A. $\frac{3}{4}$

B. $\frac{7}{10}$

C. $\frac{2}{5}$

5 - Round 5.237 to the nearest tenth.
A. 5.2
B. 5.23
C. 5.24

6 - What is 25% of 200?

A. 50

B. 40

C. 60

D. 25

7 - What is the value of y if $3y - 9 = 0$

A. 2

B. 3

C. 4

8 - Convert 5 kilometers to meters.

A. 500 meters

B. 5,000 meters

C. 50,000 meters

9 - What is the product of 12 and 9?

A. 108

B. 102

C. 98

10 - What is the value of x in the equation $3(x + 4) = 2x + 15$**?**

A. 7

B. 11

C. 3

D. 5

11 - What is -40°C in Fahrenheit?

A. -40°F

B. 0°F

C. 40°F

D. -32°F

12 - What is the solution to $2x - 4 = 10$

A. 3

B. 2

C. 7

D. 5

13 - Solve for x: $x^2 = 81$

A. 9

B. 8

C. -9

D. A and C

14 - What is the result of this operation? $15 - (3 + 2) + 7(2 + 3)$

A. 44

B. 45

C. 46

D. 54

15 - If you add 732 and 268, what do you get?

A. 990

B. 1000

C. 1020

D. 980

16 - If 15% of a number is 45, what is the number?

A. 200

B. 250

C. 300

17 - In a survey, 60% of the participants are female. If there are 30 male participants, how many participants are there in total?

A. 50

B. 60

C. 75

18 - Find the value of $2.35x + 0.12x + 0.06x$

A. 2.53

B. 2.55

C. 2.52

D. 2.50

19 - If a shirt originally costing $40 is on sale for 30% off, how much does it cost now?

A. 28$

B. 32$

C. 12$

D. 22$

20 - Convert 212°F to Celsius (C)

A. 90°C

B. 105°C

C. 100°C

21 - A product originally priced at 80$ is marked down by 25%. What is the sale price?

A. 60$

B. 55$

C. 70$

22 - Convert 150 kilograms to pounds

A. 330.69 lbs

B. 320.55 lbs

C. 310.49 lbs

23 - What is the value of x **in** $5(x-3)=20$**?**

A. 7

B. 5

C. 4

D. 6

24 - What is the decimal equivalent of $\frac{1}{8}$**?**

A. 0.125

B. 0.25

C. 0.5

D. 0.75

25 - Multiply $\frac{1}{2}$ **and** $\frac{2}{3}$

A. $\frac{1}{3}$

B. $\frac{3}{4}$

C. $\frac{2}{7}$

26 - Round 3.786 to the nearest tenth

A. 3.7

B. 3.8

C. 3.78

27 - Add 2.5 and 4.75

A. 6.55

B. 7.25

C. 7.45

28 - Subtract 0.9 from 5

A. 4.1

B. 4.0

C. 4.9

29 - Solve $3(x+2)=3x+6$

A. True for all x value

B. True only when x=0

C. True only when x=1

30 - Simplify 5^0

A. 5

B. Not allowed

C. 0

D. 1

31 - What is the result of $100 \div 0$?

A. 0

B. 1

C. Not allowed

32 - What is the least common denominator (LCD) of $\frac{1}{3}$ and $\frac{1}{4}$

A. 7

B. 11

C. 12

D. 24

33 - Simplify $(-3)^2$

A. -9

B. 9

C. 6

34 - Solve for y: $6y + 3y - 9 = 0$

A. 3

B. 6

C. 1

D. 4

35 - What is 10^{-1}?

A. 10

B. 1

C. 0.1

D. -10

36 - Convert 5 tons to pound

A. 1.000 pounds

B. 10.000 pounds

C. 5.000 pounds

37 - Solve for x: $2x + 6 = 16$

A. 2

B. 4

C. 5

D. 12

38 - Subtract $\frac{2}{3}$ **from** $\frac{5}{6}$

A. $\frac{1}{6}$

B. $\frac{3}{4}$

C. $\frac{1}{2}$

39 - If $2x + 5 = 15$**, what is x?**

A. 10

B. 5

C. 4

D. 8

40 - Convert 32°F to Celsius (C)

A. 0°C

B. 100°C

C. 32°C

D. -32°C

41 - What is the result of 3^2 **x** 3^3**?**

A. 3^6

B. 27

C. 3^5

42 - Convert 0.5 hours to minutes

A. 30 minutes

B. 55 minutes

C. 25 minutes

D. 45 minutes

43 - If 6 apples cost $3, how much do 8 apples cost?

A. 2$

B. 4$

C. 8$

D. 5$

44 - What is the value of x? $x^2 - 4x + 4 = 0$

A. 0

B. 1

C. 2

D. 3

45 - If you have a mass of 200 grams, how many kilograms do you have?

A. 2 kilograms

B. 0.2 kilograms

C. 20 kilograms

D. 0.02 kilograms

46 - Subtract 0.65 from 2

A. 1.48

B. 1.45

C. 1.35

D. 1.60

47 - If 7 meters of cloth cost 35$, how much would 14 meters cost?

A. 65$

B. 70$

C. 15$

D. 45$

48 - What is 2^3?

A. 6

B. 3

C. 9

D. 8

49 - What is the result of $144 \div 12$?

A. 10

B. 11

C. 12

50 - If a product costs 4.99$, what is the total cost of 3 products including a 10% sales tax?

A. 14.97$

B. 16.47$

C. 15.57$

D. 13.97$

FULL-LENGTH PRACTICE TESTS SECTION 1 - MATHEMATICS ANSWER KEY WITH EXPLANATIONS

1 - What is the sum of 243 and 567?

B. 810

Explanation: Adding the two numbers, 243 + 567, equals 810.

2 - What is the result of adding $\frac{1}{4}$ and $\frac{1}{2}$?

B. $\frac{3}{4}$

Explanation: To add fractions, find a common denominator. In this case, 4 is the least common multiple, making the sum $\frac{1}{4} + \frac{1}{2} = \frac{3}{4}$

3 - Simplify the fraction $\frac{10}{25}$

B. $\frac{2}{5}$

Explanation: Both numerator and denominator can be divided by 5

4 - Convert the decimal 0.75 to a fraction.

A. $\frac{3}{4}$

Explanation: 0.75 equals $\frac{75}{100}$ which simplifies to $\frac{3}{4}$

5 - Round 5.237 to the nearest tenth.

C. 5.24

Explanation: The third digit (7) is greater than 5, so you round up the second digit to 4.

6 - What is 25% of 200?

A. 50

Explanation: 25% of 200 is calculated as 0.25 x 200 = 50

7 - What is the value of y if $3y - 9 = 0$

B. 3

Explanation: Add 9 to both sides to get 3y=9, then divide by 3, so y=3

8 - Convert 5 kilometers to meters

B. 5,000 meters

Explanation: 1 kilometer is equal to 1,000 meters, so 5 kilometers is equal to 5x1,000=5,000m

9 - What is the product of 12 and 9?

A. 108

Explanation: $12 \times 9 = 108$

---

10 - What is the value of x **in the equation** $3(x+4) = 2x + 15$**?**

C. 3

Explanation: Expanding and simplifying, $3x + 12 = 2x + 15$ so x=3

---

11 - What is -40°C in Fahrenheit?

A. -40°F

Explanation: Use the formula: (°C × 9/5) + 32=°F, so (-40 °C × 9/5) + 32= -40°F

---

12 - What is the solution to $2x - 4 = 10$

C. 7

Explanation: Add 4 to both sides to get $2x = 14$ so x=7

---

13 - Solve for x: $x^2 = 81$

D. Both A and C

Explanation: Taking the square root of both sides gives $x = +9$ and $x = -9$

---

14 - What is the result of this operation? $15 - (3+2) + 7(2+3)$

B. 45

Explanation: According to PEMDAS we must first perform the operations in the parentheses: 15-5+35=45

---

15 - If you add 732 and 268, what do you get?

B. 1000

Explanation: Adding the two numbers, 732 + 268, equals 1000.

---

16 - If 15% of a number is 45, what is the number?

C. 300

Explanation: Set up the equation 0.15x = 45 and solve for x=300

---

17 - In a survey, 60% of the participants are female. If there are 30 male participants, how many participants are there in total?

C. 75

Explanation: 60% are female, so 40% are male. 40%:30=100%:x so x=$\dfrac{100 * 30}{40}$=75

---

18 - Find the value of $2.35x + 0.12x + 0.06x$

A. 2.53x

Explanation: To add decimals, align them vertically, ensuring the decimal points line up.

---

19 - If a shirt originally costing $40 is on sale for 30% off, how much does it cost now?

A. 28$

Explanation: 30% of $40 is $12. Subtract this from the original price: $40 - $12 = $28.

20 - Convert 212°F to Celsius (C)

C. 100°C

Explanation: C= $\frac{5}{9}$ (212 - 32)=100° (the boiling point of water)

21 - A product originally priced at \$80 is marked down by 25%. What is the sale price?

A. \$60

Explanation: The 25% of 80\$ is 20\$, so subtracting the discount from the original price gives 80-20=60

22 - Convert 150 kilograms to pounds

A. 330.69 lbs

Explanation: 150 x 2.20462 =330.69 lbs

23 - What is the value of x **in** $5(x - 3) = 20$**?**

A. 7

Explanation: First, distribute 5 across the parentheses and then solve: 5x-15=20,so 5x=35, then x=7

24 - What is the decimal equivalent of $\frac{1}{8}$ **?**

A. 0.125

Explanation: Dividing 1 by 8 gives a decimal value of 0.125.

25 - Multiply $\frac{1}{2}$ **and** $\frac{2}{3}$

A. $\frac{1}{3}$

Explanation: Multiply the numerators and denominators = $\frac{2}{6}$ which simplifies to $\frac{1}{3}$

26 - Round 3.786 to the nearest tenth

B. 3.8

Explanation: The second decimal place (8) is 5 or more, so you round up the first decimal place to 3.8.

27 - Add 2.5 and 4.75

B. 7.25

Explanation: Adding the two decimals directly, 2.5 + 4.75 = 7.25

28 - Subtract 0.9 from 5

A. 4.1

Explanation: Subtracting 0.9 from 5 gives 4.1

29 - Solve $3(x + 2) = 3x + 6$

A. True for all x value

Explanation: Distributing the 3 on the left side gives an equation that is identical on both sides

30 - Simplify 5^0

D. 1

Explanation: Any number raised to the power of 0 is 1

31 - What is the result of 100÷0?

C. Not allowed

Explanation: Division by zero is not allowed in mathematics

---

32 - What is the least common denominator (LCD) of $\frac{1}{3}$ and $\frac{1}{4}$

C. 12

Explanation: 12 is the smallest number both 3 and 4 can divide into evenly.

---

33 - Simplify$(-3)^2$

B. 9

Explanation: The negative sign becomes positive when squared

---

34 - Solve for y: $6y + 3y - 9 = 0$

C. 1

Explanation: Combine like terms to get $9y - 9 = 0$, then y=1

---

35 - What is10^{-1}?

C. 0.1

Explanation: A negative exponent means the reciprocal of the base raised to the absolute value of the exponent, so $10^{-1} = \frac{1}{10} = 0.1$

---

36 - Convert 5 tons to pound

B. 10.000 pounds

Explanation: 5 tons x 2000 pound/ton

---

37 - Solve for x: $2x + 6 = 16$

C. 5

Explanation: Subtract 6 from both sides to get 2x=10, then divide by 2 to solve for x, resulting in x=5

---

38 - Subtract $\frac{2}{3}$ from $\frac{5}{6}$

A. $\frac{1}{6}$

Explanation: Convert fractions to have a common denominator $\frac{5}{6} - \frac{4}{6} = \frac{1}{6}$

---

39 - If $2x + 5 = 15$, what is x?

B. 5

Explanation: Subtract 5 from both sides. $2x = 10$ so x=5

---

40 - Convert 32°F to Celsius (C).

B. 0°C

Explanation: Use the formula C=$\frac{5}{9}$(F - 32)

---

41 - What is the result of 3^2 x 3^3?

C. 3^5

Explanation: When multiplying powers with the same base, add the exponents: $3^{2+3}=3^5$

42 - Convert 0.5 hours to minutes

A. 30 minutes

Explanation: There are 60 minutes in an hour, so 0.5 x 60 = 30 minutes

43 - If 6 apples cost $3, how much do 8 apples cost?

B. 4$

Explanation: The ratio of apples to cost is constant, so 6 : 3 = 8 : x Solving for x gives x=4

44 - What is the value of x? $x^2 - 4x + 4 = 0$

C. 2

Explanation: This is a perfect square trinomial $((x-2)^2)$. Setting it equal to zero to find x

45 - If you have a mass of 200 grams, how many kilograms do you have?

B. 0.2 kilograms

Explanation: There are 1,000 grams in a kilogram, so 200 grams is equal to $200 \div 1000 = 0.2$ Kg

46 - Subtract 0.65 from 2

C. 1.35

Explanation: Subtracting the decimal 2 - 0.65 = 1.35

47 - If 7 meters of cloth cost 35$, how much would 14 meters cost?

B. 70$

Explanation: The cost is directly proportional to the length, in the specific case it is twice the length

48 - What is 2^3?

D. 8

Explanation: 2^3 means 2 multiplied by itself 3 times

49 - What is the result of 144÷12?

C. 12

Explanation: Put in column and perform the operations described in the chapter Divisions

50 - If a product costs 4.99$, what is the total cost of 3 products including a 10% sales tax?

B. 16.47

Explanation: Total cost before tax IS 3 X 4.99= 14.97$. 10% of 14.97$ is 1.479 so Total is 16.47$

FULL-LENGTH TESTS

THE MOST UP-TO-DATE COMPREHENSIVE TESTS OF THE HESI A2 EXAM

SECTION 2 - READING COMPREHENSION

FULL-LENGTH PRACTICE TESTS
SECTION 2 - READING COMPREHENSION

Start Time ....

End Time ....

Sample Text

Hand hygiene is a critical practice in all healthcare settings to prevent the spread of infections. According to the World Health Organization (WHO), proper hand hygiene is the single most effective action to stop the spread of bacteria and viruses, significantly reducing the incidence of hospital-acquired infections (HAIs).

These infections can lead to serious health complications among patients, prolonged hospital stays, and increased healthcare costs. Healthcare workers, including doctors, nurses, and support staff, are advised to perform hand hygiene at five key moments: Prior to patient contact, ahead of clean/aseptic tasks, following exposure to or the risk of body fluid contact, subsequent to patient interaction, and after making contact with the patient's environment. The use of alcohol-based hand rubs is recommended for most clinical situations due to its effectiveness against many types of pathogens and the speed of disinfection.

Despite the known benefits, compliance with hand hygiene protocols remains a challenge in many healthcare facilities. Continuous education, reminders, and the availability of hand hygiene resources are essential for improving adherence and protecting patients' health.

---

1 - What is the primary reason for practicing hand hygiene in healthcare settings?

A. To make hands smell better
B. To prevent dry skin
C. To prevent the spread of infections
D. To comply with hospital policy

---

2 - According to the WHO, what is the most effective action to stop the spread of bacteria and viruses?

A. Using gloves at all times
B. Proper hand hygiene
C. Wearing masks
D. Taking antibiotics

3 - What can result from hospital-acquired infections (HAIs)?

A. Shorter hospital stays

B. Lower healthcare costs

C. Health complications and increased healthcare costs

D. Better patient outcomes

4 - When are healthcare workers advised to perform hand hygiene?

A. Only after touching a patient

B. Before meals only

C. At the end of their shift

D. Before and after specific patient interactions

5 - What is recommended for most clinical situations for hand disinfection?

A. Soap and water

B. Alcohol-based hand rubs

C. Vinegar

D. Bleach

6 - Why is compliance with hand hygiene protocols a challenge?

A. Lack of knowledge

B. Absence of infections

C. Too many protocols

D. Limited resources and education

7 - What is essential for improving adherence to hand hygiene practices?

A. Reducing the number of patients

B. Discouraging the use of alcohol-based rubs

C. Continuous education and availability of resources

D. Increasing the cost of healthcare

8 - What are HAIs known to increase?

A. Speed of recovery

B. Patient satisfaction

C. Hospital efficiency

D. Healthcare costs

9 - What is the WHO?

A. World Health Organism

B. World Health Organization

C. Wild Health Organization

D. World Healthy Organization

Sample Text

Blood serves as the essential transport mechanism within the human body, circulating through the heart, arteries, veins, and capillaries. This complex fluid, consisting of plasma, red blood cells, white blood cells, and platelets, delivers vital nutrients and oxygen to different body areas and aids in the removal of waste. The red color of blood comes from hemoglobin in the red blood cells, which has a critical role in oxygen transport. White blood cells are pivotal in immune defense, protecting the body from infections, while platelets are key in preventing excessive bleeding by aiding in blood clotting.

The categorization of blood types hinges on specific antigens present on red blood cells, leading to the main classifications of A, B, AB, and O blood groups. These can further be categorized as positive or negative based on the Rh factor, influencing blood transfusion compatibility to avoid negative reactions. Universally, individuals with O-negative blood can donate to anyone, making them universal donors; conversely, those with AB-positive blood can receive from any donor, positioning them as universal recipients.

With an average of 5 to 6 liters of blood in the human body, it not only functions in substance transportation but also in regulating temperature and pH balance, underscoring its indispensable role in life sustenance and overall health maintenance.

10 - What is the primary function of red blood cells?

A. To fight infections

B. To clot blood

C. To carry oxygen

D. To remove waste products

11 - Which blood component is responsible for clotting?

A. Plasma

B. Red blood cells

C. White blood cells

D. Platelets

12 - How is a person's blood type determined?

A. By the color of the blood

B. By the presence or absence of certain antigens on red blood cells

C. By the volume of blood in the body

D. By the person's genetic makeup

13 - Who can receive blood from any donor?

A. Type O-negative individuals

B. Type A-positive individuals

C. Type B-negative individuals

D. Type AB-positive individuals

14 - What is the approximate volume of blood in the human body?

A. 3 to 4 liters

B. 5 to 6 liters

C. 7 to 8 liters

D. 9 to 10 liters

15 - What is the "main idea" of the article?

A. The process of blood clotting and the role of platelets.

B. The history and discovery of blood groups.

C. The critical functions and components of blood in the human body.

D. The technological advancements in blood transfusion techniques.

16 - What is the tone of this text?

A. Humorous

B. Informative

C. Suspenseful

D. Persuasive

17 - Apart from transporting nutrients and oxygen, what else does blood regulate?

A. Only body temperature

B. Only pH balance

C. Both body temperature and pH balance

D. The amount of light the body absorbs

18 - Universally, individuals with_____can donate to anyone, making them universal donors.

A. B-negative blood

B. O-negative blood

C. A-positive blood

D. B-positive blood

19 - Why is blood type compatibility important during transfusions?

A. To ensure the blood is red

B. To prevent adverse reactions

C. To match the donor's and recipient's DNA

D. To increase the volume of blood transfused

20 - What gives blood its distinctive red color?

A. Plasma

B. White blood cells

C. Platelets

D. Hemoglobin in red blood cells

Sample Text

The management of diabetes has seen significant advancements over the past few decades, revolutionizing the quality of life for patients. Traditionally, diabetes management primarily relied on insulin injections and lifestyle modifications. However, recent technological innovations have introduced more sophisticated methods of monitoring and treating this condition. Continuous Glucose Monitors (CGMs) and insulin pumps have become game-changers, providing real-time glucose levels and automating insulin delivery, respectively.

Moreover, the development of artificial pancreas systems marks a pivotal moment in diabetes care. These systems integrate CGMs and insulin pumps with an algorithm that automatically adjusts insulin delivery based on glucose readings, mimicking the function of a healthy pancreas. This technology represents a significant step towards the goal of fully automated diabetes management, reducing the burden of constant decision-making for patients.

Despite these advances, challenges remain, such as ensuring access to these technologies for all patients and addressing concerns about data privacy and the potential for technical malfunctions. Nevertheless, the trajectory of diabetes management is promising, with ongoing research and development focused on enhancing the efficacy and reliability of these technological solutions.

21 - What is the main idea of the passage?
A. The challenges associated with insulin injections
B. The evolution of technology in diabetes management
C. The lifestyle modifications required for diabetes patients
D. The history of diabetes

22 - Which of the following is not listed as a detail in the passage?
A. The creation of artificial pancreas systems
B. The introduction of CGMs and insulin pumps
C. The complete eradication of diabetes
D. The challenges of access and data privacy

23 - What is the meaning of the word "trajectory" as used in the last paragraph?
A. Direction or path
B. Speed
C. Historical background
D. Medical procedure

24 - What is the author's primary purpose in writing this text?
A. To critique modern healthcare
B. To inform about advancements in diabetes management
C. To narrate the history of diabetes
D. To sell diabetes management products

25 - Identify the overall tone of the text.

A. Pessimistic

B. Informative

C. Argumentative

D. Narrative

26 - Which of the following statements is an opinion?

A. Continuous Glucose Monitors provide real-time glucose levels.

B. Insulin pumps have automated insulin delivery.

C. The trajectory of diabetes management is promising.

D. Artificial pancreas systems adjust insulin delivery based on glucose readings.

27 - Choose the best summary of the passage.

A. Diabetes management remains unchanged and relies on traditional methods.

B. Technological advancements, including CGMs, insulin pumps, and artificial pancreas systems, have significantly improved diabetes management.

C. Diabetes can now be completely cured through modern technology.

D. Patients with diabetes no longer need to monitor their condition.

28 - Which statement would not be inferred by the reader?

A. Diabetes management requires constant decision-making by patients.

B. All patients have access to the latest diabetes management technologies.

C. Technical advancements have the potential to automate diabetes management.

D. Privacy concerns are associated with new diabetes technologies.

29 - What challenge related to diabetes management technology is mentioned in the passage?

A. A lack of patient interest in new technologies

B. The difficulty of integrating technology with traditional treatments

C. Concerns about data privacy and the potential for technical malfunctions

D. The overwhelming cost of technology development

30 - What could be inferred about the future of diabetes management from the passage?

A. It will completely eliminate the need for patient involvement.

B. It will likely continue to evolve toward more automated solutions.

C. It will regress back to more traditional methods due to technological failures.

D. It will focus exclusively on lifestyle modifications rather than technology.

31 - According to the passage, why is the integration of an artificial pancreas system significant?

A. It decreases the cost of diabetes management.

B. It allows patients to adjust their insulin doses manually.

C. It mimics the function of a healthy pancreas by adjusting insulin automatically.

D. It eliminates the need for glucose monitoring.

Sample Text

In recent years, the field of geriatric medicine has seen remarkable progress, particularly in the areas of preventive care and chronic disease management. The aging population presents unique challenges, which have spurred innovative approaches to care that emphasize quality of life and functional independence. Geriatricians now have a broader array of tools at their disposal, from advanced pharmaceuticals to specialized physical therapy regimens designed to enhance mobility and reduce fall risks.

Additionally, the integration of technology in elder care has been transformative. Telehealth services enable regular monitoring of patients' health status without the need for frequent hospital visits, which is especially beneficial for those with mobility limitations. Wearable devices can now track vital signs, detect irregularities, and alert healthcare providers in real time, offering a proactive approach to managing health issues before they escalate.

Despite these advances, accessibility to these innovations remains uneven, particularly in rural areas where resources are limited. Furthermore, the ethical implications of prolonged life expectancy and the quality of that extended life continue to prompt vigorous debate among healthcare professionals.

32 - Which of the following is not listed as a detail in the passage?
A. Integration of telehealth services.
B. Use of wearable devices in elder care.
C. Increase in healthcare funding.
D. Advanced pharmaceuticals and physical therapies.

33 - What is the main idea of the passage?
A. The challenges of training new geriatricians.
B. Advances in geriatric medicine.
C. The development of new hospitals.
D. The debate over healthcare costs.

34 - What is the meaning of the word "transformative" as used in the second paragraph?
A. Incremental
B. Problematic
C. Revolutionary
D. Insufficient

35 - What is the author's primary purpose in writing this text?
A. To entertain with stories from medical practice.
B. To inform readers about recent advances in geriatric medicine.
C. To argue against the use of technology in medicine.
D. To persuade readers to support healthcare reform.

36 - Identify the overall tone of the text.
A. Critical
B. Optimistic

C. Sarcastic

D. Neutral

37 - Which of the following statements is an opinion?

A. Telehealth services enable monitoring without hospital visits.

B. Wearable devices can track vital signs.

C. There are ethical implications of prolonged life expectancy.

D. Geriatricians use physical therapy regimens.

38 - Choose the best summary of the passage.

A. Geriatric medicine faces many new challenges that are difficult to overcome.

B. Advances in geriatric medicine have significantly improved care through new technologies and approaches to chronic disease management.

C. Most advancements in geriatric medicine have been seen only in urban areas

D. Geriatric medicine has not changed significantly in the past decade.

39 - Which statement would not be inferred by the reader?

A. Geriatric medicine benefits significantly from technological advancements.

B. All elderly patients have access to the latest medical technologies.

C. Specialized physical therapy regimens are designed to improve mobility in elderly patients.

D. Wearable devices play a crucial role in the proactive management of elderly patients' health.

40 - What role do wearable devices play in the management of elderly patients according to the passage?

A. They provide entertainment and comfort to elderly patients.

B. They track vital signs and alert healthcare providers to irregularities.

C. They are used to communicate with family members.

D. They monitor and regulate medication doses without physician oversight.

41 - What is a concern associated with the advancements in geriatric medicine as mentioned in the passage?

A. Ethical implications and accessibility of the technology.

B. The lack of technological advancements.

C. Over-reliance on family members for healthcare management.

D. The high cost of traditional medicines.

Sample Text

Nutrition plays a fundamental role in preventive health care. As medical science advances, there is a growing recognition of the connection between diet and disease prevention. Nutritionists and healthcare providers increasingly emphasize the importance of balanced diets rich in fruits, vegetables, and whole grains to combat chronic diseases such as diabetes, heart disease, and obesity.

Recent studies highlight that a nutritious diet not only helps in preventing illness but also improves overall well-being and longevity.

For instance, the Mediterranean diet, characterized by high consumption of plant-based foods, lean proteins, and healthy fats, has been linked to lower risks of cardiovascular diseases and improved mental health. Moreover, public health initiatives are focusing on educating communities about the benefits of healthy eating habits as part of a broader strategy to reduce healthcare costs and improve quality of life.

However, despite the known benefits, many populations struggle with dietary adherence due to socioeconomic factors, limited access to healthy foods, and lack of nutritional education. Addressing these barriers is crucial for the effective implementation of nutritional guidance in preventive healthcare.

42 - What is the meaning of the word 'adherence' as used in the last paragraph?
A. Avoidance
B. Ignorance
C. Resistance
D. Compliance

43 - What is the author's primary purpose in writing this text?
A. To criticize unhealthy eating habits.
B. To educate about the impact of nutrition on health.
C. To promote a specific diet.
D. To analyze socioeconomic factors affecting health.

44 - Which of the following statements is an opinion?
A. Nutrition plays a fundamental role in preventive health care.
B. Diets rich in fruits and vegetables can prevent chronic diseases.
C. Nutritious diets improve longevity and well-being.
D. Many populations struggle with dietary adherence due to socioeconomic factors.

45 - Which of the following is not listed as a detail in the passage?
A. Lean proteins are detrimental to mental health.
B. Public health initiatives aim to educate communities about nutrition.
C. Nutritional adherence can be influenced by socioeconomic factors.
D. The Mediterranean diet benefits cardiovascular health.

46 - Which statement would not be inferred by the reader?
A. Everyone has easy access to healthy foods.
B. Nutrition impacts overall health and disease prevention.
C. Socioeconomic factors can hinder nutritional adherence.
D. Public health initiatives play a role in nutritional education.

47 - What is the main idea of the passage?
A. The challenges of adopting the Mediterranean diet.
B. The benefits of nutrition in preventive health care.
C. The role of healthcare providers in treating mental health.
D. The economic impact of chronic diseases.

48 - Identify the overall tone of the text.

A. Argumentative

B. Informative

C. Pessimistic

D. Sarcastic

49 - many populations struggle with_____due to socioeconomic factors, limited access to healthy foods, and lack of nutritional education.

A. diet denial

B. dietary adherence

C. diet increase

50 - Choose the best summary of the passage.

A. Nutrition is beneficial but challenging to implement due to various barriers.

B. Dietary choices have little impact on chronic diseases.

C. Healthcare providers focus only on treatment, not prevention.

D. Nutritional education is unnecessary for public health.

FULL-LENGTH PRACTICE TESTS SECTION 2 - READING COMPREHENSION ANSWER KEY WITH EXPLANATIONS

1 - What is the primary reason for practicing hand hygiene in healthcare settings?

C. To prevent the spread of infections

Explanation: The passage identifies preventing the spread of infections as the primary reason for hand hygiene in healthcare settings.

2 - According to the WHO, what is the most effective action to stop the spread of bacteria and viruses?

B. Proper hand hygiene

Explanation: The passage mentions that proper hand hygiene is the single most effective action to stop the spread of bacteria and viruses.

3 - What can result from hospital-acquired infections (HAIs)?

C. Health complications and increased healthcare costs

Explanation: HAIs can lead to serious health complications, prolonged hospital stays, and increased healthcare costs.

4 - When are healthcare workers advised to perform hand hygiene?

D. Before and after specific patient interactions

Explanation: Healthcare workers are advised to perform hand hygiene at five key moments, including before and after touching a patient.

5 - What is recommended for most clinical situations for hand disinfection?

B. Alcohol-based hand rubs

Explanation: Alcohol-based hand rubs are recommended for most clinical situations due to their effectiveness and speed of disinfection.

6 - Why is compliance with hand hygiene protocols a challenge?

D. Limited resources and education

Explanation: The passage states that despite known benefits, compliance is a challenge due to the need for continuous education, reminders, and availability of resources.

7 - What is essential for improving adherence to hand hygiene practices?

C. Continuous education and availability of resources

Explanation: Improving adherence requires continuous education, reminders, and ensuring that hand hygiene resources are available.

8 - What are HAIs known to increase?

D. Healthcare costs

Explanation: The text indicates that HAIs lead to increased healthcare costs due to complications and prolonged hospital stays.

9 - What is the WHO?

D. World Health Organization

Explanation: The World Health Organization is a specialized UN institute for health

10 - What is the primary function of red blood cells?

C. To carry oxygen

Explanation: Red blood cells contain hemoglobin, which binds to oxygen and transports it to various parts of the body.

11 - Which blood component is responsible for clotting?

D. Platelets

Explanation: Platelets help in the clotting of blood, preventing excessive bleeding when injuries occur.

12 - How is a person's blood type determined?

B. By the presence or absence of certain antigens on red blood cells

Explanation: Blood types are determined by the presence or absence of specific antigens on the surface of red blood cells.

13 - Who can receive blood from any donor?

D. Type AB-positive individuals

Explanation: Individuals with type AB-positive blood are considered universal recipients because they can receive blood from any donor.

14 - What is the approximate volume of blood in the human body?

B. 5 to 6 liters

Explanation: The human body contains about 5 to 6 liters of blood, which circulates through the cardiovascular system.

15 - What is the "main idea" of the article?

C. The critical functions and components of blood in the human body.

Explanation: The article provides an overview of blood's essential roles, including transportation of nutrients and oxygen, removal of waste products, immune defense, blood clotting, and the significance of blood types. While it touches on various aspects of blood's functionality within the human body, the central theme revolves around its indispensable roles and components, making option C the correct answer regarding the main idea.

16 - What is the tone of this text?

B. Informative

Explanation: The text provides an educational overview of blood's components, functions, and the significance of blood types, particularly in the context of transfusions. It uses clear, direct language to impart knowledge, maintaining an informative tone throughout. There's no attempt to entertain, create suspense, or persuade, making "Informative" the best descriptor of the text's tone.

17 - Apart from transporting nutrients and oxygen, what else does blood regulate?

C. Both body temperature and pH balance

Explanation: Blood plays a key role in regulating the body's temperature and maintaining its pH balance, ensuring the proper functioning of bodily systems.

18 - Universally, individuals with_____can donate to anyone, making them universal donors.

B. O-negative blood

Explanation: As explained in the Blood types section on page 129, the O- donor is called a Universal Donor because he/she can donate to any other blood type

19 - Why is blood type compatibility important during transfusions?

B. To prevent adverse reactions

Explanation: Compatibility of blood types is crucial during transfusions to avoid adverse reactions that can occur if the donor's and recipient's blood types do not match.

20 - What gives blood its distinctive red color?

D. Hemoglobin in red blood cells

Explanation: Hemoglobin, found in red blood cells, binds to oxygen and gives blood its distinctive red color.

21 - What is the main idea of the passage?

B. The evolution of technology in diabetes management

Explanation: The text discusses the technological advancements in diabetes management, highlighting their impact on patient care.

22 - Which of the following is not listed as a detail in the passage?

C. The complete eradication of diabetes

Explanation: The passage does not mention the eradication of diabetes but focuses on managing the condition.

23 - What is the meaning of the word "trajectory" as used in the last paragraph?

A. Direction or path

Explanation: In the context, "trajectory" refers to the direction or path of progress in diabetes management technologies.

24 - What is the author's primary purpose in writing this text?

B. To inform about advancements in diabetes management

Explanation: The text aims to inform readers about recent technological advancements in managing diabetes and their implications.

25 - Identify the overall tone of the text.

B. Informative

Explanation: The tone is informative, as the passage seeks to provide details on the advancements in diabetes management without arguing a position or narrating a story.

26 - Which of the following statements is an opinion?

C. The trajectory of diabetes management is promising

Explanation: This statement expresses a hopeful viewpoint on the future of diabetes management, categorizing it as an opinion.

27 - Choose the best summary of the passage.

B. Technological advancements, including CGMs, insulin pumps, and artificial pancreas systems, have significantly improved diabetes management

Explanation: The best summary is the one that captures the essence of technological advancements in diabetes care, as described in the passage.

28 - Which statement would not be inferred by the reader?

B. All patients have access to the latest diabetes management technologies

Explanation: The passage explicitly mentions challenges such as ensuring access for all patients, implying that not all patients currently have access to these technologies.

29 - What challenge related to diabetes management technology is mentioned in the passage?

C. Concerns about data privacy and the potential for technical malfunctions

Explanation: The passage explicitly mentions that along with the advancements, there are still challenges such as data privacy concerns and the potential for technical issues that need to be addressed.

30 - What could be inferred about the future of diabetes management from the passage?

B. It will likely continue to evolve toward more automated solutions

Explanation: The passage indicates that ongoing research and the current trajectory aim to enhance the efficacy and reliability of technological solutions, suggesting that diabetes management is evolving toward more automated systems.

31 - According to the passage, why is the integration of an artificial pancreas system significant?

C. It mimics the function of a healthy pancreas by adjusting insulin

Explanation: The passage highlights the development of artificial pancreas systems as pivotal because they integrate monitoring and insulin delivery systems with an algorithm that automatically adjusts insulin, closely replicating the function of a healthy pancreas.

32 - Which of the following is not listed as a detail in the passage?
C. Increase in healthcare funding.

Explanation: The passage mentions technological integration and new medical tools, but it does not discuss any increase in healthcare funding.

33 - What is the main idea of the passage?
C. Advances in geriatric medicine.

Explanation: The passage primarily discusses the recent progress in the field of geriatric medicine, highlighting new tools and technologies that improve elderly care.

34 - What is the meaning of the word "transformative" as used in the second paragraph?
C. Revolutionary

Explanation: In this context, "transformative" describes how technology has significantly changed and improved elder care, suggesting it has had a revolutionary impact.

35 - What is the author's primary purpose in writing this text?
B. To inform readers about recent advances in geriatric medicine.

Explanation: The passage serves to educate readers about new developments in the field of geriatric medicine, emphasizing how these advances benefit elderly care.

36 - Identify the overall tone of the text.
B. Optimistic

Explanation: The tone is optimistic, as the text focuses on the positive developments in geriatric medicine and how they enhance care for the elderly.

37 - Which of the following statements is an opinion?
C. There are ethical implications of prolonged life expectancy.

Explanation: Stating that there are ethical implications involves a value judgment, making it an opinion rather than a fact.

38 - Choose the best summary of the passage.
B. Advances in geriatric medicine have significantly improved care through new technologies and approaches to chronic disease management.

Explanation: This summary accurately captures the essence of the passage, highlighting the impact of technological and medical advancements on improving geriatric care.

39 - Which statement would not be inferred by the reader?
B. All elderly patients have access to the latest medical technologies.

Explanation: The passage specifically mentions that accessibility remains uneven, particularly in rural areas, implying that not all elderly patients have access to the latest technologies.

40 - What role do wearable devices play in the management of elderly patients according to the passage?
B. They track vital signs and alert healthcare providers to irregularities.

Explanation: The passage mentions that wearable devices track vital signs, detect irregularities, and alert healthcare providers, highlighting their role in proactive health management.

41 - What is a concern associated with the advancements in geriatric medicine as mentioned in the passage?

A. Ethical implications and accessibility of the technology.

Explanation: The passage notes that while there are significant advancements, challenges like ethical implications of extended life and uneven access to technology, particularly in rural areas, remain concerns.

42 - What is the meaning of the word 'adherence' as used in the last paragraph?

D. Compliance

Explanation: In this context, 'adherence' refers to the extent to which individuals follow recommended dietary guidelines, implying compliance.

43 - What is the author's primary purpose in writing this text?

B. To educate about the impact of nutrition on health.

Explanation: The author aims to inform readers about how nutrition significantly affects preventive health care and overall well-being.

44 - Which of the following statements is an opinion?

C. Nutritious diets improve longevity and well-being.

Explanation: This statement, while it can be supported by data, remains an opinion regarding the effects of nutrition on longevity and well-being as it implies a value judgment.

45 - Which of the following is not listed as a detail in the passage?

A. Lean proteins are detrimental to mental health.

Explanation: The passage mentions the benefits of lean proteins as part of the Mediterranean diet, not their detriment.

46 - Which statement would not be inferred by the reader?

A. Everyone has easy access to healthy foods.

Explanation: The passage implies that access to healthy foods is limited for many populations, thus contradicting the idea that everyone has easy access.

47 - What is the main idea of the passage?

B. The benefits of nutrition in preventive health care.

Explanation: The passage discusses how proper nutrition plays a crucial role in preventing chronic diseases and enhancing overall health, making this the main focus.

48 - Identify the overall tone of the text.

B. Informative

Explanation: The tone of the passage is informative, providing data and insights on nutrition's role in health without arguing a position aggressively.

49 - many populations struggle with_____due to socioeconomic factors, limited access to healthy foods, and lack of nutritional education.

B. dietary adherence

Explanation: As can be seen in the text, the word that is missing is precisely the answer B

50 - Choose the best summary of the passage.

A. Nutrition is beneficial but challenging to implement due to various barriers.

Explanation: This summary accurately captures both the recognized benefits of nutrition in preventive health and the challenges in its implementation discussed in the passage.

FULL-LENGTH TESTS

THE MOST UP-TO-DATE COMPREHENSIVE TESTS OF THE HESI A2 EXAM

SECTION 3 - VOCABULARY AND GENERAL KNOWLEDGE

FULL-LENGTH PRACTICE TESTS

SECTION 3 - VOCABULARY AND GENERAL KNOWLEDGE

Start Time ....

End Time ....

1 - What does the term "benevolent" mean?

A. Hostile

B. Generous

C. Greedy

D. Miserable

2 - Choose the word that is spelled correctly and fits in the context: "The nurse must maintain accurate_____of the patient's condition."

A. reccords

B. records

C. recods

D. recoords

3 - What is the antonym of "expand"?

A. Extend

B. Enlarge

C. Contract

D. Develop

4 - Which term refers to the study of human societies and cultures and their development?

A. Anthropology

B. Psychology

C. Archaeology

D. Sociology

5 - What does the prefix "hyper-" mean in the word "hypertension"?

A. Under

B. Over

C. Between

D. Without

6 - What does the suffix "-itis" signify in the word "arthritis"?

A. Study of

B. Inflammation

C. Removal

D. Pain

7 - What does the prefix "neo-" indicate in the word "neonatal"?

A. Old

B. New

C. After

D. Before

8 - Which suffix means "the study of" when used in words like "biology"?

A. -ology

B. -otomy

C. -algia

D. -ostomy

9 - What does the prefix "anti-" mean in the word "antibiotic"?

A. Against

B. Before

C. Without

D. After

10 - What does the suffix "-ectomy" mean as used in the word "appendectomy"?

A. Visualization

B. Repair

C. Incision

D. Removal

11 - What does the term "analgesic" refer to?

A. A substance that reduces inflammation

B. A substance that relieves pain

C. A substance that promotes bleeding

D. A substance that cures infections

12 - What is the meaning of "febrile"?

A. Without fever

B. Relating to fever

C. Characterized by low temperature

D. Causing inflammation

13 - What does "hypoglycemia" refer to?

A. High blood sugar levels

B. Low blood sugar levels

C. Normal blood sugar levels

D. Fluctuating blood sugar levels

14 - Which term describes the absence of breathing?

A. Dyspnea

B. Apnea

C. Tachypnea

D. Hyperpnea

15 - Which term describes the process of visualizing the chest from the inside?

A. Angiography

B. Bronchoscopy

C. Laparoscopy

D. Radiography

16 - What does the prefix "intra-" signify in the word "intravenous"?

A. Within

B. Without

C. Beyond

D. Before

17 - Select the meaning of the underlined word in the sentence: "During the examination, the doctor noted that the patient appeared _lethargic_".

A. Energetic

B. Alert

C. Drowsy

D. Anxious

18 - What does "tachypnea" indicate?

A. Slow breathing

B. Rapid breathing

C. No breathing

D. Painful breathing

19 - Which of the following is an antonym for "benign"?

A. Malignant

B. Noncancerous

C. Harmless

D. Innocuous

20 - What does the prefix "brady-" mean in the term "bradycardia"?

A. Rapid

B. Slow

C. Irregular

D. Stop

21 - Select the meaning of the underlined word in the sentence: "After the incident, the patient was in an *acute* phase of pain and discomfort".

A. Mild

B. Manageable

C. Severe and sudden

D. Long-term

22 - Which of the following words indicates "inflammation of the liver"?

A. Hepatitis

B. Nephritis

C. Arthritis

D. Gastritis

23 - "Contagious" most nearly means:

A. Infectious

B. Isolated

C. Safe

D. Rare

24 - Which of the following root words means "bone"?

A. Oste/o

B. Hem/o

C. Gastro/o

D. Broncho/o

25 - Select the meaning of the underlined word in the sentence: "To reduce the risk of infection, the surgical area was treated with an *antiseptic* solution".

A. Cleansing

B. Infectious

C. Contaminating

D. Healing

26 - The suffix "-ectomy" indicates which medical procedure?

A. Examination

B. Enlargement

C. Surgical removal

D. Reduction

27 - Which of the following words indicates "a condition of insufficient blood flow to a body part"?

A. Ischemia

B. Hemorrhage

C. Cyanosis

D. Edema

28 - Select the meaning of the underlined word in the sentence: "The nurse administered an *analgesic* to alleviate the patient's pain after surgery".

A. Antiseptic

B. Pain reliever

C. Antibiotic

D. Sedative

29 - Which of the following root words means "heart"?

A. Gastr/o

B. Cardi/o

C. Derm/o

D. Oste/o

30 - Which of the following words indicates "blood in the urine"?

A. Hematuria

B. Hemoptysis

C. Hemolysis

D. Hematoma

31 - Which prefix means "below" or "under"?

A. hyper-

B. epi-

C. sub-

D. trans-

32 - "Palpable" most nearly means:

A. Audible

B. Visible

C. Tangible

D. Painful

33 - Select the meaning of the underlined word in the sentence: "The doctor recommended an *intravenous* antibiotic to fight the infection more effectively".

A. Oral

B. Administered into a muscle

C. Administered into a vein

D. Administered into the skin

34 - Which of the following words indicates "low blood sugar"?

A. Hyperglycemia
B. Hypoglycemia
C. Glycolysis
D. Gluconeogenesis

35 - What does the suffix "-logy" mean?

A. The study of
B. The process of
C. Pertaining to
D. Full of

36 - Select the meaning of the underlined word in the sentence: "The nurse observed that the patient was becoming increasingly _**dysphoric**_ during the assessment".

A. Calm
B. Happy
C. Anxious
D. Distressed

37 - Which of the following root words means "stomach"?

A. Hepat/o
B. Neur/o
C. Gastr/o
D. Arthr/o

38 - "Convalescence" most nearly means:

A. Deterioration
B. Recovery
C. Weakness
D. Treatment

39 - Which of the following root words means "kidney"?

A. Cardi/o
B. Nephro/o
C. Neuro/o
D. Osteo/o

40 - Select the meaning of the underlined word in the sentence: "The patient's _**chronic**_ condition required ongoing treatment over many years".

A. Severe
B. Short-lived
C. Long-lasting
D. Rare

41 - Which of the following words indicates "rapid breathing"?

A. Apnea

B. Dyspnea

C. Hyperventilation

D. Bradypnea

42 - "Sedentary" most nearly means:

A. Active

B. Restless

C. Inactive

D. Energetic

43 - The root word "hepat" refers to which body organ?

A. Heart

B. Liver

C. Stomach

D. Lung

44 - Which of the following prefixes means "before" or "in front of"?

A. sub-

B. post-

C. pre-

D. inter-

45 - Select the meaning of the underlined word in the sentence: "Upon reviewing the blood work, the physician mentioned the patient was ***anemic***".

A. Overweight

B. Having low blood sugar

C. Having a low red blood cell count

D. Having a high cholesterol level

46 - Which of the following root words means "skin"?

A. Derm/o

B. Pulmon/o

C. Myo/o

D. Nephro/o

47 - What does the term "triage" refer to in the context of nursing?

A. The process of documenting patient symptoms

B. The administration of medication

C. The process of determining the priority of patients' treatments based on the severity of their condition

D. The recovery phase after surgery

48 - "Malignant" most nearly means:

A. Harmless

B. Noncancerous

C. Cancerous

D. Unimportant

49 - Which of the following words indicates "a decrease in size of an organ or tissue"?

A. Hypertrophy

B. Hyperplasia

C. Atrophy

D. Dysplasia

50 - Select the meaning of the underlined word in the sentence: "The paramedic observed that the victim was ***tachycardic***, prompting immediate cardiac care".

A. Having a slow heart rate

B. Having a rapid heart rate

C. Lacking a pulse

D. In a stable condition

FULL-LENGTH PRACTICE TESTS

SECTION 3 - VOCABULARY AND GENERAL KNOWLEDGE

ANSWER KEY WITH EXPLANATIONS

1 - What does the term "benevolent" mean?

B. Generous

Explanation: "Benevolent" describes someone who is well-meaning and kindly, or an action meant to help others, typically indicating generosity.

2 - Choose the word that is spelled correctly and fits in the context: "The nurse must maintain accurate_____of the patient's condition."

B. records

Explanation: "Records" is the correctly spelled word fitting the context of maintaining written or saved documentation.

3 - What is the antonym of "expand"?

C. Contract

Explanation: "Expand" means to increase in size or volume; therefore, "contract," which means to decrease in size or volume, is its antonym.

4 - Which term refers to the study of human societies and cultures and their development?

A. Anthropology

Explanation: Anthropology is the study of human societies, cultures, and their development, focusing on understanding human behavior, past and present.

5 - What does the prefix "hyper-" mean in the word "hypertension"?

B. Over

Explanation: The prefix "hyper-" means excessive or over. Thus, "hypertension" refers to abnormally high blood pressure.

6 - What does the suffix "-itis" signify in the word "arthritis"?

B. Inflammation

Explanation: The suffix "-itis" is used in medical terminology to denote inflammation. Therefore, "arthritis" means inflammation of the joints.

7 - What does the prefix "neo-" indicate in the word "neonatal"?

B. New

Explanation: The prefix "neo-" means new. "Neonatal" refers to something pertaining to the newborn.

8 - Which suffix means "the study of" when used in words like "biology"?

A. -ology

Explanation: The suffix "-ology" means the study of a subject. "Biology" is the study of life.

9 - What does the prefix "anti-" mean in the word "antibiotic"?

A. Against

Explanation: The prefix "anti-" means against. "Antibiotic" refers to a substance that works against microorganisms.

10 - What does the suffix "-ectomy" mean as used in the word "appendectomy"?

D. Removal

Explanation: The suffix "-ectomy" means removal. "Appendectomy" refers to the surgical removal of the appendix.

11 - What does the term "analgesic" refer to?

B. A substance that relieves pain

Explanation: An analgesic is a type of medication used to relieve pain without causing unconsciousness.

12 - What is the meaning of "febrile"?

B. Relating to fever

Explanation: The term "febrile" is used to describe symptoms or conditions that include a fever

13 - What does "hypoglycemia" refer to?

B. Low blood sugar levels

Explanation: Hypoglycemia is a condition characterized by abnormally low levels of glucose in the blood, and is indicated by the prefix "hypo, meaning a Below or deficient

14 - Which term describes the absence of breathing?

B. Apnea

Explanation: Apnea refers to a temporary cessation of breathing, particularly during sleep

15 - Which term describes the process of visualizing the chest from the inside?

B. Bronchoscopy

Explanation: Bronchoscopy is a diagnostic technique that allows the doctor to view the airways and lungs by inserting a bronchoscope through the nose or mouth into the trachea and lungs.

16 - What does the prefix "intra-" signify in the word "intravenous"?

A. Within

Explanation: The prefix "intra-" means within. "Intravenous" means within or into a vein

17 - Select the meaning of the underlined word in the sentence: "During the examination, the doctor noted that the patient appeared ***lethargic***".

C. Drowsy

Explanation: "Lethargic" means sluggish, drowsy, or lacking energy.

---

18 - What does "tachypnea" indicate?

B. Rapid breathing

Explanation: Tachypnea is a condition marked by an abnormally high rate of breathing, commonly seen in respiratory distress.

---

19 - Which of the following is an antonym for "benign"?

A. Malignant

Explanation: While "benign" refers to conditions that are not harmful or cancerous, "malignant" refers to severe and progressively worsening conditions, often cancerous.

---

20 - What does the prefix "brady-" mean in the term "bradycardia"?

B. Slow

Explanation: The prefix "brady-" indicates slowness; bradycardia refers to abnormally slow heart rates.

---

21 - Select the meaning of the underlined word in the sentence: "After the incident, the patient was in an ***acute*** phase of pain and discomfort".

C. Severe and sudden

Explanation: "Acute" often refers to something severe and sudden in onset, such as acute symptoms or illnesses that require urgent care.

---

22 - Which of the following words indicates "inflammation of the liver"?

A. Hepatitis

Explanation: Hepatitis is the medical term for inflammation of the liver, which can be caused by viruses, toxins, or autoimmunity.

---

23 - "Contagious" most nearly means:

A. Infectious

Explanation: "Contagious" refers to a disease capable of being transmitted from one individual to another, hence it most nearly means infectious.

---

24 - Which of the following root words means "bone"?

A. Oste/o

Explanation: The root "Oste/o" is derived from the Greek word "osteon," which means bone. It is commonly used in medical terms like "osteoporosis" (a condition characterized by decreased bone density).

---

25 - Select the meaning of the underlined word in the sentence: "To reduce the risk of infection, the surgical area was treated with an ***antiseptic*** solution".

A. Cleansing

Explanation: "Antiseptic" refers to substances used to prevent the growth of disease-causing microorganisms

26 - The suffix "-ectomy" indicates which medical procedure?

C. Surgical removal

Explanation: The suffix "-ectomy" means surgical removal, as in "appendectomy"

27 - Which of the following words indicates "a condition of insufficient blood flow to a body part"?

A. Ischemia

Explanation: Ischemia refers to a reduction in blood flow to a body part, typically due to constriction or obstruction of blood vessels, which is insufficient to meet its metabolic demands.

28 - Select the meaning of the underlined word in the sentence: "The nurse administered an *analgesic* to alleviate the patient's pain after surgery".

B. Pain reliever

Explanation: "Analgesic" is a type of medication used to relieve pain.

29 - Which of the following root words means "heart"?

B. Cardi/o

Explanation: The root "Cardi/o" is derived from the Greek word "kardia," which means heart. It is used in terms like "cardiology" (the study of the heart).

30 - Which of the following words indicates "blood in the urine"?

A. Hematuria

Explanation: Hematuria refers to the presence of blood cells in the urine and can be a sign of various underlying medical conditions.

31 - Which prefix means "below" or "under"?

C. sub-

Explanation: The prefix "sub-" means below or under, as in "subcutaneous" (under the skin

32 - "Palpable" most nearly means:

C. Tangible

Explanation: "Palpable" refers to something that can be felt physically, meaning it is tangible or capable of being touched or felt.

33 - Select the meaning of the underlined word in the sentence: "The doctor recommended an *intravenous* antibiotic to fight the infection more effectively".

C. Administered into a vein

Explanation: "Intravenous" means administered through the veins.

34 - Which of the following words indicates "low blood sugar"?

B. Hypoglycemia

Explanation: Hypoglycemia is a condition characterized by an abnormally low level of glucose (sugar) in the blood.

35 - What does the suffix "-logy" mean?

A. The study of

Explanation: The suffix "-logy" means the study of, as in "biology" (the study of life).

36 - Select the meaning of the underlined word in the sentence: "The nurse observed that the patient was becoming increasingly *dysphoric* during the assessment".

D. Distressed

Explanation: "Dysphoric" means a state of unease or generalized dissatisfaction with life

37 - Which of the following root words means "stomach"?

C. Gastr/o

Explanation: The root "Gastr/o" comes from the Greek word "gaster," which means stomach. It is used in medical terms like "gastroenterology" (the study of the stomach and intestines).

38 - "Convalescence" most nearly means:

B. Recovery

Explanation: "Convalescence" refers to the time spent recovering from an illness or medical treatment, most nearly meaning recovery.

39 - Which of the following root words means "kidney"?

B. Nephro/o

Explanation: The root "Nephro/o" comes from the Greek word "nephros," which means kidney. It is used in terms like "nephrology" (the study of kidney function).

40 - Select the meaning of the underlined word in the sentence: "The patient's *chronic* condition required ongoing treatment over many years".

C. Long-lasting

Explanation: "Chronic" refers to something, especially a disease or condition, persisting for a long time or constantly recurring.

41 - Which of the following words indicates "rapid breathing"?

C. Hyperventilation

Explanation: Hyperventilation is the condition of breathing more rapidly or deeply than normal, causing excessive expulsion of circulating carbon dioxide.

42 - "Sedentary" most nearly means:

C. Inactive

Explanation: "Sedentary" refers to a way of life that involves little physical activity, thus the term most nearly means inactive.

43 - The root word "hepat" refers to which body organ?

B. Liver

Explanation: The root "hepat" is derived from the Greek word for liver, used in terms like "hepatitis" (inflammation of the liver).

44 - Which of the following prefixes means "before" or "in front of"?

C. pre-

Explanation: The prefix "pre-" means before or in front of, as in "prenatal" (before birth).

45 - Select the meaning of the underlined word in the sentence: "Upon reviewing the blood work, the physician mentioned the patient was *__anemic__*".

C. Having a low red blood cell count

Explanation: "Anemic" refers to a condition in which the blood doesn't have enough healthy red blood cells.

46 - Which of the following root words means "skin"?

A. Derm/o

Explanation: The root "Derm/o" is derived from the Greek word "derma," which means skin. This root is used in words such as "dermatology" (the study of the skin).

47 - What does the term "triage" refer to in the context of nursing?

C. The process of determining the priority of patients' treatments based on the severity of their condition

Explanation: Triage" is a critical function in nursing and emergency medical services where patients are sorted and prioritized according to the urgency of their conditions.

48 - "Malignant" most nearly means:

C. Cancerous

Explanation: "Malignant" is a medical term used to describe a severe and progressively worsening disease, primarily used to refer to cancer that is likely to be life-threatenin

49 - Which of the following words indicates "a decrease in size of an organ or tissue"?

C. Atrophy

Explanation: Atrophy is the term used to describe the partial or complete wasting away of a part of the body, indicating a decrease in the size of an organ or tissue.

50 - Select the meaning of the underlined word in the sentence: "The paramedic observed that the victim was *__tachycardic__*, prompting immediate cardiac care**".**

B. Having a rapid heart rate

Explanation: B. Having a rapid heart rate

FULL-LENGTH TESTS

THE MOST UP-TO-DATE COMPREHENSIVE TESTS OF THE HESI A2 EXAM

SECTION 4 - GRAMMAR

FULL-LENGTH PRACTICE TESTS
SECTION 4 - GRAMMAR

Start Time ....

End Time ....

1 - Choose the sentence that is grammatically correct

A. The nurse drawed blood from the patient's arm.

B. The nurse drew blood from the patient arm.

C. The nurse drew blood from the patient's arm.

D. The nurse draw blood from the patients arm.

2 - Select the sentence that correctly uses the comma.

A. Before surgery, the nurse checked the patient's vitals.

B. Before surgery the nurse, checked the patient's vitals.

C. Before surgery the nurse checked, the patient's vitals.

D. Before, surgery the nurse checked the patient's vitals.

3 - Choose the correct plural form in the sentence.

A. The nurs's duties include taking vitals.

B. The nursses' duties include taking vitals.

C. The nurses' duties include taking vitals.

D. The nurses duties include taking vitals.

4 - Choose the sentence with the correct verb tense.

A. The nurse will administered the vaccine tomorrow.

B. The nurse will administer the vaccine tomorrow.

C. The nurse will administering the vaccine tomorrow.

D. The nurse will administers the vaccine tomorrow.

5 - Identify the sentence with correct subject-verb agreement.

A. The team of doctors are reviewing the patient's history.

B. The team of doctors is reviewing the patient's history.

C. The team of doctors were reviewing the patient's history.

D. The team of doctors be reviewing the patient's history.

6 - Identify the sentence that correctly uses a plural noun.
A. The nurces station is on the second floor.
B. The nurses' station is on the second floor.
C. The nurses stations are on the second floor.
D. The nurse's stations is on the second floor.

7 - Which sentence correctly uses conjunctions?
A. The nurse needs to check the patient's heart rate and to administer medication.
B. The nurse needs to check the patient's heart rate but administer medication.
C. The nurse needs to check the patient's heart rate and administer medication.
D. The nurse needs to check the patient's heart rate also to administer medication.

8 - Which sentence uses a semicolon correctly?
A. The patient was discharged; however, he returned the next day with complications.
B. The patient was discharged; he returned the next day, with complications.
C. The patient was discharged; because he returned the next day with complications.
D. The patient was discharged; and he returned the next day with complications.

9 - Select the correct form of the verb to complete the sentence: "By the time I arrived, the nurse____already____the patient."
A. is, assessed
B. was, assessing
C. has, assessed
D. had, assessed

10 - Identify the sentence with an error in modifier placement.
A. The nurse found a patient nearly unconscious in the room.
B. Nearly, the nurse found a patient unconscious in the room.
C. The nurse nearly found a patient unconscious in the room.
D. The nurse found nearly a patient unconscious in the room.

11 - _____often take blood pressure before starting any treatments.
A. Nurses
B. Nurse's
C. Nurses'
D. Nursis

12 - Which of the following sentences correctly forms a complex sentence?
A. Although the nurse was tired, she completed her rounds.
B. The nurse was tired she completed her rounds.
C. The nurse, was tired, she completed her rounds.
D. The nurse was tired but she completed her rounds.

13 - In the sentence "The nurse who arrived late administered the medication," what is the relative clause?

A. The nurse who arrived late

B. who arrived late

C. administered the medication

D. the nurse

14 - Identify the sentence that correctly uses the past perfect tense.

A. The nurse had prepared the patient's room before they arrived.

B. The nurse has prepared the patient's room before they arrived.

C. The nurse prepared the patient's room before they arrived.

D. The nurse preparing the patient's room before they arrived.

15 - During the training, nurses learned that the_____can be critical to patient recovery.

A. Timing of Medication

B. timing of medication

C. Timing of medication

D. Timing Of Medication

16 - Identify the correct use of a modal verb in a medical instruction:

A. The doctor must reviews all the lab results.

B. The doctor must review all the lab results.

C. The doctor must reviewed all the lab results.

D. The doctor musts review all the lab results.

17 - Identify the simple predicate in the sentence: "The patient quickly recovered after the nurse administered the new medication."

A. Quickly recovered

B. Recovered

C. Administered

D. Patient

18 - The patient and_____decided on a less aggressive treatment plan.

A. I

B. me

C. myself

D. mine

19 - Which sentence correctly uses a conjunction?

A. The nurse must check the patient's blood pressure and, administer medication.

B. The nurse must check the patient's blood pressure and administer medication.

C. The nurse must check the patient's blood pressure but administer medication.

D. The nurse must check the patient's blood pressure or administering medication.

20 - Which sentence correctly uses a semicolon?

A. The patient needed bloodwork; however, the lab was closed.

B. The patient needed bloodwork; the lab was closed.

C. The patient needed bloodwork; because the lab was closed.

D. The patient needed bloodwork; and the lab was closed.

21 - _____important to check the patient's medication schedule regularly.

A. Its

B. It's

C. It

D. They're

22 - Choose the sentence that correctly uses the comparative form.

A. The surgery took fewer time than expected.

B. The surgery took lesser time than expected.

C. The surgery took less time than expected.

D. The surgery took fewest time than expected.

23 - All _____ are required to attend the annual health and safety training.

A. part and full time nurses

B. part and full-time nurses

C. part/ and full/time nurses

D. part-time and full-time nurses

24 - Select the sentence with the correct use of plural nouns:

A. The nurces provided excellent care.

B. The nurses provides excellent care.

C. The nurse's provided excellent care.

D. The nurses provided excellent care.

25 - Which punctuation correctly completes the sentence? "Before administering medication, ensure that the patient's identity___verified."

A. is

B. has

C. was

D. be

26 - Which option correctly uses a possessive adjective?

A. It's important to check the patient chart.

B. Its important to check the patient's chart.

C. It's important to check the patient's chart.

D. It's important to check the patients chart.

27 - Choose the sentence that correctly uses comparative adjectives:

A. This medicine is more safer than the one we used before.
B. This medicine is safer than the one we used before.
C. This medicine is more safe than the one we used before.
D. This medicine is safest than the one we used before.

28 - The patient thanked the nurse for_____kindness.

A. hers
B. herself
C. she
D. her

29 - Identify the sentence with correct subject-verb agreement.

A. The list of required medications include aspirin and ibuprofen.
B. The list of required medications includes aspirin and ibuprofen.
C. The list of required medications have included aspirin and ibuprofen.
D. The list of required medications are including aspirin and ibuprofen.

30 - Select the sentence that correctly uses punctuation to clarify meaning.

A. After her shift, the nurse said, "I am exhausted."
B. After her shift the nurse said "I am exhausted".
C. After her shift the nurse said, I am exhausted.
D. After her shift the nurse, said "I am exhausted."

31 - Choose the option that correctly fills the blank. The medication_____to alleviate the patient's symptoms.

A. prescribed
B. was prescribed
C. were prescribed
D. prescribe

32 - Which sentence uses a semicolon correctly in a nursing report?

A. The patient was stable; however, he required constant monitoring.
B. The patient was stable; he required constant monitoring.
C. The patient; was stable, however, he required constant monitoring.
D. The patient was stable; and required constant monitoring.

33 - Select the correct use of punctuation in the context of a list within a nursing report.

A. The patient needs rest: hydration, medication, and regular monitoring.
B. The patient needs rest, hydration, medication, and regular monitoring.
C. The patient needs: rest, hydration, medication and regular monitoring.
D. The patient needs rest; hydration; medication; and regular monitoring.

34 - Identify the sentence with the correctly placed comma.

A. Before administering medication, the nurse checked the patient's chart.
B. Before administering medication the nurse, checked the patient's chart.
C. Before administering, medication the nurse checked the patient's chart.
D. Before, administering medication the nurse checked the patient's chart.

35 - Nurses are responsible for_____to patient needs promptly.

A. responding
B. respond
C. responsive
D. response

36 - Choose the sentence that correctly uses the plural form.

A. The nurse checked the patient's vitals sign.
B. The nurse checked the patient's vital signs.
C. The nurse checked the patient's vitals signs.
D. The nurse check the patients vitals signs.

37 - It is critical that nurses monitor their patient's vital signs; _____, changes must be reported immediately.

A. because
B. after all
C. while
D. however

38 - Select the sentence that uses correct capitalization.

A. Nurse Thompson works in the Pediatric unit.
B. Nurse thompson works in the pediatric unit.
C. Nurse Thompson works in the pediatric unit.
D. nurse Thompson works in the pediatric unit.

39 - Choose the sentence with the correct use of the comma.

A. Before surgery, ensure all instruments are sterilized.
B. Before surgery ensure, all instruments are sterilized.
C. Before surgery ensure all instruments, are sterilized.
D. Before, surgery ensure all instruments are sterilized.

40 - The patient's condition _____ worsened overnight.

A. have
B. has
C. had
D. having

41 - Which sentence correctly uses capitalization for a medical term?
A. The Nurse administered a dose of Epinephrine.
B. The nurse administered a dose of epinephrine.
C. The nurse administered a dose of Epinephrine.
D. The Nurse administered a dose of epinephrine.

42 - Select the sentence with the correct verb tense.
A. The doctor recommends that the nurse administers the vaccine.
B. The doctor recommend that the nurse administers the vaccine.
C. The doctor recommends that the nurse administer the vaccine.
D. The doctor recommended that the nurse administers the vaccine.

43 - The nurses' lounge is_____the second floor.
A. at
B. in
C. on
D. by

44 - Choose the sentence with the correct plural possessive form.
A. The nurses' lounge was renovated last month.
B. The nurse's lounge were renovated last month.
C. The nurses lounge was renovated last month.
D. The nurses's lounge was renovated last month.

45 - Which sentence correctly uses an indefinite pronoun?
A. Anybody are welcome to attend the health seminar.
B. Anyone are welcome to attend the health seminar.
C. Anyone is welcome to attend the health seminar.
D. Any persons are welcome to attend the health seminar.

46 - Identify the sentence that correctly uses a relative clause.
A. The surgeon who performed the operation was highly experienced.
B. The surgeon, that performed the operation, was highly experienced.
C. The surgeon which performed the operation was highly experienced.
D. The surgeon, who performed the operation was highly experienced.

47 - It was clear that the nurse_____her notes thoroughly before the meeting.
A. prepared
B. prepares
C. was prepared
D. prepare

48 - Which sentence correctly uses a possessive adjective?

A. She checked her patients' charts.

B. She checked hers patients' charts.

C. She checked she patients' charts.

D. She checked hers patients charts.

49 - Select the sentence that uses correct capitalization.

A. Nurse Thompson reported to the Intensive Care Unit.

B. Nurse thompson reported to the intensive care unit.

C. Nurse Thompson reported to the Intensive care unit.

D. Nurse Thompson reported to the intensive care unit.

50 - Everyone in the unit must complete_____charts before lunch.

A. their

B. there

C. they're

D. them

FULL-LENGTH PRACTICE TESTS
SECTION 4 - GRAMMAR
ANSWER KEY WITH EXPLANATIONS

1 - Choose the sentence that is grammatically correct.
C. The nurse drew blood from the patient's arm.
Explanation: The correct sentence uses the past tense "drew" and the possessive "patient's" to show that the arm belongs to the patient.

2 - Select the sentence that correctly uses the comma.
A. Before surgery, the nurse checked the patient's vitals.
Explanation: A comma is used after an introductory phrase or clause like "Before surgery."

3 - Choose the correct plural form in the sentence.
C. The nurses' duties include taking vitals.
Explanation: "Nurses'" is the correct plural possessive form indicating that the duties belong to multiple nurses.

4 - Choose the sentence with the correct verb tense.
B. The nurse will administer the vaccine tomorrow.
Explanation: Future simple tense "will administer" is correctly used for actions that will occur in the future.

5 - Identify the sentence with correct subject-verb agreement.
B. The team of doctors is reviewing the patient's history.
Explanation: "Team" is a collective noun treated as singular when the group is considered a whole, hence "is" is the correct verb.

6 - Identify the sentence that correctly uses a plural noun.
B. The nurses' station is on the second floor.
Explanation: "Nurses'" is the correct plural possessive form indicating that the station belongs to the nurses.

7 - Which sentence correctly uses conjunctions?
C. The nurse needs to check the patient's heart rate and administer medication.
Explanation: The conjunction "and" correctly connects two related actions without additional words.

8 - Which sentence uses a semicolon correctly?
A. The patient was discharged; however, he returned the next day with complications.
Explanation: A semicolon is correctly used before transitional phrases like "however" when they link two independent clauses.

9 - Select the correct form of the verb to complete the sentence: "By the time I arrived, the nurse ___ already ___ the patient."

D. had, assessed

Explanation: The past perfect tense "had assessed" is appropriate here to indicate that the action was completed before another past action.

10 - Identify the sentence with an error in modifier placement.

C. The nurse nearly found a patient unconscious in the room.

Explanation: This sentence incorrectly implies that the nurse almost found a patient, rather than describing the patient's condition. It should say, "The nurse found a nearly unconscious patient in the room."

11 -_____ often take blood pressure before starting any treatments.

A. Nurses

Explanation: "Nurses" is the plural form needed here to indicate more than one nurse performing the action.

12 - Which of the following sentences correctly forms a complex sentence?

A. Although the nurse was tired, she completed her rounds.

Explanation: A complex sentence has at least one independent clause and one dependent clause. "Although the nurse was tired" is the dependent clause, and "she completed her rounds" is the independent clause.

13 - In the sentence "The nurse who arrived late administered the medication," what is the relative clause?

B. who arrived late

Explanation: The relative clause "who arrived late" provides additional information about "the nurse." It is dependent as it cannot stand alone.

14 - Identify the sentence that correctly uses the past perfect tense.

A. The nurse had prepared the patient's room before they arrived.

Explanation: The past perfect tense ("had prepared") is correctly used to describe an action completed before another past action.

15 - During the training, nurses learned that the_____can be critical to patient recovery.

C. Timing of medication

Explanation: Only the first word and proper nouns should be capitalized in a phrase.

16 - Identify the correct use of a modal verb in a medical instruction:

B. The doctor must review all the lab results.

Explanation: "Must" is a modal verb used to express necessity, followed by the base form of the verb "review."

17 - Identify the simple predicate in the sentence: "The patient quickly recovered after the nurse administered the new medication."

B. Recovered

Explanation: The simple predicate is the main verb of the sentence, which in this case is "recovered," describing what the patient did.

18 - The patient and_____decided on a less aggressive treatment plan.

B. me

Explanation: After a preposition like "and," the object pronoun "me" is correct.

19 - Which sentence correctly uses a conjunction?

B. The nurse must check the patient's blood pressure and administer medication.

Explanation: The conjunction "and" correctly joins two related actions without additional punctuation or changes in verb form.

20 - Which sentence correctly uses a semicolon?

A. The patient needed bloodwork; however, the lab was closed.

Explanation: A semicolon is correctly used before a transition word ("however") linking two independent clauses.

21 - _____important to check the patient's medication schedule regularly.

B. It's

Explanation: It's" is a contraction for "it is," which is necessary here for the verb "to be."

22 - Choose the sentence that correctly uses the comparative form.

C. The surgery took less time than expected.

Explanation: "Less" is used for comparative non-count nouns, and "time" is non-countable.

23 - All _____ are required to attend the annual health and safety training.

D. part-time and full-time nurses

Explanation: The correct use of hyphens in "part-time and full-time" clarifies that both groups of nurses are meant.

24 - Select the sentence with the correct use of plural nouns:

D. The nurses provided excellent care.

Explanation: "Nurses" is the correct plural form of "nurse," and "provided" is the correct past tense verb form for the plural subject.

25 - Which punctuation correctly completes the sentence? "Before administering medication, ensure that the patient's identity___verified."

A. Is

Explanation: The sentence requires the present tense "is" for a general procedural instruction, fitting the context of ongoing and routine actions in nursing tasks.

26 - Which option correctly uses a possessive adjective?

C. It's important to check the patient's chart.

Explanation: "It's" is the contraction for "it is," and "patient's" is the correct possessive form indicating the chart belongs to the patient.

27 - Choose the sentence that correctly uses comparative adjectives:

B. This medicine is safer than the one we used before.

Explanation: "Safer" is the correct comparative form of the adjective "safe."

28 - The patient thanked the nurse for_____kindness.

D. her

Explanation: "Her" is the possessive adjective needed to modify the noun "kindness."

29 - Identify the sentence with correct subject-verb agreement.

B. The list of required medications includes aspirin and ibuprofen.

Explanation: The subject "list" is singular, so the singular verb "includes" is correct.

30 - Select the sentence that correctly uses punctuation to clarify meaning.

A. After her shift, the nurse said, "I am exhausted."

Explanation: The comma after "shift" sets off the introductory phrase, and the quotation marks correctly enclose the spoken words.

31 - Choose the option that correctly fills the blank. The medication_____to alleviate the patient's symptoms.

B. was prescribed

Explanation: "Was prescribed" correctly uses the passive voice to indicate that the medication was given by someone (implied to be a healthcare provider).

32 - Which sentence uses a semicolon correctly in a nursing report?

A. The patient was stable; however, he required constant monitoring.

Explanation: A semicolon is correctly used before "however" when it links two independent but related clauses.

33 - Select the correct use of punctuation in the context of a list within a nursing report.

B. The patient needs rest, hydration, medication, and regular monitoring.

Explanation: This sentence lists elements of care that should be separated by commas, with the final comma before "and" (Oxford comma) used for clarity.

34 - Identify the sentence with the correctly placed comma.

A. Before administering medication, the nurse checked the patient's chart.

Explanation: A comma is used after introductory phrases or clauses to set them off from the main clause.

35 - Nurses are responsible for_____to patient needs promptly.

A. responding

Explanation: The gerund "responding" is needed after the preposition "for."

36 - Choose the sentence that correctly uses the plural form.

B. The nurse checked the patient's vital signs.

Explanation: "Vital signs" is the correct plural form referring to indicators such as heart rate, temperature, and blood pressure.

37 - It is critical that nurses monitor their patient's vital signs;_____, changes must be reported immediately.

D. however

Explanation: "However" is used to introduce a contrasting statement, which is appropriate in this sentence.

38 - Select the sentence that uses correct capitalization.

C. Nurse Thompson works in the pediatric unit.

Explanation: Proper nouns (names) like "Nurse Thompson" are capitalized, and "pediatric unit" is not a proper noun so remains lowercase.

39 - Choose the sentence with the correct use of the comma.

A. Before surgery, ensure all instruments are sterilized.

Explanation: A comma is used after introductory phrases or clauses.

40 - The patient's condition_____worsened overnight.

B. has

Explanation: The contraction "has" is the correct form to use with the singular subject "patient's condition" in present perfect tense, indicating a change over time.

41 - Which sentence correctly uses capitalization for a medical term?

B. The nurse administered a dose of epinephrine.

Explanation: Medical terms such as "epinephrine" are not capitalized unless they are brand names or at the beginning of a sentence.

42 - Select the sentence with the correct verb tense.

C. The doctor recommends that the nurse administer the vaccine.

Explanation: The subjunctive mood is used with "recommends" for suggestions or demands, hence "administer" without 's'.

43 - The nurses' lounge is_____the second floor.

C. on

Explanation: "On" is the preposition used to indicate specific floors of a building.

44 - Choose the sentence with the correct plural possessive form.

A. The nurses' lounge was renovated last month.

Explanation: "Nurses'" is the correct plural possessive form, indicating that the lounge belongs to multiple nurses.

45 - Which sentence correctly uses an indefinite pronoun?

C. Anyone is welcome to attend the health seminar.

Explanation: "Anyone" is an indefinite pronoun that requires a singular verb form, "is," in this context.

46 - Identify the sentence that correctly uses a relative clause.

A. The surgeon who performed the operation was highly experienced.

Explanation: "Who" is the correct relative pronoun for referring to people, and no comma is needed in this restrictive clause.

---

47 - It was clear that the nurse_____her notes thoroughly before the meeting.

A. prepared

Explanation: "Prepared" is the correct past tense verb needed here to indicate the action was completed before the meeting.

---

48 - Which sentence correctly uses a possessive adjective?

A. She checked her patients' charts.

Explanation: "Her" is the correct possessive adjective modifying "patients'," which is correctly used as a possessive plural noun.

---

49 - Select the sentence that uses correct capitalization.

D. Nurse Thompson reported to the intensive care unit.

Explanation: Proper nouns like names are capitalized, but common nouns and generic places (like "intensive care unit") are not unless part of a specific name.

---

50 - Everyone in the unit must complete_____charts before lunch.

A. their

Explanation: "Their" is the possessive pronoun needed to show ownership of the charts by everyone.

FULL-LENGTH TESTS

THE MOST UP-TO-DATE COMPREHENSIVE TESTS OF THE HESI A2 EXAM

SECTION 5 - BIOLOGY

FULL-LENGTH PRACTICE TESTS
SECTION 5 - BIOLOGY

Start Time ....

End Time ....

1 - What is the basic unit of life in all living organisms?
A. Atom
B. Molecule
C. Organelle
D. Cell

2 - Which organelle is responsible for producing ATP, the energy currency of the cell?
A. Golgi apparatus
B. Mitochondria
C. Nucleus
D. Ribosome

3 - What type of cell lacks a defined nucleus and organelles bound by membranes?
A. Eukaryotic
B. Archaea
C. Prokaryotic
D. Multicellular

4 - During which phase of mitosis do chromosomes align at the cell's equator?
A. Prophase
B. Metaphase
C. Anaphase
D. Telophase

5 - Which process describes the synthesis of RNA from a DNA template?
A. Translation
B. Replication
C. Transcription
D. Mutation

6 - What is the primary function of the ribosomes in a cell?

A. DNA replication

B. Protein synthesis

C. Lipid metabolism

D. Detoxification

7 - Which is a function of the smooth endoplasmic reticulum?

A. Synthesizing proteins

B. Breaking down carbohydrates

C. Detoxifying chemicals

D. Packaging DNA

8 - What structure in plant cells captures energy from sunlight to produce glucose in a process called photosynthesis?

A. Chloroplast

B. Mitochondrion

C. Nucleus

D. Peroxisome

9 - Which type of cell division results in four genetically unique daughter cells?

A. Mitosis

B. Binary fission

C. Meiosis

D. Interphase

10 - Which term describes the diffusion of water across a selectively permeable membrane?

A. Osmosis

B. Active transport

C. Endocytosis

D. Exocytosis

11 - What type of cells form the human body?

A. Bacterial cells

B. Eukaryotic cells

C. Archaeal cells

D. Viral particles

12 - Which organelle is primarily involved in the detoxification of medications in liver cells?

A. Lysosome

B. Smooth endoplasmic reticulum

C. Mitochondrion

D. Golgi apparatus

13 - How do nerve cells transmit signals to other cells in the body?

A. Through direct contact with each target cell

B. Via releasing hormones into the bloodstream

C. By generating electrical impulses transmitted along axons

D. Through passive diffusion of ions

14 - What is the primary purpose of red blood cells in the circulatory system?

A. To fight infections

B. To regulate blood pH

C. To transport oxygen

D. To clot blood

15 - Which structure within the cell is responsible for synthesizing proteins?

A. Nucleus

B. Ribosome

C. Endoplasmic reticulum

D. Mitochondria

16 - During which stage of the cell cycle does DNA replication occur?

A. G0 phase

B. G1 phase

C. S phase

D. M phase

17 - What process do cancer cells often undergo to spread from one part of the body to another?

A. Apoptosis

B. Necrosis

C. Mitosis

D. Metastasis

18 - What is the function of the Golgi apparatus in a cell?

A. Producing ATP

B. Synthesizing lipids

C. Modifying, sorting, and packaging proteins

D. Digesting cellular waste

19 - Which part of the brain controls heart rate, respiration, and blood pressure?

A. Cerebrum

B. Cerebellum

C. Hypothalamus

D. Brainstem

20 - Which cellular process is primarily responsible for genetic diversity during sexual reproduction?

A. Mitosis

B. Binary fission

C. Meiosis

D. Budding

21 - What is the primary function of white blood cells in the human body?

A. To carry oxygen to tissues

B. To clot blood

C. To combat infections

D. To remove carbon dioxide from the body

22 - Which hormone regulates the metabolism of glucose in the body?

A. Adrenaline

B. Insulin

C. Cortisol

D. Estrogen

23 - Where does gas exchange occur in the human body?

A. Trachea

B. Bronchi

C. Diaphragm

D. Alveoli

24 - What type of tissue connects muscles to bones?

A. Tendons

B. Epithelial tissue

C. Cartilage

D. Ligaments

25 - Which cellular process results in the production of daughter cells with half the number of chromosomes of the parent cell?

A. Binary fission

B. Transcription

C. Meiosis

D. Mitosis

FULL-LENGTH PRACTICE TESTS
SECTION 5 - BIOLOGY
ANSWER KEY WITH EXPLANATIONS

1 - What is the basic unit of life in all living organisms?

D. Cell

Explanation: The cell is the smallest unit of life capable of performing all life processes, making it the fundamental building block for all living organisms.

2 - Which organelle is responsible for producing ATP, the energy currency of the cell?

B. Mitochondria

Explanation: Mitochondria are known as the "powerhouses" of the cell because they generate most of the cell's supply of adenosine triphosphate (ATP), which is used as a source of chemical energy.

3 - What type of cell lacks a defined nucleus and organelles bound by membranes?

C. Prokaryotic

Explanation: Prokaryotic cells, such as bacteria, lack a defined nucleus and membrane-bound organelles, with their DNA floating freely within the cell.

4 - During which phase of mitosis do chromosomes align at the cell's equator?

B. Metaphase

Explanation: During metaphase, chromosomes align at the cell's equator, preparing for separation into two daughter cells.

5 - Which process describes the synthesis of RNA from a DNA template?

C. Transcription

Explanation: Transcription is the process by which the information in a strand of DNA is copied into a new molecule of messenger RNA (mRNA).

6 - What is the primary function of the ribosomes in a cell?

B. Protein synthesis

Explanation: Ribosomes are cellular structures responsible for protein synthesis, translating mRNA into polypeptide chains.

7 - Which is a function of the smooth endoplasmic reticulum?

C. Detoxifying chemicals

Explanation: The smooth endoplasmic reticulum is involved in various metabolic processes, including the detoxification of chemicals in the cell.

8 - What structure in plant cells captures energy from sunlight to produce glucose in a process called photosynthesis?

A. Chloroplast

Explanation: Chloroplasts are the sites of photosynthesis in plant cells, containing chlorophyll that captures light energy to synthesize glucose.

9 - Which type of cell division results in four genetically unique daughter cells?

C. Meiosis

Explanation: Meiosis is a type of cell division that reduces the chromosome number by half, creating four genetically unique gametes.

10 - Which term describes the diffusion of water across a selectively permeable membrane?

A. Osmosis

Explanation: Osmosis is the process by which water molecules move across a selectively permeable membrane from a region of lower solute concentration to higher solute concentration.

11 - What type of cells form the human body?

B. Eukaryotic cells

Explanation: Human cells are eukaryotic, characterized by a nucleus and membrane-bound organelles, differentiating them from prokaryotic cells like bacteria.

12 - Which organelle is primarily involved in the detoxification of medications in liver cells?

B. Smooth endoplasmic reticulum

Explanation: The smooth endoplasmic reticulum (ER) in liver cells plays a crucial role in metabolizing and detoxifying various substances, including medications.

13 - How do nerve cells transmit signals to other cells in the body?

C. By generating electrical impulses transmitted along axons

Explanation: Nerve cells (neurons) transmit signals through electrical impulses called action potentials, which travel along axons to other cells, such as other neurons or muscle cells.

14 - What is the primary purpose of red blood cells in the circulatory system?

C. To transport oxygen

Explanation: Red blood cells are primarily responsible for carrying oxygen from the lungs to body tissues and transporting carbon dioxide back to the lungs for exhalation.

15 - Which structure within the cell is responsible for synthesizing proteins?

B. Ribosome

Explanation: Ribosomes are cellular structures where proteins are synthesized, reading mRNA sequences to assemble amino acids into proteins.

16 - During which stage of the cell cycle does DNA replication occur?

C. S phase

Explanation: DNA replication occurs during the S (synthesis) phase of the cell cycle, ensuring each new cell receives a complete set of genetic information.

17 - What process do cancer cells often undergo to spread from one part of the body to another?

D. Metastasis

Explanation: Metastasis is the process by which cancer cells spread from the original tumor site to other parts of the body, forming new tumors.

18 - What is the function of the Golgi apparatus in a cell?

C. Modifying, sorting, and packaging proteins

Explanation: The Golgi apparatus is involved in modifying, sorting, and packaging proteins for secretion or use within the cell.

19 - Which part of the brain controls heart rate, respiration, and blood pressure?

D. Brainstem

Explanation: The brainstem regulates vital involuntary functions such as heart rate, respiration, and blood pressure.

20 - Which cellular process is primarily responsible for genetic diversity during sexual reproduction?

C. Meiosis

Explanation: Meiosis is a type of cell division that reduces the chromosome number by half and includes mechanisms such as crossing over and independent assortment, which contribute to genetic diversity in offspring.

21 - What is the primary function of white blood cells in the human body?

C. To combat infections

Explanation: White blood cells (leukocytes) are crucial components of the immune system. They play a significant role in defending the body against both infectious disease and foreign invaders.

22 - Which hormone regulates the metabolism of glucose in the body?

B. Insulin

Explanation: Insulin is a hormone produced by the pancreas that regulates glucose levels in the blood. It helps cells absorb glucose to be used for energy or stored, playing a key role in managing blood sugar levels.

23 - Where does gas exchange occur in the human body?

D. Alveoli

Explanation: Gas exchange in humans occurs in the alveoli, small sac-like structures located at the ends of the respiratory bronchioles in the lungs. Here, oxygen from inhaled air is exchanged for carbon dioxide from the blood.

24 - What type of tissue connects muscles to bones?

A. Tendons

Explanation: Tendons are strong, flexible bands of fibrous connective tissue that attach muscles to bones, facilitating the movement of bones when muscles contract.

25 - Which cellular process results in the production of daughter cells with half the number of chromosomes of the parent cell?

C. Meiosis

Explanation: Meiosis is a type of cell division that reduces the chromosome number by half through two rounds of division, resulting in four daughter cells. This process is critical for producing gametes (sperm and eggs) in sexually reproducing organisms.

FULL-LENGTH TESTS

THE MOST UP-TO-DATE COMPREHENSIVE TESTS OF THE HESI A2 EXAM

SECTION 6 - CHEMISTRY

FULL-LENGTH PRACTICE TESTS
SECTION 6 - CHEMISTRY

Start Time ....

End Time ....

1 - What is the primary purpose of a catalyst in a chemical reaction?

A. To increase the temperature of the reaction
B. To decrease the reaction rate
C. To provide an alternative reaction pathway with a lower activation energy
D. To act as a reactant

2 - Which state of matter has a definite volume but no definite shape?

A. Solid
B. Liquid
C. Gas
D. Plasma

3 - What happens to the temperature of a substance during a phase change when heat is added?

A. It increases continuously.
B. It decreases.
C. It remains constant.
D. It first increases, then decreases.

4 - Which of the following is true about isotopes?

A. They have different numbers of protons.
B. They have different numbers of electrons.
C. They have different numbers of neutrons.
D. They are different elements.

5 - What type of bond is formed when electrons are transferred from one atom to another?

A. Ionic bond
B. Covalent bond
C. Metallic bond
D. Hydrogen bond

6 -Which term describes the amount of solute that can be dissolved in a solvent at a given temperature?

A. Solubility

B. Saturation

C. Concentration

D. Permeability

7 - What is the process called in which liquid water changes into water vapor?

A. Condensation

B. Evaporation

C. Sublimation

D. Deposition

8 - In the healthcare setting, why is understanding the pH of solutions important?

A. It influences the taste of medications.

B. It affects the stability and absorption of medications.

C. It alters the color of medications.

D. It changes the scent of solutions.

9 - Which of the following best describes a chemical property?

A. Density

B. Color

C. Flammability

D. Boiling point

10 - What type of chemical reaction involves the exchange of ions between two compounds?

A. Synthesis reaction

B. Decomposition reaction

C. Single displacement reaction

D. Double displacement reaction

11 - What is the normal pH range of human blood?

A. 5.5-6.5

B. 7.35-7.45

C. 6.5-7.5

D. 8.0-9.0

12 - Identify the compound with a molecular bond likely to be found in the human body.

A. NaCl

B. H_2O

C. O_2

D. All of the above

13 - The pH of gastric acid in the stomach is typically around 2.0. What does this indicate about gastric acid?

A. It is weakly acidic.

B. It is strongly acidic.

C. It is weakly basic.

D. It is strongly basic.

14 - What determines the chemical properties of an element?

A. The number of protons

B. The number of neutrons

C. The distribution of electrons

D. The position in the periodic table

15 - What is required to initiate a combustion reaction?

A. Water

B. Oxygen

C. Carbon dioxide

D. Nitrogen

16 - What type of chemical reaction is involved in the process of electrolysis?

A. Decomposition

B. Synthesis

C. Double displacement

D. Single displacement

17 - How does the atomic number affect the position of an element on the periodic table?

A. It determines the element's group number.

B. It specifies the period of the element based on its electron shells.

C. It places the element sequentially from left to right based on increasing atomic number.

D. It dictates whether the element is a metal, metalloid, or nonmetal.

18 - Which bond is characterized by the electrostatic attraction between positively and negatively charged ions?

A. Covalent bond

B. Ionic bond

C. Dipole-dipole interaction

D. Metallic bond

19 - In which reaction do electrons transfer from one reactant to another?

A. Synthesis

B. Combustion

C. Oxidation-reduction

D. Neutralization

20 - What is an example of a reversible chemical reaction?

A. Combustion of gasoline

B. Electrolysis of water

C. Decomposition of potassium chlorate

D. Synthesis of ammonia by the Haber process

21 - Which process describes the conversion of glucose to energy within cells?

A. Photosynthesis

B. Transcription

C. Fermentation

D. Cellular respiration

22 - Which element is most essential for the transport of oxygen in blood?

A. Carbon

B. Iron

C. Sodium

D. Chlorine

23 - What is Avogadro's number?

A. The number of particles in 1 mole of a substance

B. The number of protons in an atom

C. The maximum number of electrons in an energy level

D. The constant pressure value for an ideal gas

24 - What is a synthesis reaction?

A. A reaction where a single compound breaks down into two or more simpler substances.

B. A reaction where two or more substances combine to form a new compound.

C. A reaction where an element replaces another in a compound.

D. A reaction where ions are exchanged between two reactants.

25 - What characterizes a neutralization reaction?

A. Formation of water

B. Release of a gas

C. Production of a base

D. Production of an acid

FULL-LENGTH PRACTICE TESTS
SECTION 6 - CHEMISTRY
ANSWER KEY WITH EXPLANATIONS

1 - What is the primary purpose of a catalyst in a chemical reaction?
C. To provide an alternative reaction pathway with a lower activation energy
Explanation: A catalyst speeds up a chemical reaction without being consumed by lowering the activation energy needed for the reaction to proceed, thus increasing the rate of the reaction.

2 - Which state of matter has a definite volume but no definite shape?
B. Liquid
Explanation: Liquids have a definite volume that does not change with the shape of the container but have no definite shape and will take the shape of their container.

3 - What happens to the temperature of a substance during a phase change when heat is added?
C. It remains constant.
Explanation: During a phase change, the temperature of a substance remains constant as the added energy is used to change the state of the substance rather than increasing its temperature.

4 - Which of the following is true about isotopes?
C. They have different numbers of neutrons.
Explanation: Isotopes are variants of a particular chemical element that have the same number of protons and electrons but different numbers of neutrons.

5 - What type of bond is formed when electrons are transferred from one atom to another?
A. Ionic bond
Explanation: Ionic bonds form between atoms when electrons are transferred from one atom to another, creating ions that are held together by electrostatic forces.

6 - Which term describes the amount of solute that can be dissolved in a solvent at a given temperature?
A. Solubility
Explanation: Solubility is the maximum amount of solute that can dissolve in a solvent at a specific temperature.

7 - What is the process called in which liquid water changes into water vapor?

B. Evaporation

Explanation: Evaporation is the process in which liquid water changes into water vapor, typically occurring at the surface of the liquid.

8 - In the healthcare setting, why is understanding the pH of solutions important?

B. It affects the stability and absorption of medications.

Explanation: The pH of solutions can significantly influence the stability, solubility, and absorption of medications in the body, affecting their efficacy and safety.

9 - Which of the following best describes a chemical property?

C. Flammability

Explanation: A chemical property involves the ability of a substance to undergo a specific chemical change; flammability is a chemical property because it describes how easily a substance can burn in the presence of oxygen.

10 - What type of chemical reaction involves the exchange of ions between two compounds?

D. Double displacement reaction

Explanation: A double displacement reaction involves the exchange of ions between two compounds to form two different compounds, typically resulting in the formation of a precipitate, gas, or water.

11 - What is the normal pH range of human blood?

B. 7.35-7.45

Explanation: The normal pH range for human blood is tightly regulated between 7.35 and 7.45, ensuring optimal functioning of enzymatic reactions and overall metabolic processes.

12 - Identify the compound with a molecular bond likely to be found in the human body.

D. All of the above

Explanation: NaCl (table salt), H_2O (water), and O_2 (oxygen) are all compounds with bonds found in the human body, serving various essential biological functions.

13 - The pH of gastric acid in the stomach is typically around 2.0. What does this indicate about gastric acid?

B. It is strongly acidic.

Explanation: A pH of around 2.0 is highly acidic, which helps in the digestion of food and killing of ingested pathogens.

14 - What determines the chemical properties of an element?

C. The distribution of electrons

Explanation: The chemical properties of an element are primarily determined by the distribution of electrons, especially the electrons in the outermost shell, as these are the ones involved in chemical bonds and reactions.

15 - What is required to initiate a combustion reaction?

B. Oxygen

Explanation: A combustion reaction requires oxygen to burn the fuel, which typically results in the release of heat, light, carbon dioxide, and water.

16 - What type of chemical reaction is involved in the process of electrolysis?

A. Decomposition

Explanation: Electrolysis involves a decomposition reaction where an electric current breaks down compounds into their elements or simpler compounds.

17 - How does the atomic number affect the position of an element on the periodic table?

C. It places the element sequentially from left to right based on increasing atomic number.

Explanation: The periodic table is organized by increasing atomic numbers from left to right. This arrangement allows elements with similar chemical properties to align in the same columns, known as groups or families. The atomic number increases sequentially as you move from one element to the next across the table, reflecting an increase in the number of protons in the nucleus.

18 - Which bond is characterized by the electrostatic attraction between positively and negatively charged ions?

B. Ionic bond

Explanation: An ionic bond is formed between a metal and a non-metal. It is characterized by the transfer of electrons from the metal atom to the non-metal atom. The resulting electrostatic attraction between the oppositely charged ions holds the compound together, as seen in common salts like sodium chloride ($NaCl$).

19 - In which reaction do electrons transfer from one reactant to another?

C. Oxidation-reduction

Explanation: Oxidation-reduction (redox) reactions involve the transfer of electrons from one reactant (the reducing agent) to another (the oxidizing agent), leading to changes in oxidation states.

20 - What is an example of a reversible chemical reaction?

D. Synthesis of ammonia by the Haber process

Explanation: The synthesis of ammonia by the Haber process is a reversible reaction where nitrogen and hydrogen gases react under pressure to form ammonia, which can decompose back into the original reactants under different conditions.

21 - Which process describes the conversion of glucose to energy within cells?

D. Cellular respiration

Explanation: Cellular respiration is the metabolic process in which cells convert glucose and oxygen into energy (ATP), releasing carbon dioxide and water as byproducts.

22 - Which element is most essential for the transport of oxygen in blood?

B. Iron

Explanation: Iron is a key component of hemoglobin, the protein in red blood cells that binds to oxygen and transports it throughout the body.

23 - What is Avogadro's number?

A. The number of particles in 1 mole of a substance

Explanation: Avogadro's number, approximatel 6.022×10^{23}, is the number of atoms, ions, or molecules present in one mole of any substance.

24 - What is a synthesis reaction?

B. A reaction where two or more substances combine to form a new compound.

Explanation: A synthesis reaction is a type of chemical reaction in which two or more reactants combine to form a single product. It is typically represented by A + B --> AB.

25 - What characterizes a neutralization reaction?

A. Formation of water

Explanation: Neutralization is a type of chemical reaction where an acid and a base react quantitatively with each other.

FULL-LENGTH TESTS

THE MOST UP-TO-DATE COMPREHENSIVE TESTS OF THE HESI A2 EXAM

SECTION 7 - HUMAN ANATOMY AND PHYSIOLOGY

FULL-LENGTH PRACTICE TESTS

SECTION 7 - HUMAN ANATOMY AND PHYSIOLOGY

Start Time ....

End Time ....

1 - What is the primary function of the smooth muscle tissue found in the human body?

A. To pump blood through the heart
B. To facilitate voluntary movements
C. To contract and relax for various involuntary functions
D. To transmit electrical impulses throughout the body

2 - What is the role of the cerebellum in the human brain?

A. It controls voluntary movements and balance.
B. It is involved in the processing and interpretation of sensory input.
C. It regulates heart rate and respiratory rate.
D. It manages emotional responses and memory formation.

3 - Which organ is primarily responsible for filtering blood and forming urine?

A. Liver
B. Kidneys
C. Heart
D. Lungs

4 - What is the function of alveoli in the respiratory system?

A. To pump blood through the body
B. To filter blood
C. To exchange gases between the air and the blood
D. To produce vocal sounds

5 - What type of blood cells are primarily involved in immune response?

A. Erythrocytes
B. Platelets
C. Leukocytes
D. Plasma cells

6 - What is the main function of the axial skeleton?

A. To facilitate movement

B. To produce blood cells

C. To protect vital organs

D. To store lipids

7 - During which phase of the cardiac cycle do the ventricles fill with blood?

A. Systole

B. Diastole

C. Contraction

D. Relaxation

8 - Where does hematopoiesis primarily occur?

A. Heart

B. Bone marrow

C. Spleen

D. Liver

9 - What is the role of osteocytes in bone tissue?

A. To provide energy for bone remodeling

B. To act as mechanosensors and coordinate the bone remodeling process

C. To connect bone to muscles

D. To resorb bone matrix

10 - The neuron is integral to the nervous system for its role in:

A. Producing hormones

B. Transmitting electrical signals

C. Filtering blood

D. Contracting muscles

11 - What is the primary function of neurons in the nervous system?

A. To provide structural support

B. To produce hormones

C. To transmit information via electrical and chemical signals

D. To regulate blood flow

12 - What is the main function of the lymphatic system?

A. To coordinate bodily functions

B. To transport nutrients to cells

C. To maintain fluid balance and support immune functions

D. To produce movement and generate heat

13 - What role does the hypothalamus play in the endocrine system?

A. It secretes enzymes that digest proteins.

B. It regulates the pituitary gland and hormone release.

C. It produces antibodies to fight infections.

D. It controls skeletal muscle contractions.

14 - Which type of tissue is primarily responsible for body movement?

A. Epithelial tissue

B. Connective tissue

C. Muscle tissue

D. Nervous tissue

15 - Which part of the brain is responsible for processing visual information?

A. Cerebellum

B. Medulla oblongata

C. Occipital lobe

D. Frontal lobe

16 - What is the primary role of red blood cells?

A. To clot blood

B. To defend against pathogens

C. To transport oxygen

D. To regulate heart rate

17 - Which gland produces insulin?

A. Thyroid

B. Adrenal

C. Pancreas

D. Pituitary

18 - What type of joint allows for rotational movement around a single axis?

A. Pivot joint

B. Saddle joint

C. Hinge joint

D. Ball-and-socket joint

19 - Which of the following best describes the primary function of epithelial tissue?

A. To contract and enable movement

B. To transmit nerve impulses

C. To cover and protect body surfaces

D. To connect and support body structures

20 - Which structure in the digestive system is responsible for absorbing nutrients?

A. Esophagus

B. Large intestine

C. Stomach

D. Small intestine

21 - Which type of neuron is responsible for transmitting sensory information from sensory receptors to the central nervous system?

A. Motor neurons

B. Interneurons

C. Neuroglia

D. Sensory neurons

22 - What is the role of osteoblasts in bone remodeling?

A. Breaking down bone tissue

B. Transporting nutrients

C. Forming new bone tissue

D. Secreting hormones

23 - What barrier protects the brain by preventing the passage of harmful substances from the blood?

A. The blood-brain barrier

B. The cerebral cortex

C. The lymphatic barrier

D. The meninges

24 - Which hormone is primarily involved in the fight-or-flight response?

A. Insulin

B. Estrogen

C. Adrenaline

D. Leptin

25 - What hormone regulates calcium levels in the blood?

A. Thyroxine

B. Insulin

C. Cortisol

D. Parathyroid hormone

FULL-LENGTH PRACTICE TESTS

SECTION 7 - HUMAN ANATOMY AND PHYSIOLOGY

ANSWER KEY WITH EXPLANATIONS

1 - What is the primary function of the smooth muscle tissue found in the human body?
C. To contract and relax for various involuntary functions
Explanation: Smooth muscle tissue is primarily found in the walls of hollow organs such as the stomach, intestines, and blood vessels.

2 - What is the role of the cerebellum in the human brain?
A. It controls voluntary movements and balance.
Explanation: The cerebellum is a part of the brain located under the cerebrum at the back of the skull. Its primary functions include coordinating voluntary movements and maintaining posture and balance.

3 - Which organ is primarily responsible for filtering blood and forming urine?
B. Kidneys
Explanation: The kidneys filter waste products and excess substances from the blood, forming urine to excrete these wastes, helping to regulate blood pressure, electrolyte balance, and red blood cell production.

4 - What is the function of alveoli in the respiratory system?
C. To exchange gases between the air and the blood
Explanation: Alveoli are tiny sacs within the lungs where oxygen from inhaled air is exchanged for carbon dioxide in the blood, a crucial process for respiratory function.

5 - What type of blood cells are primarily involved in immune response?
C. Leukocytes
Explanation: Leukocytes, or white blood cells, are the main type of cell involved in the immune response, protecting the body against infections and foreign invaders.

6 - What is the main function of the axial skeleton?
C. To protect vital organs
Explanation: The axial skeleton includes the skull, vertebral column, and rib cage, which primarily provide support and protection for the brain, spinal cord, and thoracic cavity organs.

7 - During which phase of the cardiac cycle do the ventricles fill with blood?

D. Diastole

Explanation: Diastole is the phase of the cardiac cycle when the heart muscle relaxes and the ventricles fill with blood coming from the atria.

8 - Where does hematopoiesis primarily occur?

B. Bone marrow

Explanation: Hematopoiesis, the process of blood cell production, primarily occurs in the bone marrow found in the hollow centers of bones.

9 - What is the role of osteocytes in bone tissue?

B. To act as mechanosensors and coordinate the bone remodeling process

Explanation: Osteocytes, mature bone cells, act as mechanosensors that regulate bone remodeling in response to mechanical stress and communicate with osteoblasts and osteoclasts to maintain bone density.

10 - The neuron is integral to the nervous system for its role in:

B. Transmitting electrical signals

Explanation: Neurons are specialized cells designed to transmit information throughout the body in the form of electrical and chemical signals, crucial for coordinating bodily functions.

11 - What is the primary function of neurons in the nervous system?

C. To transmit information via electrical and chemical signals

Explanation: Neurons are specialized cells designed to transmit information throughout the body, facilitating communication between different parts of the body by electrical and chemical signals.

12 - What is the main function of the lymphatic system?

C. To maintain fluid balance and support immune functions

Explanation: The lymphatic system helps to maintain fluid balance by returning excess tissue fluid to the bloodstream and supports immune functions by transporting white blood cells and handling foreign bodies and pathogens.

13 - What role does the hypothalamus play in the endocrine system?

B. It regulates the pituitary gland and hormone release.

Explanation: The hypothalamus controls many body functions via the endocrine system by regulating the pituitary gland, which in turn controls other endocrine glands to secrete hormones that influence metabolism, growth, and other functions.

14 - Which type of tissue is primarily responsible for body movement?

C. Muscle tissue

Explanation: Muscle tissue is specialized for contraction, which is essential for all types of body movements. It includes skeletal muscle (voluntary movements), cardiac muscle (heart contractions), and smooth muscle (involuntary movements in internal organs).

15 - Which part of the brain is responsible for processing visual information?

C. Occipital lobe

Explanation: The occipital lobe, located at the back of the brain, is primarily responsible for visual processing, including the interpretation of colors and shapes.

16 - What is the primary role of red blood cells?

C. To transport oxygen

Explanation: Red blood cells, or erythrocytes, are primarily responsible for carrying oxygen from the lungs to the body's tissues and returning carbon dioxide to the lungs for exhalation.

17 - Which gland produces insulin?

C. Pancreas

Explanation: The pancreas produces insulin, a hormone that helps regulate blood glucose levels by facilitating the uptake of glucose into cells.

18 - What type of joint allows for rotational movement around a single axis?

A. Pivot joint

Explanation: Pivot joints allow for rotation around a single axis. An example is the joint between the first and second cervical vertebrae in the neck, which allows for the rotation of the head.

19 - Which of the following best describes the primary function of epithelial tissue?

C. To cover and protect body surfaces

Explanation: Epithelial tissue forms the lining of internal organs and the outer layer of skin, providing a barrier against microorganisms, physical injuries, and fluid loss.

20 - Which structure in the digestive system is responsible for absorbing nutrients?

D. Small intestine

Explanation: The small intestine is the site of most chemical digestion and nutrient absorption. Its inner surface is highly folded to increase surface area, enhancing nutrient uptake.

21 - Which type of neuron is responsible for transmitting sensory information from sensory receptors to the central nervous system?

D. Sensory neurons

Explanation: Sensory neurons carry signals from the outer parts of your body (periphery) into the central nervous system.

22 - What is the role of osteoblasts in bone remodeling?

C. Forming new bone tissue

Explanation: Osteoblasts are cells that form new bone tissue, playing a key role in the growth, maintenance, and repair of bones.

23 - What barrier protects the brain by preventing the passage of harmful substances from the blood?

A. The blood-brain barrier

Explanation: The blood-brain barrier is a selective barrier that prevents most substances in the blood from entering the brain, thereby protecting it from toxins and pathogens.

24 - Which hormone is primarily involved in the fight-or-flight response?

C. Adrenaline

Explanation: Adrenaline, also known as epinephrine, is a hormone released by the adrenal glands that increases heart rate, expands air passages of the lungs, and mobilizes energy, preparing the body for rapid action.

25 - What hormone regulates calcium levels in the blood?

D. Parathyroid hormone

Explanation: Parathyroid hormone (PTH) is secreted by the parathyroid glands and plays a crucial role in regulating serum calcium levels by increasing bone resorption and enhancing calcium absorption from the diet.

FULL-LENGTH TESTS

THE MOST UP-TO-DATE COMPREHENSIVE TESTS OF THE HESI A2 EXAM

SECTION 8 - PHYSICS

FULL-LENGTH PRACTICE TESTS
SECTION 8 - PHYSICS

Start Time ....

End Time ....

1 - What is the unit of force in the International System of Units?
A. Joule
B. Pascal
C. Newton
D. Watt

2 - Which of the following is not a vector quantity?
A. Velocity
B. Acceleration
C. Speed
D. Force

3 - What does Newton's First Law of Motion state?
A. F = ma
B. For every action, there is an equal and opposite reaction.
C. The force of gravity is inversely proportional to the square of the distance between two masses.
D. An object will remain at rest or in uniform motion unless acted upon by an external force.

4 - Which law explains how current and voltage are related in a circuit?
A. Ohm's Law
B. Coulomb's Law
C. Newton's Second Law
D. Kepler's Law

5 - What is acceleration?
A. The rate at which velocity changes over time
B. The total distance traveled by an object
C. The rate at which displacement changes over time
D. The resistance to change in motion

6 - Which of the following is true about scalar quantities?

A. They have both magnitude and direction.

B. They only have magnitude.

C. They include examples like velocity and force.

D. They are represented by arrows.

7 - What does the term 'kinematics' focus on?

A. The forces causing motion

B. The energy of moving objects

C. The motion of objects without considering the forces causing the motion

D. The interactions between moving objects

8 - Which quantity is affected by the gravitational force between two objects?

A. Mass

B. Color

C. Speed

D. Weight

9 - What is necessary for a wave to be classified as a longitudinal wave?

A. The disturbance is perpendicular to the direction of wave travel.

B. The disturbance is parallel to the direction of wave travel.

C. It must travel through a vacuum.

D. It is composed of transverse motions.

10 - What does Coulomb's Law relate to?

A. The force between magnetic poles

B. The force between two point charges

C. The resistance in an electrical circuit

D. The acceleration due to gravity

11 - What is the primary purpose of the scientific method in physics?

A. To publish experimental data

B. To form untestable hypotheses

C. To explore observations and test hypotheses

D. To argue theoretical physics without evidence

12 - Which quantity is considered a fundamental measure in physics?

A. Weight

B. Volume

C. Time

D. Density

FULL-LENGTH TESTS   273

13 - Newton's second law of motion states that force is the product of mass and what other quantity?

A. Velocity

B. Acceleration

C. Speed

D. Distance

14 - What type of wave requires a medium through which to travel?

A. Light wave

B. Radio wave

C. Sound wave

D. Gamma ray

15 - In the context of circular motion, what force is directed toward the center of the circle?

A. Centripetal force

B. Centrifugal force

C. Gravitational force

D. Electrostatic force

16 - Which statement about vectors and scalars is true?

A. Scalars have magnitude and direction.

B. Vectors have only magnitude.

C. Speed is a vector quantity.

D. Displacement is a vector quantity

17 - Which law of motion introduces the concept of inertia?

A. Newton's First Law

B. Newton's Second Law

C. Newton's Third Law

D. Hooke's Law

18 - What does the slope of a velocity-time graph represent?

A. Displacement

B. Acceleration

C. Velocity

D. Speed

19 - What is the SI unit for power?

A. Joule

B. Newton

C. Watt

D. Pascal

20 - What is the term for the number of cycles of a wave that pass a point per unit of time?

A. Amplitude

B. Wavelength

C. Frequency

D. Speed

21 - What physical quantity is measured in ohms?

A. Resistance

B. Conductance

C. Inductance

D. Capacitance

22 - Which formula represents Ohm's Law?

A. $V = IR$

B. $P = IV$

C. $F = ma$

D. $E = mc^2$

23 - In terms of wave motion, what does the term 'amplitude' describe?

A. The distance covered by the wave

B. The energy transferred by the wave

C. The maximum height of the wave

D. The speed of the wave

24 - What is the correct expression for kinetic energy?

A. $KE = \frac{1}{2} mv^2$

B. $KE = mv^2$

C. $KE = \frac{1}{2} mgh$

D. $KE = mgh$

25 - What is the principle that changing magnetic fields can induce an electric current called?

A. Coulomb's Law

B. Ampère's Law

C. Ohm's Law

D. Faraday's Law of Electromagnetic Induction

FULL-LENGTH PRACTICE TESTS
SECTION 8 - PHYSICS
ANSWER KEY WITH EXPLANATIONS

1 - What is the unit of force in the International System of Units?
C. Newton
Explanation: Force is measured in Newtons. A Newton is defined as the force needed to accelerate 1 kilogram of mass at the rate of 1 meter per second squared.

2 - Which of the following is not a vector quantity?
C) Speed
Explanation: Speed is a scalar quantity because it has magnitude but no specific direction. Velocity, acceleration, and force are vector quantities because they describe both magnitude and direction.

3 - What does Newton's First Law of Motion state?
D. An object will remain at rest or in uniform motion unless acted upon by an external force.
Explanation: Newton's First Law, also known as the Law of Inertia, states that an object at rest stays at rest and an object in motion continues in motion with the same speed and in the same direction unless acted upon by an unbalanced force.

4 - Which law explains how current and voltage are related in a circuit?
A. Ohm's Law
Explanation: Ohm's Law states that the current through a conductor between two points is directly proportional to the voltage across the two points and inversely proportional to the resistance between them. It is mathematically expressed as $V = IR$.

5 - What is acceleration?
A. The rate at which velocity changes over time
Explanation: Acceleration is a vector quantity that describes how quickly an object's velocity changes. It includes changes in speed and/or direction.

6 - Which of the following is true about scalar quantities?
B. They only have magnitude.
Explanation: Scalar quantities have magnitude but no direction, such as temperature, energy, speed, or mass.

Hesi A2 Study Guide

7 - What does the term 'kinematics' focus on?

C. The motion of objects without considering the forces causing the motion

Explanation: Kinematics is the study of motion without considering its causes. It deals with the concepts of velocity, acceleration, displacement, and time.

8 - Which quantity is affected by the gravitational force between two objects?

D. Weight

Explanation: Weight is the force of gravity acting on an object's mass. Unlike mass, which is constant, weight can change depending on the gravitational pull at a specific location.

9 - What is necessary for a wave to be classified as a longitudinal wave?

B. The disturbance is parallel to the direction of wave travel.

Explanation: In longitudinal waves, the particles of the medium move parallel to the direction that the wave travels, typical of sound waves.

10 - What does Coulomb's Law relate to?

B. The force between two point charges

Explanation: Coulomb's Law quantifies the amount of force between two stationary, electrically charged particles. The force is directly proportional to the product of the electrical charges and inversely proportional to the square of the distance between them.

11 - What is the primary purpose of the scientific method in physics?

C. To explore observations and test hypotheses

Explanation: The scientific method is a systematic process used to explore observations, answer questions, and test hypotheses, forming the basis of scientific inquiry.

12 - Which quantity is considered a fundamental measure in physics?

C. Time

Explanation: Time, along with length and mass, is a fundamental physical quantity that forms the basis for many other measurements in physics.

13 - Newton's second law of motion states that force is the product of mass and what other quantity?

B. Acceleration

Explanation: Newton's second law defines force as the product of mass and acceleration ($F = ma$), describing how the velocity of an object changes when it is subjected to an external force.

14 - What type of wave requires a medium through which to travel?

C. Sound wave

Explanation: Sound waves are mechanical waves and require a medium, such as air, water, or solids, to travel through, unlike electromagnetic waves like light and radio waves.

15 - In the context of circular motion, what force is directed toward the center of the circle?

A. Centripetal force

Explanation: Centripetal force is the force that keeps an object moving in a circular path and is directed toward the center around which the object moves.

16 - Which statement about vectors and scalars is true?

D. Displacement is a vector quantity

Explanation: Displacement is a vector quantity because it includes both magnitude and direction, unlike speed, which is a scalar and has only magnitude.

17 - Which law of motion introduces the concept of inertia?

A. Newton's First Law

Explanation: Newton's First Law, also known as the Law of Inertia, states that an object at rest stays at rest and an object in motion stays in motion with the same speed and in the same direction unless acted upon by an unbalanced force.

18 - What does the slope of a velocity-time graph represent?

B. Acceleration

Explanation: The slope of a velocity-time graph indicates the acceleration of an object. It represents the rate of change of velocity over time.

19 - What is the SI unit for power?

C. Watt

Explanation: The watt is the SI unit of power, which measures the rate of energy transfer equivalent to one joule per second.

20 - What is the term for the number of cycles of a wave that pass a point per unit of time?

C. Frequency

Explanation: Frequency is defined as the number of cycles of a wave that pass a point per unit of time, typically measured in hertz (Hz).

21 - What physical quantity is measured in ohms?

A. Resistance

Explanation: Resistance measures how much a material opposes the flow of electric current and is measured in ohms (Ω).

22 - Which formula represents Ohm's Law?

A. $V = IR$

Explanation: Ohm's Law states that the voltage (V) across a conductor is equal to the current (I) through it multiplied by the resistance (R) of the conductor.

23 - In terms of wave motion, what does the term 'amplitude' describe?

C. The maximum height of the wave

Explanation:

24 - What is the correct expression for kinetic energy?

A. $KE = \frac{1}{2} mv^2$

Explanation: The kinetic energy (KE) of an object is given by the formula $KE = \frac{1}{2} mv^2$ where m is mass and v is velocity, representing the energy an object possesses due to its motion.

25 - What is the principle that changing magnetic fields can induce an electric current called?

D. Faraday's Law of Electromagnetic Induction

Explanation: Faraday's Law of Electromagnetic Induction describes how a changing magnetic field within a circuit induces a voltage across the circuit, generating an electric current.

TAKE YOUR GIFTS AND YOUR FURTHER FULL-LENGTH TESTS

We've reached the end of this book, but our journey together continues. As promised at the start, with your purchase, you've unlocked access to six comprehensive tests, flashcards, round-the-clock support through our Facebook community, and much more.

We recognize the pivotal role these exams play in your healthcare career. It's our mission to ensure you not only pass your exam on the first try but also achieve an excellent score.

I understand the balancing act between work, personal life, and family commitments can make finding time to study a significant challenge. That's precisely why we've crafted a manual to provide a comprehensive study guide, aimed at simplifying your preparation process.

With the bonuses and detailed guidance included, your performance will soar. By practicing with materials that closely simulate the actual exam conditions, you'll gain both accuracy and speed, leading to outstanding results.

So, what are you waiting for? Scan the QR code and claim your bonuses now.

Begin your journey to success today!

I'D LOVE TO HEAR YOUR THOUGHTS!

Don't forget to leave a review on Amazon. Your support is crucial for my ongoing work and helps me keep providing fresh content. It takes just a minute, but the impact is tremendously valuable to me. Reviewing is easy—just log into Amazon, scan the QR code provided, and share your feedback.

Made in the USA
Columbia, SC
26 September 2024

43079727R00154